International Library of Psychology
Philosophy and Scientific Method

REASONS AND FAITHS

REASONS AND FAITHS

An Investigation of Religious Discourse, Christian and Non-Christian

by

NINIAN SMART

LONDON
ROUTLEDGE & KEGAN PAUL

First published in 1958
by Routledge & Kegan Paul Limited
Broadway House, 68-74 Carter Lane
London EC4V 5EL

Reprinted 1965
Reprinted 1971

Reproduced and Printed in Great Britain by
Redwood Press Limited
Trowbridge & London

ISBN 0 7100 3155 6

TO
LIBUSHKA

Contents

Preface

THE general aim of this book is to describe the nature of religious doctrines and concepts. But not just those of theism (the main preoccupation of philosophers of religion in the past), but also those of important and different faiths, notably Buddhism and Hinduism. Comparisons here are not, I hope, odious, but illuminating. Conversely it may be that a philosophical inquiry into religious concepts can be of use in the comparative study of religion (which, under its more fashionable title 'the history of religions', can often issue in unrelated chains of indigestible facts). Regarding the philosophical side of this book, it will be obvious that much I have written is rather unoriginal; and I should like to acknowledge my debt here to the work of modern philosophers. In general, I have not loaded the book with references to those whose views and arguments have influenced me. As for the facts of religion, I have tried, at least where the more important theses are being propounded, to give adequate documentation. It will be seen in general, though, that I owe much (even where I differ sharply from them) to Rudolf Otto and Evelyn Underhill.

A complication in a Janus-faced book such as this is that I have had to refer to non-Western concepts, and this involves the use of, in particular, some Sanskrit and Pāli terminology. Apart from the text, the Index gives brief explanations of these expressions, so that the reader, where he has a doubt, may swiftly resolve it. The Bibliography is a list of the modern works cited in the text.

In addition to the general acknowledgements of debt expressed above, I should like to thank my mentors in these subjects, and especially Professor J. L. Austin of the University of Oxford, who supervised my postgraduate work there, and Professor Paul Tedesco, of Yale University, under whom, all too briefly, I first studied Pāli. Also I am deeply grateful to Professor H. D. Lewis, of the University of London, who read the greater part of the book in manuscript and gave me much careful and illuminating advice.

London, 21 June 1958 NINIAN SMART

I have taken advantage of the second printing of this book to make some very minor corrections.

Birmingham, 2 December 1964 N. S.

Introduction

I. THE MAIN AIM OF THIS BOOK

NIETZSCHE remarked that 'the best that philosophy can offer is possibilities'.[1] Many philosophers would be inclined to agree with this assertion if it were interpreted to mean that philosophy is primarily the attempt to solve logical or conceptual problems: for example the problem whether it is self-contradictory to say both that a man's action is free and that it was determined by previous events. On this view, philosophers are not concerned directly with the facts but rather with the way we speak about the facts. But others might take exception to Nietzsche's remark on the ground that the philosopher is concerned to establish certain general facts about the world, and to discover not merely what it is possible to say but also what is the case. Fortunately, such disagreements about the nature of philosophy need not worry us unduly, on two counts. For first, the activity of philosophizing flourishes on discord; and second (more relevantly for the present investigation), there is perhaps a general willingness to concede that linguistic analysis, the method which the former of the above parties tends to favour, is a fruitful pursuit for philosophers even if not the only or the principal one. Provided, that is, it is directed to important and not trivial areas of discourse. Perhaps, then, there would be a fair measure of agreement that an investigation of the discourse of religion (which could hardly be thought unimportant) would be in some degree useful; and such an enquiry is the object of this book.

The task of describing a certain field of discourse, such as the language of science or of morals or of religion, has, apart from its intrinsic interest, a philosophical rationale. For many conceptual problems arise through treating the concepts of one field of discourse as though they belonged in another—as when 'good' is taken to be quite similar in logic to 'red' and to denote an albeit peculiar empirical property. This wider task corresponds to the narrower one of trying to elucidate the nature of concepts

[1] *Human-all-too-Human*, ch. iii.

within a field of discourse which are philosophically troublesome—as, for instance, is the expression 'mind' when it is treated as if it is on a logical par with 'body': a temptation made easy by the close juxtaposition of these two concepts when we are talking about people and animals.

It would, however, be idle to suppose that the kind of description herein attempted, namely the general description of religious discourse, is simple or straightforward or indeed likely to be undisputed; and it is best to show forth its peculiarities by pointing to what can very loosely be called the 'method' used in it.

II. PHILOSOPHY, AND THE PHILOSOPHY OF RELIGION, IS HIGHER ORDER

It is useful to make a somewhat crude distinction between higher and lower-order utterances. Thus the statement 'The Lord is my shepherd' is lower order, but the remark ' "The Lord is my shepherd" is synthetic (in the sense that its truth cannot be seen by considering simply the meanings of expressions used in it)' is higher order: it is a statement about a statement, not a straight statement. However, not all utterances about utterances are philosophical and so it would not do simply to say that the difference between philosophy and science, morals, etc., is that in the latter fields we just talk whereas in the former we talk about the talk. Rather, philosophical remarks about language have a special flavour: they seek to classify statements and expressions in special ways, to characterize them as having certain properties relevant to two main questions—namely (1) how we confirm the truth, correctness, etc., of statements, commands, etc.; and (2) how statements, etc., are logically connected or disconnected. As for (2), it is obvious that connections between statements, etc., hold or fail to hold irrespectively of the actual truth or falsity of the particular statements considered. And therefore in this respect the philosopher is a neutral in any disputes about what is the case. As for (1), it is to be noted that remarks about the confirmation of statements and so on point to general canons of acceptability: particular statements are treated, then, not by themselves but in the bosom of their families. The philosopher is not worried as to whether the birds are singing, but what sort of a statement 'The birds are singing' may be. Hence in this respect also the philosopher is a neutral.

His attitude can be characterized briefly as 'higher-order neutralism'. His task is not to establish particular truths (however wide-ranging these may be), but to elucidate their nature.

Unfortunately, the distinction between higher- and lower-order statements (as applied in a philosophical context) often looks vague, and there are certainly occasions upon which it is hard to tell whether a pronouncement is philosophical or not. But the fact that there is an area of vagueness is no good ground for abandoning the distinction, for we do not for like reason jettison the distinction between town and country. Moreover, the spirit of the contrast weighs more than the letter: we must always *try* to be clear as to whether we are engaged in conceptual elucidation in the philosophical manner or merely upon the establishment of truths in religion, science or what you will. If there is a doubt, we must look to see what problem the doubt conceals.

There is this difficulty about the contrast too: that since questions about confirmation and logical connection involve questions about the validity of grounds and arguments, and since people's beliefs rest ultimately on grounds and arguments, philosophical decisions on these matters will, if publicized, tend to alter in some cases people's beliefs. Higher-order utterances will, that is, affect lower-order beliefs. Is this not like the neutral power which sells arms to one side? Yet the objection scarcely blurs the contrast, since the mistakes corrected are still logical and not factual errors: and it is not the philosopher's job to establish the truth or falsity of the grounds or premisses upon which beliefs are held. Nevertheless, since procedures of reasoning have the function of guiding people to true beliefs, etc., the scrutiny of these by the philosopher may perform a vital service. And the philosopher, though remote from lower-order enquiries in one respect, need not be thought to be conducting investigations that are without significance to non-philosophers—provided that, as we said earlier, he is realistic enough to investigate the logic of concepts that play an important role in non-philosophical discourse. He is not like the philologist for whom all words are equal.

From what has been said, it will be clear that the word 'philosophy' here is being used in such a way that it would be misleading to count natural theology (often regarded as part of the philosophy of religion) as philosophy: for the main object of natural theology is to establish the truth of such claims as that God exists and that God has such-and-such attributes. It is therefore a lower-order activity, though it throws up logical problems that *are* the province of the philosopher. By the same token, it will make sense in only an unsatisfactory use of 'philosophy' to speak of 'the philosophy of the Christian religion', 'the philosophy of Buddhism', etc. If someone were to object that this is an unfortunate restriction on the use of the word 'philosophy', it can only be said that there seem to be two different activities, viz. analysis and the establishment of general truths about the world, and therefore there should be two names. 'Philosophy' is here being reserved for the former; perhaps 'metaphysics' can be suitably used for the latter. It might then be sensible to talk of 'the metaphysics of Christianity', etc. And as a gloss on the distinction, it is worth pointing out that this linguistic recommendation is not intended to carry with it the suggestion that those who are generally called 'philosophers' should necessarily refrain from doing metaphysics: for the following reasons—(1) the attempt to establish metaphysical truths throws up in its course many logical problems and is hence not only interesting to but also better undertaken by the philosopher; (2) it is not politic to attempt in any rigid way to direct intellectual labour; and (3) just as in political philosophy there are interesting and important points to be made in a reasoned way which are not strictly philosophical ones but which are as well done by the informed philosopher as anyone else, so it is possible there are certain metaphysical enquiries where the same holds good: at any rate, given the traditions in these matters that we have it is unpractical and unwise to make a sweeping recommendation that a certain activity is *tabu* for a man merely because he bears the label of 'philosopher'. But these remarks should be read in the light of a thesis which I hope in some measure to establish, viz. that many metaphysical claims are disguised religious claims. When, then, I talk of the philosophy of religion, by this is meant an investigation of religious concepts in a spirit of higher-order neutrality.

III. HIGHER-ORDER NEUTRALISM AND PHILOSOPHY

This neutralism may at first appear unfortunate—for it seems to lead to the result that all the writings, utterances and activities of religion will be equal as data. This lack of criticism would itself seem to lead to a kind of lower-order attitude. And it is a common charge against so-called 'ordinary language' philosophers that they are committed by their very approach to adopting current beliefs enshrined in ordinary discourse; and that therefore their professed neutrality is unsubstantial and uncritical. The complaint may be met at least partly by the following general replies and by some further ones especially applicable to the philosophy of religion.

(i) In general, there is some error caused by the slogan-wise use of 'ordinary language'. A better but emptier expression would be 'non-philosophical' language (the emptiness does not matter too much, since it is largely philosophizing that shows us what philosophy is, and before this is seen, only hints can be given). For example, philosophers of science are much concerned with highly sophisticated and technical concepts employed in physics and elsewhere—and these are rarely counters of common conversation. 'Ordinary' at any rate should not be taken to mean 'everyday'—but since it almost inevitably suggests this sense it is a bad expression to use for the purpose. But an important part of the force of the slogan that we should turn to ordinary language is that thereby the air is cleared of gratuitous philosophical and metaphysical obscurities (since these often result from odd but unobviously odd uses of ordinary concepts). Still, it may well be that sometimes (for instance, in the analysis of moral utterances) philosophers tacitly accept prevalent standards, allowing these to appear in heavy analytic disguise. But the remedy for this is greater vigilance and candour; for such errors may readily be removed once we are in a position to distinguish between the question as to how one *would* justify a belief and the question whether *in fact* the belief *is* justified. Thus a philosophical description of ordinary discourse may often be stylized: one takes as a model an instance where it is indubitably correct usage to say, e.g. 'I know that P', though it may turn out on a wider survey that ordinary parlance and ordinary claims to knowledge are sometimes inconsistent or confused. This leads to the second reply.

(ii) Common ways of speaking sometimes enshrine philosophical mistakes (as could be claimed, for instance, about fatalistic beliefs embodied in modes of parlance such as 'the iron grip of destiny'). This special class of usages, together with those crude and vague ways of talking about language itself which are often found in common speech (e.g. the common distinction between 'abstract' and 'concrete') are ones for which the philosopher would of course wish to supply remedies. He often has to tidy, and thus occasionally to legislate. But what we do does not matter if we know what it is we are doing, so that as long as philosophers show clearly what is legislation and what is not, there will be no confusion (though there may be disagreements about the legislation, but such differences will be above-board).

IV. NEUTRALISM IN THE PHILOSOPHY OF RELIGION

As to the philosophy of religion, the charge that philosophical neutralism is a sham may perhaps more easily be answered, though the reply involves taking up a new approach to this field of enquiry. This may be summed up in the slogan: The philosophy of religion is intimately linked to the comparative study of religions. The best way of uncovering the style of religious utterances is by looking at the whole range of doctrines and practices presented in the world's great faiths. It is thus that the canons for evaluating religious pronouncements (as true or false, correct or incorrect, etc.) become clearer. Later we shall see not only why this is so, but additional reasons why the comparative study of religions is of particular interest to the philosopher. Now a peculiar feature of religion is that it is presumptuous and ineffectual to sit down coolly and in a study to excogitate some scheme of salvation or some spiritual theory of the universe. Only extraordinary and spiritually gifted men are the communicators of fundamental doctrines and these, if learnt at all, are learnt in living and experience. Hence it is not amiss—and surely not cowardice—to count as genuinely important messages the pronouncements of the great religions: if anything in religion is true it is likely that something like the truth will be found there, and we cannot rely on ourselves to devise novel alternative doctrines. Before we have arrived at a more lucid understanding, it is reasonable to give heed to those pragmatic tests whereby the great religions are adjudged to be such. By selecting these as his models, the philosopher is armed with a two-edged sword. On the one hand, he defends himself against the charge of counting all religious utterances as equal, even the most frivolous or lunatic. On the other hand, he has sufficient variety to maintain his attitude of neutralism—he examines different faiths but not with the object of determining which is true. Moreover, the variety of doctrines bears other fruits: thereby he is not misled into supposing that one faith or group of faiths necessarily gives a correct picture of religious discourse (as though all religious language, for instance, must sooner or later involve reference to God: a mistake that would be engendered easily in the West, by the fact that Western tradition has been deeply acquainted only with the Judaic group of faiths).

But some might argue that this programme for the philosophy of religion seems to involve the assumption that there *are* criteria of truth (correctness, etc.) in spiritual discourse; whereas it is quite possible that religious utterances, like some metaphysical ones, are vacuous, just because there are no such ways of deciding between them. On examination, may it not turn out that talk about God and so on is without content? Now first, I believe that this view is mistaken; and second it provides a temptation to be eschewed. The temptation is this: that we feel like stopping to argue the issue and thus are swept on into generalities before any attempt is made to describe in any detail the style of religious discourse. This is dangerous, since thereby it is all too easy to misconstrue what is being discussed: polemics present a snare. In any event, the attempt to assimilate religious utterances to certain vacuous metaphysical propositions rests mainly on two points, one true but by no means persuasive here, the other false. The first is the undoubted fact that the criteria of spiritual correctness, if any, are lacking in the directness and public convincingness of those found in empirical or even moral argument. But their looseness is not such that nothing could count for or against a religious utterance, and they thus avoid the vacuity of certain metaphysical doctrines. Consequently, spiritual claims, though they may all be false, are not without content. However, it must be conceded that there may not only be dispute as to the truth of religious claims but also as to the criteria: hence, it is open to anyone to say that the neutralist approach, with its tendency towards presuming that there are genuine criteria, is possibly misleading. But at least this may be replied: the description of alleged criteria, the description of the way religious truths are held to be confirmed, will at any rate throw a little light on what sort of truths religious truths are supposed to be. A second reason for assimilating religious and metaphysical statements is that certain religious entities, such as God, the Tao, Brahman, etc., are seemingly locked for ever beyond ordinary experience in the way the metaphysical substrate is. And so utterances about God would appear likewise vacuous. However, an examination of spiritual doctrines and especially of the manner in which, in a given creed, they are linked together, reveals that at worst these entities are in a position not unlike the theoretical constructs of science. Moreover, even though there may in fact be no evidence for the existence of such entities, it is by no means obvious that it should in principle be impossible for there to be such. But again, whether or not these dogmatic replies, foreshadowing theses to be developed in the later discussions, are justified, it is not politic—as has been said above—to discuss these general issues before passing in review the doctrines of a number of faiths and the settings in which they appear. It should be added, however, that the charge that religious claims are like metaphysical ones should not be castigated too heavily, for religious thinkers, especially in the West, have often argued for certain of their beliefs metaphysically and are themselves both victims and propagators of an illusion. But since these points can only be brought out as we proceed with our enquiry, the foregoing remarks are intended merely as hints serving to justify initially the line of approach here adopted. To sum up: the neutralism of the philosopher is preserved, at least in spirit, by taking into account a number of well-known alternative systems of belief and by refraining from arguing from any one of them. All that is attempted is to describe the types of grounds which would be appropriate if one were to try to confirm spiritual truths. This task involves the wider one of showing what sort of truths such truths would be.

It is here perhaps that the history of religions is most helpful to the philosopher. For hitherto Western philosophers have tended to have in mind, when speaking of religion, a group of fairly closely allied faiths (Christianity, Islām, Judaism); and yet it is not fortuitous that other faiths, of a rather different though not entirely dissimilar flavour—such as Hinduism and Taoism, are called *religions*. Just as expanding intercourse with non-Greek neighbours in the sixth and fifth centuries B.C. stimulated the Greeks to philosophical discussion of the nature of moral rules—simply because it was brought home to them that there were alternative moral beliefs on many matters; and as too the discovery of non-Euclidean geometries in the last century led to a reappraisal of the status of mathematics—so too the increasedly sympathetic and accurate awareness in this century of impressive non-Western religions (mainly as a consequence of the endeavours of orientalists in the last hundred years or so) can conduce to a fructifying discussion of the character of spiritual concepts. We now have a reasonably correct understanding of Eastern religions and have moreover outgrown the inclination to interpret them as lower forms of Christianity (a tendency fostered, of course, by missionary enterprise, for it is neither unnatural nor wholly unreasonable within a certain context to seek in another man's faith the foundations on which to build a comprehension of Christian doctrine; but outside such a context of conversion, the procedure tends to lead to distortions). But the comparative study of religions does more than broaden the philosopher's outlook. For in other fields the philosopher sometimes must, in the course of his investigations, invent examples of logically possible situations, etc. (e.g. it is logically possible that the table in front of me will suddenly vanish). This is easy enough in dealing with everyday concepts such as *table*; but how can one tell whether an allegedly possible religious doctrine would count as a religious doctrine at all? As was said above, we are not at liberty to sit down and work out schemes of salvation. But fortunately the study of religions affords us a wider range of possible doctrines than would occur to one brought up blinkered in one culture.

Further ways in which comparative religion affords the philosopher illuminations will, I hope, emerge in outline in the following account of certain terminological proposals which I wish to make and which require for their explanation a more substantial preview of the aims and claims of this book.

V. TERMINOLOGY: PROPOSITIONS AND LANGUAGE-FRAMES

First, two general proposals to facilitate the explanation of the others. There is lacking a general word to cover statements, commands, questions, exclamations, etc., i.e. the various types of employments of sentences (here I adhere to P. F. Strawson's distinction between sentence and statement—that is to say, we can distinguish between a sentence such as 'I am old' and the statements made by different people on different occasions using this sentence[1]—and to its analogues). Since religious utterances are by no means always statements it would ease expression if some generic term were found ('utterance' itself being unsuitable since there are no written utterances). I intend to use 'proposition'

[1] *Introduction to Logical Theory*, pp. 3–4, 9–12.

for this purpose, since the evils of the term have been sufficiently advertised to render it harmless. It follows of course that the usual definition of proposition (such that 'proposition' is convertible with 'capable of being true-or-false or true only') will not apply, since commands, for instance, cannot be true or false. It will therefore be appropriate, on this use of 'proposition', to contrast the sentence 'Oh what a beautiful morning!' with the proposition, i.e. the utterance of this sentence on a particular occasion by a language-user. But since it is somewhat cumbrous to refer to the class of such utterances (with similar import on similar occasions and expressed in the use of the said sentence), 'proposition' will also on legitimate occasions be used to stand for both the particular example and its brothers. Thus 'Oh what a beautiful morning' could be said to be an expressive proposition: and this would be a succinct way of saying that there is a class of exclamatory propositions made by the use of the sentence 'Oh what a beautiful morning' which are expressive (of joy, etc., at the morning). But this should be understood with the lurking proviso in the background that the same sentence can be used to assert dissimilar propositions.

Second, we need some word to characterize an area of discourse, or language-stratum (as Dr. F. Waismann says[1]), in which fall propositions of a certain kind—for example, material-object statements, morals, poetry, art-criticism, religion: these each present different areas of discourse. Since the use of 'stratum' gives rise to a picture of the mutual relationships of the different areas to which there is no need to commit ourselves, I shall use 'frame' for this purpose. Thus we say that: 'The boiling point of water is 100 degrees Centigrade' and 'Thou shalt not kill' belong to different language-frames (more simply: to different frames). The general object of this book, then, is to exhibit the style of propositions in the spiritual frame.

VI. TERMINOLOGY: 'SPIRITUAL' AND 'RELIGIOUS'

It is advisedly that I speak of it as the spiritual rather than the religious frame of language, and for the following reasons. (1) 'Religion' is sometimes defined by reference to a God or gods, and yet there are some doctrinal systems which include no such notion or

[1] See his essay 'Language Strata' in *Logic and Language* (Second Series), ed. A. G. N. Flew, pp. 11 ff.

only have it in a shadowy form; for this reason Buddhists sometimes deny that Buddhism is a religion.[1] Nevertheless, we would probably all concede that Buddhist doctrines can be called *spiritual*. (2) A religion has to be to some extent institutionalized before taking on the title, and yet we often find sentiments expressed by metaphysicians and poets, among others (as for instance by Spinoza and Aeschylus), which although they might not be called religious doctrines (belief in which would be binding within a community), yet lie unmistakably within the orbit of spiritual discourse. Indeed, as already stated, a thesis which I would wish later to develop is that many metaphysical assertions have mainly a spiritual point, heavily obscured often enough by the kind of arguments urged on their behalf. Plotinus would be a good example of a writer whose work is mainly concerned with spiritual matters, though in one sense at least of 'religion' Neo-Platonism would not be called a religion. Nevertheless, though the word 'spiritual' might be less misleading than 'religious' in such contexts, it has a not altogether satisfactory flavour when used outside its ordinary habitat in devotional manuals, etc., and therefore I shall continue to use the words 'religion' and 'religious' in a broad sense to characterize the area of investigation. But the points made above, in regard to the narrower senses of the words, should be kept in mind.

VII. DOCTRINAL SCHEMES

Now it is a noticeable feature of religions that they possess a body of doctrine, a system of propositions linked together which are taken to be true (and belief in which constitutes one of the criteria for being counted an adherent of the religion). Sometimes these propositions are summed up briefly in a creed and sometimes

[1] 'Buddhism, it is often said, is not a religion. In the Western sense of the word *religion*, this is perhaps true; for Buddhism denies the existence of a creator-god to whom we owe honour and reverence.' From an article on *Gratitude* by the Lord Abbot Kosho Otani, *The Middle Way*, Vol. XXIX, No. 4 (Feb., 1955), p. 154. Söderblom has remarked (ERE, vi. 731, art. on *Holiness*): 'The attaching of undue importance to the conception of divinity has led to the exclusion from the realm of religion of (1) phenomena at the primitive level . . . (2) Buddhism and other higher forms of salvation and piety which do not involve belief in God. The only sure test is holiness.' But the last remark needs qualification, for the root type of the holy is the numinous, whereas it is only the secondary type (morally pure, etc.) which figures centrally in the above-mentioned higher forms of salvation. But, of course, the main point holds good.

expanded at length in the sermons and catechisms whereby the faithful are instructed. These propositions hang together and in many cases one of them cannot be understood save in the light of some or all the others. Their impact is, that is, affected by what other propositions are jointly asserted. For example, in Christianity propositions about the Creator (often made by using sentences with which similar assertions are made by Jews and Muslims) have a force different from the analogous claims made in Judaism and Islām, for they are not fully understood unless we advert to what is preached about the Son. Much as colours in a painting take on different effects according to the juxtaposition of other colours (a fact which constitutes one ground for calling works of art 'organic'), so the same sentence takes on different meanings according to the doctrinal context in which it is used. Further, some of the propositions may in some sense be said to follow from some of the others. It would, however, be absurd to consider such a system of spiritual propositions as analogous in any close way to a deductive system such as Euclidean geometry. Putting it crudely, in the latter the relations between propositions are rigid, in the other loose. In the one case we can speak of entailment, but rarely if ever can we do this with regard to spiritual propositions.[1] Consequently, the word 'system' already gives a false impression, and therefore I shall use the phrase 'doctrinal scheme' for those propositions which taken together constitute the main doctrines of a faith. 'Scheme' is negatively appropriate in that it does not suggest deductive orderliness, and positively so in that it smacks a little of arrangement and, as we shall find, there is some element of aesthetic arrangement about the way different segments of a doctrinal scheme come to hang together. Thus we can speak of 'the Christian doctrinal scheme', 'the doctrinal scheme of the *Bhagavadgītā*', etc. The use of this piece of terminology is important because it will frequently remind us that it is rather useless and sometimes genuinely harmful to discuss spiritual propositions in isolation. Thus the disputes about arguments for the existence of God will seem less important, since it will be apparent that the claim that God exists can only be understood by reference to many, if not all, other propositions in the doctrinal scheme from which it is extrapolated. As has been remarked apropos of the question 'Do electrons exist?', it serves to question a whole theory;

[1] I am not here considering, of course, trivial entailments such as the fact that 'Christ is God and the Holy Ghost is God' entails 'Christ is God'.

so 'Does God exist?' questions a whole doctrinal scheme.[1] Or rather, since different doctrinal schemes share sentences about a Creator God, it questions a class of doctrinal schemes. However, it would be wrong to be beguiled by terminology into supposing (a common fault) that we can discuss the propositions of a doctrinal scheme without looking also not only to the surrounding pronouncements which throw light on them, but also to the religious activities which give them life and point. Without the latter I believe it is impossible to gain any sure philosophical insight into the nature of spiritual propositions; and for this reason would be apprehensive of the wrong impression likely to be created by saying that the present study is an investigation of religious language. A lesson of great importance which contemporary philosophers have learnt is that the setting of an utterance can be of the greatest philosophical importance (hence the sentence-statement distinction, which I generalize as the sentence-proposition distinction, is efficacious in guiding us past common but subtle traps). The root of many confusions is due to the failure to see that the same sentence can be used on different occasions for quite different purposes, and thus it may be that a sentence used to make a philosophical or metaphysical assertion misleads us because in an ordinary context it would normally be used to assert an obvious truth, though it by no means follows that in a bizarre context this would be the case. This is one main reason why in philosophy 'the spoken is superior to the written word'. For by cross-questioning we can find out what a puzzling claim amounts to—the force of an utterance is often created by later answers. A good example of this superiority is found when the analytic-synthetic distinction

[1] ' "There is such a quality as mass" is nonsense, unless it means merely to affirm the consequences of a mechanical theory'—F. P. Ramsey, *Foundations of Mathematics*, p. 261. And further, with regard to the way one proposition in a scheme affects the others and consequently the sense of the key terms, compare a similar situation in deductive systems: 'The premisses of the deductive system represented by the initial formulae of the calculus, must be taken as a whole; and . . . the growth of the theory by the addition of a new premiss affects all the other premisses'—R. B. Braithwaite, *Scientific Explanation*, p. 81. It should however be remarked that the notion of *premiss* is hardly applicable to doctrinal schemes, though there are some more or less central propositions from which others in a loose manner follow (perhaps it is best to say the former *suggest* rather than *imply* the latter); and indeed the discovery that an inference suggested by these more central propositions is allowable (and not, say, conducive to heresy) throws light on the sense of these propositions in a way in which the performance of an inference in a deductive system does not throw light on the sense of the premisses.

is examined closely. For it is statements, not sentences, which in a primary sense can be said to be analytic, since it is chiefly by considering the answers given to crucial questions that we can judge a statement to be analytic or synthetic. More generally, it is by an understanding of the *situations* in which a sentence might be used that we come to appreciate its 'logical style' (though there are objections to the loose use of 'logic' and 'logical' in much current philosophical discourse, slogan-wise it has a point). These remarks apply with even greater force than usual to the investigation of spiritual language. There is little hope indeed, for example, of comprehending the point of many utterances by mystics unless we pay attention to the context of behaviour and experience of those who make the utterances. Again, to gain an inkling of the nature of the concept *God* it is surely requisite to look to the worshipping activities that surround, so to speak, belief in the divine. So it would be distressingly mistaken to regard the propositions of a doctrinal scheme in unnatural loneliness; their spirit becomes manifest only in the company of the peripheral utterances and activities.

VIII. LOGICAL STRANDS IN DOCTRINAL SCHEMES

Although, then, one main task of the philosopher is to reveal the manner in which doctrinal schemes are to be established, etc., and although he may do this by comparing and contrasting the discourse of the spiritual frame with other areas of language, even this modest descriptive task is not fully described in this way. For the subtleties of the situation are greater than might at first appear. Not only are there, so to say, macroscopic differences between the language of the spirit and other types of speech but there are microscopic divergencies within the former. It will be found upon investigation that many doctrinal schemes are woven together, as it were, from differing logical strands. For there are considerable divergences between the fashion in which propositions about God the Creator (the object of praise and worship) are established and that in which mystical claims are to be confirmed. Again, the style of propositions about an incarnate deity is different from either of the above two kinds of proposition. Further and notoriously, religious doctrines are connected with moral assertions and these latter also diverge from the style of the above three types of spiritual proposition. These distinctions within the spiritual frame have to be accounted for just as much as the macroscopic contrasts, and so the belief that there is just one analysis of spiritual propositions is quite illusory. Although it is only in a discursive manner that the internal differences can be clearly illuminated, that there are such contrasted strands can be seen without too much reflection before such an investigation. First, it seems that claims about a Creator God 'beyond' the world of sense experience would find their support if any in general features of the world, or would find at least part of their support there; by looking to the starry skies above men gain an inkling of the divine grandeur. On the other hand, the mystical path is, so to speak, directed inward, and in so far as any confirmation of such claims as mystics make can be given, it is at least partly exhibited in their glorified behaviour. Further, the claim that some human is divine draws its plausibility largely from the character and historical circumstances of the chosen one. Moreover, coupled with the three kinds of claims there are three sorts of demands. Men are constrained to worship the concealed One beyond the world; but mysticism in its pure form is not a sort of worship: asceticism and meditation are the hall-marks of this activity. Finally, imitation and discipleship are joined closely to belief in an incarnate deity. Of course, these contrasts are obscured by the fact that in Christianity all three strands are to be found, delicately interwoven, and we find in Brāhmanism, for instance, an impressive conjunction of the worship and mystical strands. Thus the above remarks are crude not only because they merely prefigure that which must be exhibited discursively and in detail; but also because the genius of some doctrinal schemes lies precisely in their success in weaving together what I have called the different strands, even though their epistemological characters are distinct. And thus, in view of what has already been said about the organic nature of such doctrinal schemes—that the sense of a proposition is altered, so to speak, by its environment, by what other propositions are its neighbours—it is not surprising that it is difficult to separate out convincingly these different elements. Fortunately for the philosopher, however, the history of religions affords examples of comparatively simple doctrinal schemes which can be used as models of single strands. Thus Lesser Vehicle Buddhism is a conspicuous instance of an almost purely mystical religion; while Islām (not here counting the Ṣūfīs, who indirectly confirm my claim for they proved so difficult to accommodate to Islamic orthodoxy) is a good example of the worshipper's faith. Almost all the doctrine concerns the object of worship and the relations thereof to men while in Theravāda Buddhism the central concept, nirvāṇa, is a state to be achieved by moral and mystical self-discipline. Thus the philosopher can gain real help from the study of religions, and this in two ways. (1) The very situation that he finds suggests to him naturally the contrasts between strands which I have in mind. (2) Such distortion as he inflicts upon complex doctrinal schemes in pointing separately to different logical elements which the scheme has subtly mingled together can be excused by appeal to comparisons evident from the history of religions. It is a bad metaphor to say that analysis (like dissection) must kill; but in the present instance there is certainly a danger, despite the above-mentioned excuses, that the separating out of the strands will present a wrong picture; the organic nature of the complex doctrinal schemes will be hidden from view. Nevertheless, it is a necessary task if insight here is to be attained, and the philosopher undertakes it fortified by historical comparisons and by his own promise to introduce correctives after the job is done. Philosophy at any rate is a delicate activity, for the drawing of comparisons always involves using slightly unsuitable models: the rather is not the utterly alike and the somewhat is not the completely different.

IX. THE PHILOSOPHY OF RELIGION NOT IRREVERENT

It is convenient at this point to mention another hazard besetting us and arising from the very fact that religion is the subject of enquiry. In speaking about religious propositions sometimes we seem to be irreverent, for philosophizing has that neutral air and this may look out of place when we are talking about something which by its very nature seems incapable of dispassionate treatment, where even neutrality may look blasphemous. For a higher-order remark may seem to be lower order. For instance, the trivial assertion that the concept *God* is a spiritual concept might strike some as about God, and we are not accustomed to trivial remarks about God. But because philosophical remarks are not reverent it does not follow that they are irreverent for higher-order statements are neither reverent nor irreverent. But of course the trouble is not removed simply by saying this. For as plain men we use language in unreflective ways and it all seems natural to us; but then some time an odd note is struck and what we say though straightforward and common suddenly seems odd. Once we are in this philosophical frame of mind, even the obvious and everyday takes on a flavour of strangeness; so much more does the mysterious and supernatural which we have hitherto half-comprehended. Thus the language of worship with which we have hitherto been familiar seems to suffer a sea-change as we step back to contemplate it. And we are liable to find that philosophical discussion, which often appears absurd enough when we talk about tables and chairs and flowers, may frequently seem blasphemous when we are probing utterances about the divine. Nevertheless, any offence caused is unintended, since the philosopher's aim is neither to praise nor to fail to praise, neither to pray nor refrain from praying. His words, to repeat, are intended neither to be reverent nor irreverent.

But maybe someone, bred in the fashionable theology of today, will have a deeper repugnance to the programme herein proposed. For unless, he will say, we are already committed in some way to a faith, we shall not understand it. Thus a neutralist approach (where beliefs, if held, are suspended, viewed as it were from above and not from within) will necessarily fail. Religion is not the sort of thing you can stand back from. Such an objection, however, rests on a mere half-truth. It is true that we must have had some fairly extensive experience of religion and religious activities in order to have a rough comprehension of the point of religious utterances (and this will indeed be evident if my thesis that from these activities the doctrines draw their life is correct) But it follows neither that one should believe in some creed at the time of philosophizing in order to give a reasonably accurate account of what the creed amounts to nor that such belief would necessarily help the philosopher. For often the strength of conviction will make philosophy appear trivial, or more dangerously it will tempt one into substituting apologetics for analysis. (This is not of course to say that apologetics is an ill-conceived pursuit, but it is not philosophy; and—to repeat—that type of general apologetics that goes under the name of Christian philosophy or Buddhist philosophy, etc., is ill-named.) Perhaps, however, a broadly religious disposition might help a philosopher to greater insight (as scientific expertise aids the philosopher of science—though religiosity is not, of course, a kind of expertise); but even this is hardly a safe thing to say, and is liable to result in intellectual pharisaism. Enough then on this topic.

I have used the expressions 'strand' and 'logical strand' to stand for differing elements in doctrinal schemes and hope that its rough use is now evident. This is my final terminological proposal.

X. SUMMARY

The first main job of the philosopher of religion can now be represented as the description of the character of doctrinal schemes (and in general of religious discourse) in such a way as both to compare and contrast these with other language-frames and to show the differences and connections between logical strands within the religious frame. This jargon is but a row of pegs on which slogans are hung and the slogans merely foreshadow the beginnings and ends in any philosophizing contained in this work. The slogans are:

(i) Each language-frame has its own family characteristics;

(ii) the propositions of religion are to be understood in their doctrinal contexts;

(iii) the doctrines find their life in the activities surrounding them;

(iv) there are differing strands within religious discourse.

Slogans, however, without their explanation are barren, and to this discursive task we now proceed. The manner of progress will be somewhat circuitous, and only later will the woods be seen among the trees. In this fashion the temptation to begin by arguing general theses, a common fault among philosophers, will be avoided. For they are at best slogans, and slogans are only a kind of proleptic shorthand. Their applications, what it is that they sum up—these are what is important. Nevertheless, the discursive investigations which follow will be seen to be in their own manner crude in comparison with the richness and subtlety of spiritual discourse and the variegation of the spiritual life. Moreover, although I shall at some points attempt to indicate how philosophical metaphysics—for instance Thomism—has superimposed itself, so to speak, upon religious discourse, my main concern is with what I believe to be the more central aspects of the latter. And to this extent also I am guilty of crudity. Yet despite the immense disproportion between the rich profundity of religious doctrines and the bludgeon-like analysis herein offered, there is some advantage in presenting a relatively simple account. For an analysis professedly offering clarification should not, perhaps, obscure itself through too much proliferation of detail. Still, it is not always easy to find the right balance here.

I propose to begin the discussion by considering one or two texts from the *Upaniṣads* touching on Brahman. The reason for starting there is twofold. First, the Brahman-Ātman doctrine is one which illustrates rather clearly the distinction between two strands of spiritual discourse, and this distinction is vital to most of the other things which one needs to say about doctrinal schemes. The second reason is that the very fact that this is written in English is likely to mean that most of those who read it will have been brought up under the aegis of Western civilization, and so will be less offended by our treatment of religious propositions garnered from a non-Western religion. Less offended on two scores: first, because neutralism seems less unnatural when we are speaking of an alien (yet respected) faith; second, because we shall not immediately be touching on the reader's own faith and so the unintended flavour of blasphemy will not immediately be tasted.

I

The Object of Worship

I. BRAHMAN IS BOTH FAR AND NEAR

REFERRING to Brahman, the *Īśa Upaniṣad* remarks:

> It is both far and near; It is within all this and It is outside all this.[1]

Similarly, the *Muṇḍaka Upaniṣad* says:

> Vast, divine, of unimaginable form, subtler than the subtle, It shines forth, farther than the far, yet close at hand.[2]

And the *Chāndogya Upaniṣad* in like vein:

> This is my Self within the heart, tinier than a rice-grain, tinier than a barley corn, or a mustard-seed, or a grain of millet, or the kernel of a grain of millet. This is my Self within the heart, greater than the earth, greater than the atmosphere, greater than the sky, greater these worlds.[3]

These paradoxical pronouncements fulfil such a number of functions that by understanding the gist of them one can penetrate to the heart of the philosophy of religion. In particular they exhibit two logical strands woven into spiritual discourse which it is desirable to unravel.

II. BRAHMAN AND SPATIAL PREDICATES

One of the superficial accomplishments of these propositions is the indication that spatial predicates do not apply to Brahman in any straightforward fashion. Indeed a function of many paradoxes is to draw attention to new uses of language—new uses which may have the effect of changing significantly men's attitudes on the topics dealt with. For example there are the words:

> For whosoever will save his life shall lose it; but whosoever shall lose his life for my sake and the gospel's, the same shall save it.[4]

[1] *Īśa Upan.*, 5.
[2] III.1.7.
[3] III.14.3. Cp. *Kaivalya Upan.*, 19–20.
[4] *Mark*, viii.35.

But we do not take Jesus to be contradicting himself; and neither is the author of the *Īśa Upaniṣad*.

But why do spatial predicates not apply to Brahman? Partly because Brahman is not, so to say, an empirical object. Thus it is incorrect to suppose that, in a literal sense, one can see Brahman (or God or Allah or the Tao or etc.). As the *Kaṭha Upaniṣad* puts it:

> His form is not visible: no one whatever sees Him with the eye.[1]

And the *Śvetāśvatara Upaniṣad*:

> There is no image of Him whose name is Great Glory.[2]

But yet at the same time it is said that the divine *can* be seen. For instance, the *Kaṭha Upaniṣad* says:

> Though the Self is concealed in all beings and is not obvious, It can be seen by subtle seers, through their subtle discernment.[3]

(The Self, in Brāhmanist teaching, is identical with Brahman, the source and sustainer of the world, for reasons which we shall try to explain.) And Suso speaks too of an immediate view or apprehension of the Deity.[4] Instances of such language can be multiplied. So we meet another paradox: that the invisible can be seen.[5] This is so because in any ordinary sense of these perceptual verbs, Brahman cannot be seen, heard, felt, etc.,[6] but in an extraordinary sense, It can. And the first thing we wish to discover is why Brahman is not in some *ordinary* sense perceptible, for this will help us to see why propositions about Brahman are not simple empirical ones.

III. BRAHMAN IS NOT SIMPLY EMPIRICAL BECAUSE HOLY

One reason why propositions about Brahman are not simply empirical is that the major concepts of religion, such as *holy* and *sacred*, are not employed simply in a descriptive way. The reference to these as 'major' may stand in need of justification, since the key concepts of spiritual discourse seem to be those like *God*, *Allah*,

[1] II.3.9. [2] IV.19. [3] I.3.12.

[4] *Leben*, liv, p. 277.

[5] Also the (voice of the) divine can be heard, it is said, and it is also possible to have contact with the divine, but tasting and smelling do not seem appropriate analogies (though see *Milindapañha*, IV.8.73–4, in regard to nirvāṇa).

[6] Cp. *Bṛhadāraṇyaka Upan.*, III.4.2.

Brahman, *Ātman*, *Tao*, *nirvāṇa*—those that hold a central place in doctrinal schemes. However, expressions like 'holy' and 'sacred' have a peculiar importance in that not only are they used to characterize religious entities and persons, but also serve to cordon off in a rough and general manner the spiritual domain from others. Hence the special significance in the history of the philosophy of religion of Rudolf Otto's *The Idea of the Holy*. Thus those who believe in God would regard it as somehow superfluous or analytic to say that He is holy—this is what religious entities are supposed to be.

Now to say that something is holy is not just to ascribe to it a property like redness or hardness. People sometimes speak of religious experiences, and though there is room to believe that what they have in mind is quite a variety of types of events, it is clear that these are frequently experiences of awe or dread, and it is not unlikely that part of what is meant by saying that a thing is holy is that it is apt to or ought to give rise to such reactions. Thus, in the *Kaṭha Upaniṣad*, even the world is described as standing in awe of Brahman:

> All this world, whatever exists, comes from and moves in life: a great fear, an upraised thunderbolt. . . . Through fear of Him, fire burns and the sun burns: through fear of Him, Indra and wind and death, the fifth, speed to and fro.[1]

The holy inspires terror, dread, fear, awe, wonder, etc., and therefore is terrible, dreadful, fearsome, awful, wonderful, etc. (Unfortunately, as becomes readily apparent, such words speedily lose their solemnity: bad coinage soon drives out good, cp. 'fantastic', 'out of this world', and the other current candidates for debasement.) This list immediately reveals some mundane analogues of the holy, such as the wonderful and the marvellous, and it is perhaps useful to examine these.

IV. REASONS WHY 'WONDERFUL', ETC., SEEM DESCRIPTIVE

To say of something ordinarily that it is wonderful or marvellous is not to describe it, just as to say of something that it is good or beautiful is not so to do; and yet these predicates *seem* to be descriptive ones like 'red' and 'hard', for a number of reasons. (1) The majority of sentences in which expressions like 'wonderful' occur are not distinguished grammatically from those which *are* used

[1] II.3.2–3. For a similar sentiment, *Taittirīya Upan.*, II.8.1.

descriptively. Thus 'The rose is red' (a model for sentences that are used descriptively) is structurally similar to 'The rose is wonderful'. (2) There are certain criteria for applying the predicates, the criteria varying with the subject. In some contexts it is easy to think of the predicate as being shorthand for those characteristics whose presence makes the predicate applicable. For example, a woman is beautiful if she possesses some conjunction of characteristics drawn from the relevant set. To say that she has these is often to describe (not always, for often the criteria include 'aesthetic attributes' such as fine bone structure, and to say that she has *fine* bone structure is not simply a descriptive pronouncement). And so the claim that a woman is beautiful acquires a descriptive flavour. Especially so if the hearer or utterer has in mind some ideal instance and takes the proposition to be asserting that there is a similarity between the person referred to and the ideal instance. (3) There is an inverted-commas use of the expressions. Thus 'This picture is beautiful' may sometimes be taken to mean 'Experts/everyone/etc. judge this picture to be beautiful'. In such cases it is clearer to write the sentence 'This picture is "beautiful" ', with the inverted commas to signalize that it is really being used to talk about a judgment and not to express one (though this way of writing it might also seem too much to indicate irony; but the fact that this is so points to the fundamental appropriateness of the suggestion). The genuine and inverted-commas uses shade into one another; so that sometimes it is rather like a descriptive statement of fact to say that a picture is beautiful. (4) Since in declaring a thing to be wonderful one is making a claim, as is clear from the fact that men argue over the application of such predicates, it is tempting to say that such a proposition is 'objective' and that wonderfulness is an 'objective property'. Now certainly in one sense it is, but if the paradigm for objective properties is, say, redness or hardness, the temptation can be harmful—for it might lead one into supposing that wonderfulness is indeed like redness, only more nebulous. But this involves an insufficient distinction between the two types of predicates. For the objectivity of wonderfulness does not stem from the situation (which does not obtain, as we can see from imaginative reflection) that these words stand for observable properties, but from the fact that there are commonly agreed criteria for their application. It is because we can appeal to such canons that the predicates can be used absolutely: the user alone does not determine their application (as though men could play a common game in which each man invented his own rules). But there are two qualifications here: (*a*) when it is said that 'wonderful' does not stand for an observable property, it is meant that there is no property over and above the properties making its application appropriate which it stands for. But this is not to say that there is nothing about the object to make it wonderful apart from the properties that we may mention as conducing to its wonderfulness. And (*b*) wonderfulness is not (save perhaps in the near quotes use of 'wonderful') like humanity, a complex attribute (for 'human' too is objective because there are complex canons for its application). In ascribing wonderfulness one is not merely (or even) ascribing an appropriate complex of properties.

V. 'WONDERFUL', ETC., FUNCTION IN EXCLAMATORY PROPOSITIONS

In fact, the job of one who wishes to persuade another of the wonderfulness or marvellousness of a landscape is often performed by allusive exclamation. 'Just look at those colours', for instance. It is allusive by being an imperative serving to draw one's attention to something; it is exclamatory, in that it evinces excitement, etc. Thus the task of showing the respects in which the landscape is wonderful is done in an expressive manner, for indeed it is an exclamation that the allusions have to support. We note, incidentally, that allusive imperatives would be appropriate in a similar situation where the truth of a descriptive proposition is at stake, when one man draws the attention of another to properties of an object serving to establish its claim to some empirical complex property. But away from the object, where it is being described to another, we notice a difference between pure descriptive and exclamatory propositions—'You should have seen the colours!' we might say about the sunset. That it is an exclamation to say that the sunset is wonderful is seen from the fact that the reply 'Yes, it is marvellous' in a tired, bored voice would hardly be thought to show proper agreement and appreciation. Agreeing that it is wonderful tends to take the form of an echoing exclamation (there are as many types of 'Yes' as there are types of proposition).

Now an important and obvious feature of exclamations is that they are to be regarded as part of the behaviour of the exclaimer. But are not assertions so too? Not in the same intimate way, for the words of exclamation are in some measure like smiles and frowns, of which we say that they *express* feelings. A descriptive statement on the other hand does not express a situation but describes it. Unfortunately unclarity is induced by the double status of the word 'fact', for it is common enough to say that a statement expresses a fact—what is really meant is that the words express a true statement which describes a state of affairs. And therefore, when we say that some form of words express feelings, we must not be taken to mean that it describes feelings, as though 'It is wonderful' describes my feelings on being confronted by something wonderful; it is the target of wonder, not the observer, which is wonderful. Yet it is not right to say that a sentence like 'That sentence is wonderful' is used simply as part of the reaction of marvelling.

VI. EXCLAMATORY PROPOSITIONS ARE NOT JUST SEGMENTS OF REACTIONS

As stated earlier, to declare something to be wonderful is to make a claim, and one would be unhappy if others did not react in the same manner as oneself. Usually, this type of declaration is persuasive, and success consists in getting the other to react in the appropriate manner. Thus the exclamatory question 'Isn't that landscape wonderful?' serves as a convenient model for exclamatory propositions in so far as they both express and invite. Thus they are part of one's reaction to a target and containing a call to others to react likewise. (There is, perhaps, for this reason some temptation to label such propositions 'subjective', for without rational beings there would be no targets; but it does not follow that a lifeless universe would not be wonderful or the reverse, since the relativity of the target is a logical, not a contingent, fact.)

Second, with regard to the notion of a reaction; the use of this word may suggest that the causal connection between the target and the person is the essence of the wonderfulness (or etc.) of the target. That is, to state that X is wonderful to A is simply to say that X causes certain changes in A. Now doubtless there is some causal connection between X and A (in many cases, though an imagined target might be an exception to this, or a very peculiar instance of it); but to describe it we would have to switch over to the language of physics and physiology and would not employ that of aesthetics (just as in an analogous case, we would have to switch from the language of sense-perception). Clearly the question 'What makes you think that the landscape is wonderful?' is answerable by one who has no scientific knowledge and is in fact answered by adducing (not causes but) reasons why the landscape strikes one as wonderful. So the word 'react' here is not used in a simple causal way.

It is no objection to the view that exclamatory expressions invite or call for similar reactions from others that we utter them sometimes to ourselves when alone. Such a use is in a way parasitical —we use *words* to express our feelings to ourselves because we are in the habit of using such words. But in important ways it is *not* parasitical, for (*a*) the existence of public rules for the application of exclamatory predicates gives us a procedure for determining the truth or falsity of such propositions, and so their utterance may express decisions to ourselves; and (*b*), more vitally, the expressive element in the proposition is considerably sophisticated, for the words themselves greatly enrich the subtleties both of behaviour and discrimination. A courtier can cringe much more subtly and delicately than a dog. The use of exclamatory supports to a claim allows us to pick out the features found striking in virtue of which the claim seems correct.

Summing up in rough outline: (*a*) the use of these predicates fits intimately into certain kinds of behaviour such as marvelling; and they express feelings in a way analogous to that in which smiles, frowns, etc., express feelings (and moods, etc.). (*b*) They show at what target the behaviour is directed. (*c*) They precisify behaviour in two main ways: for by learning the use of these predicates one increases the possibility of accurately directed appropriate reactions; and also one can show more clearly to others what the reaction is and at what directed. (*d*) They call for similar reactions from others, in accordance roughly with publicly agreed canons. The facts that the propositions in which the predicates occur are expressive, that they refer to targets and that such predicates are laudatory (or the reverse) make it clear that to declare something to be wonderful (or etc.) is not (in the paradigm sense of 'describe') to describe it. But it should be added that the existence of publicly recognized (or recognizable) criteria, changing chameleon-fashion with the type of subject to which they are applied, is ground for calling these predicates 'objective'.

VII. THE REMARKS ABOUT 'WONDERFUL', ETC., RELEVANT TO 'HOLY'

These remarks apply in a general fashion to the major concepts of spiritual discourse. First, because we can see that the latter belong to the same continuum of expressions ('wonderful', 'amazing', 'awe-inspiring', 'dread', 'holy', 'sacred') and the reactions belong to a similar continuum ('wonder', 'amazement', 'awe', 'dread', 'fear'). To speak of there being a continuum here is not, incidentally, to deny that there may be a 'critical point'. Second, the spiritual predicates tally with the points made above. (*a*) They fit into behaviour intimately (either the spontaneous amazement at the mysterious and dread or the more formal ceremonial of worshipping). Thus to say that God is holy is properly to express a reaction of abasement before the divine (so it is not the sort of thing to be said casually and conversationally). (*b*) Propositions of praise indicate the target at which they are directed (and, as we shall observe, *to which* they are directed). (*c*) The use of the predicates precisifies behaviour (thus we learn to distinguish religious from other fear). (d) They call for similar reactions from others. Thus Rudolf Otto has said: 'The numinous cannot be "taught" –it must be awakened from the spirit'.[1] Doubtless he used inverted commas round 'taught' to show that it is used in the special sense of imparting information: the numinous cannot be taught as a piece of history is taught. For to say that something is holy is not to impart information, save in that peculiar manner adverted to above where the form of words usually employed to *express* a judgment is used to assert that the judgment is held by some or most people or etc., as when the Ganges is described as a river holy to the Hindus. To say something is holy is to call for the words 'Holy, holy!' from another. Thus we may say that the primary use of such expressions is to praise, etc., and to express fear and awe. And second, outside the ceremony and the numinous situation, it both does this and calls for like reactions from others.

The simple analogue of marvelling will not quite do, in that religious awe is often expressed in a most complicated way—in the form of ceremonial worship and sacrifice, for example. But the similarities are brought out in a startling manner by the *Kena Upaniṣad*:

> Of this Brahman, there is this teaching: When lightning flashes forth, Aaah! When the eyes wink, Aaah! [2]

[1] *The Idea of the Holy*, p. 67. [2] IV.4, quoted in Otto, p. 192.

And so it is not surprising that the reaction to the numinous is often expressed without the use of words or by such mysterious cries as OM (in Brāhmanism)[1] 'Halleluiah', etc. It is also understandable that men of diverse nations could understand the Apostles when they spoke with tongues.[2]

VIII. DIFFERENCES BETWEEN THE HOLY AND THE WONDERFUL

But at the same time we must note the differences between the reactions expressed in worship and marvelling at the wonderful. (*a*) Worship is usually enjoined as a regular practice: so it is not simply a spontaneous expression of feeling, as when we exclaim in surprise. True, there are occasions when religious awe and dread are evinced in this manner, as were Job's, when Yahweh appeared to him out of a whirlwind,[3] but most often such expression occurs

[1] This sound plays a considerable part in Upaniṣadic writings and is used as a symbol for Brahman, cp. *Chāndogya Upan.*, I.4.5: 'he who knowing it thus praises this syllable' (n.b. *akṣaram* can either mean 'syllable' or 'imperishable'/'uncompounded') 'takes refuge in that syllable, in the immortal fearless sound, and having entered it, he becomes immortal, even as the gods become immortal'. In *Aitareya Brāhmaṇa*, V.32, it is treated as expressing the essence of the Vedas and of the universe. Its more usual liturgical use was as a response by the offering priest (*adhvaryu*) to each Ṛg-Vedic verse uttered by the reciting priest (*hotṛ*) and thus roughly equals 'Amen'. And so its employment as a symbol for Brahman is not unlike the use made of 'Amen' by St. John the Divine in *Revelations*, iii.14: 'These things saith the Amen, the faithful and true witness, the beginning of the creation of God' (I owe this comparison to J. N. Rawson, *The Kaṭha Upaniṣad*, pp. 102–3)—and compare *Isaiah*, lxv.16 ('the God of Amen'). Deussen maintains that it is essentially the unknowableness of the first principle of the universe that 'Om' is meant to express, and both Rawson and Radhakrishnan (apud *Kaṭha Upan.*, I.2.16) object that the word, having a liturgical use, expresses the numinous. But the two views can be reconciled by pointing to the two-sidedness of Brahman (as the object of worship and as the Ātman or Self within): 'Om' is used to express on the one hand the mysteriousness of the adorable reality behind the world and on the other the ineffability of the mystical realisation of the Ātman. Deussen was, of course, wrong to overlook the sound's liturgical origin. For the general subject of what Otto calls 'numinous sounds', see App. III to his *The Idea of the Holy* (pp. 190–3).

[2] *Acts*, ii.6–11. The author confuses glossolalia with speaking many foreign languages. Cp. I *Cor*. xiv.2: 'For he that speaketh in an unknown tongue speaketh not unto men but unto God; for no man understandeth him; howbeit in the spirit he speaketh mysteries.' Thus in one sense of 'understand' their 'words' could not be understood; but yet listeners could understand the point (so to speak) of their utterance. Hence the division of opinion among the audience.

[3] *Job*, xl.3ff.

outside the ritual. We are not indeed to suppose that the God-fearing man is necessarily one who is frequently attacked by gusts of dread. Thus it would be wrong to look on religious fear just as a short-term agitation or disposition to such. Or rather, since there are occasions upon which the feeling of dread before the holy is called 'religious fear', we should say that 'religious fear' in a very common sense does not refer to a short-term agitation or disposition to such. For the injunction 'Fear the Lord' does not, it seems, command us to have particular feelings or otherwise the imperative could be repudiated on the ground that such control of feeling is not in our power. (It may of course be that there is a use of 'feel' such that it is appropriate to say such things as 'You ought to feel fear of the Lord': but this is like 'You ought to feel grateful', which does not enjoin us to have certain specific feelings. However, under some circumstances 'You ought to feel grateful' is used to evoke feelings, and so too sometimes with 'Fear the Lord'. But evoking is not enjoining.) But it is thought to be a sufficient indication of God-fearingness that a man sincerely takes part in the worship of the Lord and extends the appropriate attitudes into his daily life (of this connection between worship and conduct much more has to be said later). Thus fear of the Lord can in part be enjoined, since it is clear that the ritual of worship (sacrifice, etc.) which expresses it can be enjoined. But can the sincerity in worship be enjoined? Neither can sincerity in the observance of any rule: this grows with obedience and understanding.

(*b*) In general, there is a difference in spirit between worshipping and marvelling (at a landscape, etc.). First, in respect of atmosphere—there is more bias in the former towards the side of dread and even horror, as Otto has shown. Second, there is a difference of degree in the intensity of the reaction. And this for two reasons: (i) The divine is considered to be intrinsically far more impressive than the beautiful or marvellous. Whether this is so can only be decided by judgment through experience. (ii) Attitudes to the divine affect, or are meant to affect, our whole way of life, whereas, although we may deplore someone's lack of responsiveness to beautiful scenery, we would not be inclined to think of this as a *radical* defect of behaviour. The regular ceremonial service tends to inculcate fear of the Lord throughout one's living and to unite men in a common feeling for the sublime mysteries of (and beyond) the world. As a by-product of the latter comes a common way of regarding moral problems and so a cementing of society under a common code of moral rules; but of this aspect of the matter we shall not now speak, since it is misleading at this point to emphasize it, for one would misunderstand the gist of religion by considering it as morality tinged with emotion. Obviously, of course, religion and morality are tightly interwoven, but spiritual utterances differ from moral ones. It is clearly wrong to think of the *point* of religious doctrines as being the inculcation of good behaviour, since it would then be superfluous to ask whether they are correct or not and patently this is a legitimate question.

(*c*) Another respect in which praise differs from the expression of wonderment is that the former is addressed *to* its target, not merely directed at it. Thus in most ceremonies the object of worship is addressed in the second person singular (though the third person is sometimes used honorifically, speaking to the Deity being thought itself presumptuous: cp. third person speech, to persons of higher rank—a phenomenon observable in many languages). This involves, seemingly, the belief that the divine can hear, in some sense of 'hear' the worship expressed, and this involves regarding the target as in some manner sentient. Thus another model would be homage paid by a suitor to his monarch (expressing his admiration, etc.). As to the sense in which the divine target is sentient, this we shall leave over until the present account of why the object of worship is not simply an empirical entity is completed.

IX. MAIN CIRCUMSTANCES FOR THE USE OF 'HOLY', ETC.

We can set down the main circumstances for the use of such expressions as 'holy' as follows:

(*a*) As part of the exclamatory reaction to a numinous target—though often enough, if the experience is overwhelming, speechlessness would be more natural, as in the following story about Caitanya:

> When overcome by ecstasy in the temple at Gaya, he said: 'Leave me alone. I am no longer fit for the world. Let me go to the Vrindā-groves to find out Krishna, my Lord and the Lord of the universe.' On his return to Navadvīpa he strove to tell what he had seen but could find no words.[1]

[1] Quoted from J. Estlin Carpenter, *Theism in Medieval India*, p. 440. The passage has been slightly abbreviated.

(*b*) To give an exclamatory report of such an experience at a later time (see the story above).

(*c*) In the ordinary ceremonial of worship to express the correct religious awe and to give praise.

(*d*) Outside the ceremonial, in order to express praise, etc., in one's daily life (this being regarded as an extended form of worship).

(*e*) (Overlapping with the above) to indicate the way all men ought to react towards the divine.

Perhaps we should say that the spontaneous ascription of holiness is the fount from which all the more formal behaviour flows, for although it is by no means obvious that every worshipper has had some such overwhelming experience, nevertheless he would probably have some intimations of holiness. Moreover, those that have the powerful reactions tend to be spiritual leaders and so show by their powers of expression the glories of the numinous.[1]

X. BRAHMAN IS BY DEFINITION HOLY

If the above rough account of the nature of expressions such as 'holy' and 'sacred' is correct, the claim that X is holy is not just a descriptive proposition. Further, there is a case for saying that 'Brahman is holy' is analytic. Indeed, 'Brahman' *means* 'sacred power/energy'—originally that created and employed in the Vedic sacrifice. As Rawson remarks: 'More and more Brahman comes to the fore, not merely as a power attached to prayer or sacrifice, gods or nature, but as the highest principle of the universe, the *mysterium tremendum*, the one mysterious, supremely great and adorable reality'.[2] If so, it will at once be obvious that Brahman is not simply an empirical object. Or rather, since the material mode of speech is deceptive, that propositions about Brahman are not simply empirical or descriptive ones. But the analyticity of the above proposition is peculiar. For it is not prima facie self-contradictory to deny that Brahman is holy. Nevertheless it is odd, for it is self-contradictory both to believe in Brahman or God and to deny It or Him to be holy. More generally: it is self-contradictory to believe in God and to deny that he ought to be worshipped. For the ascription of holiness either expresses

[1] E.g. prophets. And running through the Cabbalistic *Zohar* is the notion of the *tzaddik* who can by the force of his personality bring his fellow-creatures into communion with God (M. Simon, *Jewish Religious Conflicts*, p. 78). And in general we are well aware of the necessity for the preacher.

[2] *The Kaṭha Upaniṣad*, p. 25.

worship or implies that it is due. In fact the proposition 'Brahman is not holy' would perform a peculiar function. For normally when we refer to something, its existence is assumed. On the other hand 'Brahman is not holy' would serve sharply to bring in doubt the propriety of a whole doctrinal scheme, including the crystallizing belief that Brahman exists. And thus belief in God or etc. is not like ordinary belief in the existence of something (e.g. fairies or unicorns). Of these peculiarities in religious belief we shall treat later. Though there is, then, some use for 'God is not holy', etc., to believe that there is a God is to commit oneself to the proposition that God ought to be worshipped. Thus the fifth of the Thirteen Articles of Maimonides, summarizing the Jewish faith, declares God 'alone to be worshipped' (this follows after articles declaring him to be Creator, One, Incorporeal, Eternal). If then these propositions are analytic in this way it is intrinsically true that Brahman, God, etc., are not simply empirical objects, and so their divinity is not to be seen in the way sense-qualities are to be seen. This could be one reason for saying that Brahman is not to be seen in the ordinary sense of 'seen'.

XI. FURTHER WAYS IN WHICH BRAHMAN IS NOT TO BE SEEN

But people have worshipped the sun, and the sun is to be seen. Thus in the *Bṛhadāraṇyaka Upaniṣad* we read:

> Gārgya said: 'That person there in the sun, him indeed do I worship as Brahman.' Ajātaśatru said: 'Do not speak to me about him. I worship him as sovereign, as the head and monarch of all beings . . .'[1]

So it does not seem absurd to say that a god can, in a straightforward sense, be seen. To see the sun as a god is more than simple seeing, yet it is still true that there is a simple seeing of the sun and the sun is a god. Divinity on this view, which is consistent with all that has been said so far, can be ascribed to a perceptible object. And indeed we may observe many instances of such an ascription (here I am not speaking of human beings' possessing divinity—e.g. Christ—for this is in a different strand of religious discourse and brings with it rather different problems).

But though it is not logically absurd to say that a perceptible entity is divine, there are two as it were *theoretical* reasons which

[1] II.1.2. Ajātaśatru is here leading Gārgya up to an understanding of Brahman as transcendent—he is willing to worship the sun, but not as Brahman.

make any divine object which is perceptible in some degree unsatisfactory. But as is hinted at above this remark does not apply to incarnate deities. And since the second of these has reference to the nature of mystical experience, with which we are not yet ready to deal, I shall at this point consider the first.

The particular kind of marvelling involved in worship is linked to a doctrinal scheme and it is not possible properly to understand many of the propositions employed in praise without acquaintance with the scheme. Now the structure of a doctrinal scheme is often determined by several different sorts of consideration, only one of which will be its appropriateness as a setting for worship (and even this may be omitted, as, e.g., in Theravāda Buddhism, for worship plays little or no part here.[1] Nevertheless the consideration is important in those schemes where the strand appears. For—putting the matter in the mildest fashion—worship is an activity to which many people are inclined, and it expresses something not otherwise expressible (summed up as 'the sense of the numinous': whether it is *worth* expressing rests upon a complex of justifications which we shall consider when we come to discuss the verification of doctrinal schemes). There are certain things which impress people powerfully: the majesty of the nightscape, the thunderstorm, the seeming transitoriness of human existence, the beauty and pain of life, the strangeness that anything should exist at all. These impressions give rise to odd musings, though not ordinary metaphysical ones, for their point is not connected (directly at any rate) with philosophical problems: many religious people believe that the external world is not fully real—Śaṅkara, Nāgārjuna, Plotinus *et al.*; but it is not on philosophical arguments alone or primarily that this belief is based, for otherwise such arguments would merely induce *aporia* as Zeno's did. Different things have impressed different generations of men: once they found thunder and lightning outlandish and mysterious; now perhaps we are more astonished at the beauty of a snow-crystal. But whatever it is that we do find marvellous, a monotheistic or monistic scheme[2]

[1] I.e., not officially. See later, p. 58.

[2] I use 'monism' as a suitable word to label non-dualistic Brāhmanism (i.e. Brāhmanism as understood by Śaṅkara), since it is the view that only one entity is real, Brahman-Ātman, and the empirical universe is mere appearance—'in highest truth' the world is unreal. But the view is not far removed from pantheism, since the existence of an *apparent* universe is ascribed to Brahman's miraculous power of transformation (*māyā*). As we shall see, pantheism and monotheism are not far removed either.

attempts to link up these astonishments in a remarkable way. The nightscape and the thunder are signs of God's glory, yet the world is in some measure ephemeral, for could not God sweep it away in the twinkling of an eye? Yet we are not to despair at the transitoriness of human life, for that insight leads too to God.

> For the invisible things of him from the creation of the world are clearly seen, being understood by the things that are made, even his eternal power and Godhead.[1]

And:

> The heavens declare the glory of God; and the firmament sheweth his handywork.[2]

If there is anything which is marvellous or sublimely mysterious, there is something behind it more mysterious; and at that we marvel by worshipping.

Now the holy and mysterious in religion is something which tends to be marked off: religious people tend to treat sacred and holy objects as screened and hidden away.[3] It is necessary to keep that which is worshipped at a distance—the behaviour appropriate to a mysterious target is circumspect. The great gulf fixed between the worshipper and the object of worship is expressed in the abasement of the worshipper, literally, and by the linguistic substitute of praise. Hence the sense of sin afflicting the devotee, for sin is the contrary of holiness (though 'sin' has moral connotations with which we are not primarily concerned here). Now if a doctrinal scheme not only has to give a picture of the world which portrays in some measure its wonders and strangenesses but also has to be

[1] *Romans*, i.20. [2] *Psalms*, xix.1.

[3] Thus, Hebrew *qadosh*, 'holy', has the root meaning of 'separate', with which compare Latin *sacer*, connected with Greek *σαός*, *σῶος*, 'safe', 'whole', 'intact'. And too, with 'whole', 'untouch-ed/-able' compare German *heilig* and 'holy', connected with 'hale'. Similarly *tabu* from *tapui* 'to mark thoroughly'. *ὅσιος* means something set apart for the use or service of God (Chrysostom on *St. John*, 82.1), but also for evil objects (Procopius of Gaza on *Deut.* xxii.9). Cp. also *sanctus* (root SAC = Gk. *'ΑΓ* as in *ἅγιος*, *ἁγνός* and in *ἅζομαι* 'to worship', 'stand in awe of', with which is connected Sanskrit *YAJati* 'to sacrifice'). The sense of 'holy' as morally pure is secondary (see G. L. Prestige, *God in Patristic Thought*, pp. 21 ff.). For the ambivalence of awe see G. Van der Leeuw, *Religion in Essence and Manifestation*, pp. 48–9; this ambivalence is understandable in that the sacred and holy is to be avoided. For the screening of sacred objects, cp. the Ark of the Covenant, the Reserved Sacrament, etc.

framed in the spirit of worship, then it has to depict the holy as somehow screened off from human gaze.

XII. PHENOMENA THEMSELVES AS THE SCREEN

In a monistic or monotheistic scheme, in place of a picture of the world containing a number of independently holy and mysterious objects, we have a unitary world behind which lies a single mystery, of which the sublime and awe-inspiring features of the universe are regarded as traces. The primitive notion of a holy object as screened from human gaze and as requiring to be kept so is extended to the case where phenomena themselves are regarded as concealing Brahman (or God, etc.). This extension of the notion has two phases, the first phase being the way in which a unitary picture of the world arises; the second being the way in which the unitary world is seen as concealing Brahman. It should be said that the language here employed is not intended to suggest that the extension of the notion of the holy as screened necessarily occurs in an historical sequence of two phases, (though there is for instance ample evidence of the evolution of Vedic religion from polytheistic to monistic, this process being preceded by a belief in *ṛta* or cosmic order[1]). Nor is it suggested that a scheme containing the unified view is *necessarily* superior to one which is polytheistic, though there are general grounds for supposing this to be so.

XIII. FIRST PHASE OF THE EXTENSION OF THE SCREEN-CONCEPT: ONE WORLD

In the words of the *Īśa Upaniṣad*, Brahman is not only far but outside all this. In the *Upaniṣads* and other Sanskrit writings the words 'all this' (*sarvam idam*) are used to refer to the world (i.e. the cosmos or universe). But what the world *is* is in some measure unclear. We might for instance suppose that all this is everything

[1] The move from polytheism to monism occurred via monarchianism (Varuṇa placed in an exalted position among the other gods—though the cult strangely collapsed) and kathenotheism (the worship of one god at a time as supreme), which is not far from the identification of all gods as one, as in the hymn ascribed to Dīrghatamas (*Ṛg Veda*, I.164), which contains the verse 'They call it Indra, Mitra, Varuṇa and Agni/And also heavenly beautiful Garūtman:/The Real is One, though sages name it variously—/ They call it Agni, Yama, Mātariśvān' (vs. 46). Cp. *Bṛhadāranyaka Upan.*, III.9. The concept *ṛta* (cosmic and moral order) was especially associated with Varuṇa, and later tended to be replaced by *dharma*.

that there is. But this is hardly helpful, since (i) Brahman is said to exist[1] and is outside all this:[2] so there will be something that exists apart from everything that there is; and (ii) 'everything that there is' seems a logically malformed phrase, for 'exists' is not a (logical) predicate and hence the expression 'that there is' does not define a class in the way 'blue' does. 'Everything blue' is intelligible; 'everything existent' is not (at least immediately). Nor do we get out of the difficulty by saying that the world is everything which is perceptible, since this last expression, like 'existent', is an ontological quasi-predicate, and the same argument will apply. However, as we shall see, this interpretation is not too far from the truth. Nor is the world the universe in the scientific sense. The concept *universe* is used by cosmologists in a different way from the use of *sarvam idam* in the *Upaniṣads*. For example, Śaṅkara plausibly (at least) interprets Upaniṣadic doctrines in an idealistic sense and maintains that all this does not really exist: it is illusion (*māyā*). But to say that the world is unreal would presumably mean, if 'the world' is here equivalent to 'the universe' as used by cosmologists, that the concept *universe* has no genuine instance: this would be a shorthand way of saying that cosmological theories which employ this concept are unsatisfactory (see note to p. 13). This seems far from Śaṅkara's meaning, for a scientific picture of reality has little directly to do with salvation (*mokṣa*). A correct religious view on the other hand is highly relevant to this purpose, but is unimportant in the matter of scientific explanation. Where

[1] Cp. *Kaṭha Upan.*, II.3.12–13: 'How can he be apprehended except by him who says "He is"? He should be apprehended only as existent . . .' However 'existent' and other ontological expressions have a special use (see pp. 132–147).

[2] True, Brahman is frequently declared to be all this, and this signalizes a pantheistic doctrine. But (1) as we shall have occasion to point out, pantheism is not too far removed from monotheism, in that the pantheos does not really *consist in* trees, brooks, stars, tables and other bits of the world, but is rather the underlying reality in all this, the *satyasya satyam* 'the reality of reality' (i.e. the essence of the empirical world). And (2) in the *Upaniṣads* such things as this are said: that B. is all this and more (*Īśa Upan.*, 1; *Śvetāśvatara Upan.*, III.14.6), a point naïvely expressed in *Ṛg Veda*, X.90, the famous *Puruṣa-sūkta*, where it is asserted of the supreme cosmic Person that all beings constitute one-quarter of him, while three-quarters is in heaven (cp. *Chāndogya Upan.*, III.12.6). So also with some monotheistic believers: 'God fills all things; He contains but is not contained. To be everywhere and nowhere is His Property and His alone.' (Philo, *The Confusion of Tongues*, 136): and pseudo-Athanasius, *Sermo Major de Fide*, 29: God contains everything and alone is uncontained.

For references to B. is all this, see *Chānd. Upan.*, III.14.1, VII.25.2; *Bṛhadāraṇyaka Upan.*, II.4.6.

the two sometimes cross in an embarrassing way is in cases where 'the universe is unreal' is used to mean that scientific investigation is an unimportant or nugatory activity. But why should not 'all this' and 'the universe' refer to the same entity? There might sometimes be a point in saying this, but (1) 'refer to the same thing' may be misleading, since it suggests the picture of the universe as an entity and this is already a queer way of regarding it; and (2) the two concepts have different roots and milieus, or ones which can largely be described independently. Further, and obviously, to say that Brahman is outside all this is to use 'outside' in a way inadmissible in scientific discourse, since containers (things one can be outside of) are in space and space is not a container.

However, it is significant that in Sanskrit the world is all *this*. Now 'this' is an indexical expression whose application becomes manifest in the circumstances of its utterance. To see what is being referred to it is necessary to observe or imagine the situation of the utterer and the direction in which he points (or nods or looks and so on). The typical situation in Brāhmanism under which 'all this' is used is roughly as follows:[1]

The spiritual instructor is trying to lead his pupil on to insight, and sweepingly points to the natural environment, uttering such words as 'All this is Brahman'.[2] But at what shall we understand him to be pointing? At the visible scenery, or beyond it to the hills which lie behind the nearest range? Probably just at the visible scenery, but in a special way. For the all this at which he points is, so to speak, only an instance of a wider all this. Consider an analogous example, the proposition, 'There is no time like the present'. This does not mean (as we might suppose on the ground that any time is a candidate for being the present) 'There is no time like any time'. Nor does it mean, when uttered at 8.55 a.m. on 12 July 1964, that this time is a special moment in history (like the time of the Crucifixion in Christian eyes). The feeling that this is a general pronouncement, not a particular one, is correct. Roughly, its sense is equivalent to 'Do it NOW' as used in a general way. This latter sentence is employed to make the point that whenever we have a task on hand 'Do it now' is the correct injunction. But though it makes this point it does not state it, for it is not an assertion (or an injunction) about an injunction. But it does no harm to distinguish between 'Do it now'$_1$ and 'Do it now'$_2$,

[1] See *Philosophies of India*, by H. Zimmer, p. 372.
[2] See note to p. 36.

the former being the general maxim and the latter the injunction appropriate on a particular occasion, so long as it is remembered that the latter may be used in such a way that it is obvious that an unstated appeal to the general maxim is being made. We may then describe the situation as follows: 'Do it now'$_1$, by taking the form of a particular proposition and by being used with general reference, serves to show that under generally understood conditions 'Do it now'$_2$ is the correct injunction. Such propositions may be called 'self-generalizing particular propositions'; and 'Brahman is all this' can be counted as one of these. The *guru* points to the visible scenery in such a way as to indicate that under all appropriate circumstances Brahman is all this. 'All this' does not then stand for a visible conglomeration of entities, and still less for a class, but its application is given in the conditions under which sentences containing it may be used appropriately. It is not easy to state precisely what these conditions are, but a few hints may be dropped:

(*a*) It is usual to use natural phenomena as examples of all this, but the way in which they are selected is different from the way we might divide physical and biological phenomena from others (for these are the ones susceptible of description and explanation by the physicist and biologist; but the aesthetic attributes of phenomena interest the spiritual man strongly). Thus F. W. Robertson:

> It is true, even literally, that the darkness reveals God: every morning God draws the curtain of the garish light across His eternity and we lose the Infinite. We look down on earth instead of up to heaven, on a narrower and more contracted spectacle . . . smallness, instead of vastness. 'Man goes forth unto his work and unto his labour till the evening'; and in the dust and pettiness of life we seem to cease to behold Him: then at night he undraws the curtain again, and we see how much of God and Eternity the bright distinct day has hidden from us. Yes, in solitary, silent, vague darkness the Awful One is near.[1]

For a wider selection of the marvellous, the *Śvetāśvatara Upaniṣad*:

> You are the dark-blue bird, you are the green one with red eyes. You are (the cloud) with lightning in its womb. You are the seasons and the oceans. Without beginning you are to be found everywhere . . .[2]

[1] *Ten Sermons*, point 2, quoted in Otto, *The Idea of the Holy*, App. XI, pp. 220–1.

[2] *Śvetāśvatara Upan.*, IV.4.

(*b*) Second, the utterance should occur in a setting of tranquillity: indeed it is required that the Brahman student should undergo quite severe ascetic and moral training before he is considered suitable for instruction in spiritual matters.[1] In this way the force and point of the assertion is not obscured by extraneous matters, by the 'dust and pettiness of life'. Similarly it is difficult to display the glories of scenery to one who is agitated and preoccupied (but his failing to see the glories does not count against the proposition that it *is* glorious, since he is not fulfilling the correct conditions).

The assertion, then, that Brahman is all this, made under appropriate circumstances, provides an example to show the truth of the general claim that Brahman is all this: the world is, so to speak, a series of panoramas.

But furthermore, the world is, in spiritual discourse, frequently regarded as a finite whole. And indeed some will say that finiteness is the characteristic of this-worldly phenomena, as opposed to the *infinity* of the divine. The world is, on this view, a finite object or series of objects which can be pictured as the product of (transformation of, etc.) God (Brahman, etc.). Often this sense of the unity of all things is expressed emphatically by mystics—but for the moment we are leaving mystical experience on one side and wish merely to elucidate the type of doctrine which arises out of worship. Now it was stated earlier that one formal advantage of monism or monotheism is that instead of being faced with a number of independent and discrepant mysteries, all the wonder and sublimity of the natural world is traced back to a single divine source. This tracing back is clearly not an ordinary causal explanation, although God may be said to be the First Cause; but

[1] Thus Śaṅkara describes the antecedent conditions for the study of B. as follows: the discrimination of the eternal from the non-eternal; the renunciation of all desire to enjoy the fruit of one's actions; the acquirement of tranquillity and self-restraint and the other means (viz. discontinuance of religious ceremonies, patience in suffering, ability to concentrate and faith); and the desire for final release. Comm. on the *Vedānta-Sūtras*, I.1.1 (SBE, XXXIV, p. 12). For the need of a *guru*, see *Kaṭha Upan.*, I.ii.8–9: 'Taught by an inferior man he cannot be understood . . . Unless taught by one who knows Him as himself, there is no going thither . . . Not by reasoning is this apprehension attainable, but, dearest, taught by another is it well understood.' Rawson (*The Kaṭha Upaniṣad*, p. 84) comments: 'One of the things Hinduism has always most strongly insisted is the need for a . . . spiritual teacher. This has sometimes been extravagantly and unintelligently stated, but in essence it is correct and follows from the very nature of religious truth'. There is also a long tradition in India of choosing a beautiful natural environment for meditation, etc.

if a cause a different sort of cause from an ordinary cause. Nevertheless God is said to be the Maker of all things; and this fact does point to something which we might expect on other grounds.

The way of unifying sublime and wonderful phenomena is to show that they are connected; and since empirical connections between events have no immediate relevance to aesthetic judgments, we cannot produce a causal hypothesis to cover all cases of wonderfulness in a manner which would explain them: indeed the notion of explanation appears discordant here. So that the unification to be achieved in a spiritual account of the world will be non-scientific. What sort of unification, then, can we expect?

A hint as to the answer can be found by considering artistic composition. A work of art is in a sense organic and in roughly the following manner: Elements in a work have a mutual effect evidenced in two main ways: (*a*) the appearance of each within the whole is not independent, since its appearance would be different with different neighbours or in isolation; (*b*) the criticism of detail largely involves showing how it does or does not contribute to the general pattern; and so the *reason* for detail lies mainly in its contribution to the whole effect. Particular beauties, then, can be linked together if it can be shown that they fit into a general pattern. Thereby their value most likely will be enhanced, for not only would they possess intrinsic beauty but also collectively would exhibit a beautiful pattern. We may expect the same with sublime and holy objects: in so far as it is possible to unify them, they will be shown to be part of a sublime or holy pattern. It may or may not be the case that there *is* such a pattern in the world, but the unity of the world must be of this sort if it exists. Hence the essence of the Argument from Design is not its exhibition of teleology in the universe, but its aesthetic appraisal of the world as a single mysterious work. This partly accounts for the special manner in which the world is finite, for it is regarded as an organic particular, for the purposes of this kind of aesthetico-spiritual judgment: it is the glory of one Lord that the heavens declare.

When it is said that Brahman is outside all this (i.e. that all this conceals Brahman, its source), this self-generalizing particular proposition, as has been stated, exhibits the world as a series of panoramas. In saying that it is unified, we are adverting to its organic sublimity. The model of the world as a series of panoramas suggests the useful comparison that this unity is found in the theme running through the different scenes, a theme of holy portents.[1] For we need to remind ourselves that the types of situation in which it is said 'Brahman is all this', etc., are diverse (thus Addison's hymn and Blake's *Tyger* would be examples of quite different illustrations[2]). Further, there is an extension of the notion of design beyond the harmonies of creation to the lives of individuals and peoples.

XIV. SECOND PHASE OF THE EXTENSION OF THE SCREEN-CONCEPT: THE ONE MYSTERY

Since the fear of the divine involves awed admiration, it also involves an attitude of humility, which is partly expressed as recognition of one's sinfulness, for the holiness of the target is reflected in the unholiness of the worshipper. Thus Arjuna, after the awful theophany of Kṛṣṇa in the *Bhagavadgītā*, declares:

> Thou art the father of the world of things that move and of things that do not move: thou art its honoured and most reverend teacher . . . Therefore bowing and prostrating my body I beg grace from thee, adorable Lord . . . I am overcome with joy at seeing what has not been seen before, yet my mind shakes with fear . . . Be gracious, O Lord of Gods.[3]

But although it is one of the aims of the worshipper to purify himself, thereby increasing his likeness to the divine, a possibility guaranteed in the Judaic religions by the doctrine that man is made in the image of God, he cannot as a worshipper genuinely entertain the belief that he himself is holy, and he signalizes his own profanity by keeping at a distance from that which is holy. To do otherwise is sacrilege (or if it is linguistic interference, i.e. treating the sacred as mundane or ordinary, blasphemy)—for which reason, those who have to deal intimately with a sacred object require to be consecrated first. In a primitive manner, the distance can be maintained by screening the object, so that the worshipper cannot defile it even by looking at it; or if it is unscreenable, like the sun, he bows his head as a sign that he is not bold enough to look on it. Thus he shows his inadequacy for giving the overwhelming praise due to the divine.

[1] (Referring to the works of creation) 'Lo! herein verily are portents for people who take thought' *Koran*, xiii.3.

[2] Two examples quoted by J. W. Harvey in App. X to the *Idea of the Holy*.

[3] XI.43–5.

But although men's behaviour towards copses and mountain-peaks and strange stone objects and the wind and rivers and trees and stars may express in a very powerful way the sense of the mysteriously sublime, there are certain disadvantages attached to limited holy objects. (i) Some of them may be disfigured or destroyed in such a way that they are seen to lose their sanctity, especially if their numinous power is understood in a material way; (ii) their limitedness is an obstacle to simplicity and generality of religious belief: in polytheistic faiths we have a conglomeration of often fratricidal deities, at best only loosely connected by common descent from, or submission to, a chief god, a *primus inter pares*; (iii) if it be the case that we are justified in regarding the world as a finite whole, then a polytheistic picture has the disadvantage of militating against the unified view, and hence tending to distort the truth.

Consequently, if we accept the first phase, it is natural to regard the finite world as containing or concealing not many mysteries but one mystery. But to have the world pointed out as a single composite entity does not by itself at all convey the mysteriousness of the situation. To be an adequate target for worship, the divine must be unobvious and impervious to full exploration. It is therefore represented as veiled from us (and so needing to reveal itself) in some manner as the sacred object in the temple is veiled. Our praise and wonder is more adequately expressed if we speak of the sublime and marvellous and awe-inspiring features of the world not as exhibiting their own divinity but as signs or traces of something divine which lies beyond. So the divine becomes transcendent and phenomena become themselves a veil screening our gaze from the object of worship. But the roots of transcendence are often hidden from us by the opaque latinity of the word, which is properly understood through the *trans-*, the special sense here of 'beyond'; for holiness and transcendence are intimately connected, as Clement of Alexandria saw:

> What product of builders and masons and mechanical craft could be holy? Are not they better thinkers who regard the sky and the firmament, and the whole universe and totality of things, as a worthy manifestation of God's transcendence? [1]

It may also be noted that the technical-looking distinction between

[1] *Strom.*, 7.5, quoted in G. L. Prestige, *God in Patristic Thought*, p. 26. Cp. *Strom.*, 4.23, 148.1: As we marvel at the creation we sanctify (i.e. ascribe holiness to) the Creator (Prestige, *ibid.*, p. 23).

subject and object in philosophical theology is to be understood too by reference to worship.

It must be emphasized that the transcendence of a divine object is quite different from the peculiar metaphysical account of substances, etc., as 'underlying' appearances. For the point of saying that the divine lies *beyond* phenomena arises out of the formal requirements of worship, i.e. out of a particular way of expressing our reactions to the numinous in the world; whereas the metaphysical pronouncements spring mainly from logical and quasi-logical difficulties—though, of course, philosophers' motives are often mixed: Plato's Theory of Forms, for example, fulfilled a religious function as well as its other functions in epistemology and the analysis of meaning; and was transmuted into a thoroughly religious doctrine by Plotinus, who was not to the same degree interested in logical and epistemological problems. The picture of the divine as beyond or behind the world is a model whereby is expressed the fullest possible sense of the mystery gleaming in the finite world, and this is not at all the usual purpose of a philosophical doctrine.

XV. THE MODEL OF THE DIVINE BEYOND PHENOMENA ATTENUATES THE DISTINCTION BETWEEN PANTHEISM AND MONOTHEISM

The distinction between pantheism (as a religious doctrine) and monotheism is not, in one sense, as great as might at first be supposed, in view of what has been said above. For the spiritually important part of the pantheos (so to speak) is that which is concealed; although phenomena are the expression of the pantheos, He is properly the spirit lying within, behind, beyond or above them. For even if Brahman is all this, It is also concealed and lies deeper than physical objects. Thus there are various root analogies to describe the relation between Brahman and them:

> He who abides in all beings, yet is within all beings . . . and rules all beings from within.[1]
>
> *Brahman* is beyond space. . . .[2]

And Brahman encircles everything, is around everything:

> It stands embracing everything in the world.[3]

[1] *sarvebhyo bhutebhyo antaraḥ: Bṛhadāraṇyaka Upan.*, III.7.15.
[2] *para ākāšād: ibid.*, IV.4.20.
[3] *loke sarvam āvṛtya tiṣṭhati: Śvetāśvatara Upan.*, III.16.

We may put the matter crudely thus: that the divine is imagined as *beyond* phenomena when the latter are conceived two-dimensionally, and *within* them when they are thought of three-dimensionally, and *around* or *above* when they are considered as a finite conglomeration. (*Beyond* and *above* are the usual spatial analogies for the description of the place of a monotheistic God.) Nevertheless, there are important differences between the two types of doctrine, which it will be necessary to touch on later: save that it can be noted at this stage that the monotheistic view *exalts* God more, and there is therefore a difference in degree of numinous expressiveness in the monotheistic doctrines. Since inadequately magnifying views are looked on by one who worships a Supreme God as blasphemous, a difference in degree will look *intense*, and in this sense it would be misleading to dismiss the distinction between the two types of doctrines as unimportant. Wrong doctrines are, to the theist, blasphemous because the improper expression of praise lies in the continuum wherein also lies disrespect towards the holy: though it is sometimes doubtful whether agnostic non-participation in worship lies there also.

XVI. THE SCREEN-MODEL, IF CORRECT, IS INELUCTABLY TRUE

It is not to be thought that the model of the divine lying *beyond* the world is an 'as if' one, a useful fiction to do a certain job. It may be a *false* model, but it is not a fictional one, even though we recognize that it is only a model. It is a model in so far as 'beyond' (etc.) is being used analogically and not literally.[1] But it is not fictional,

[1] A rough distinction between the analogical and the literal can be drawn as follows:

A word may have two or more uses (W_1 and W_2 and . . .) in different areas of discourse. Thus suppose that 'S is W_1' and 'T is W_2' represent two sentences belonging to different areas of discourse: then the following possibilities obtain:

(i) 'W_2' can be translated by some word belonging to area II;
(ii) 'W_1' can only be translated by words belonging naturally to some other area and used secondarily in area II;
(iii) It cannot be translated at all.

Then, under (i), 'W_2' is said to be *metaphorical*—a 'mere metaphor', as it is said; for it can be replaced by literal speech); if (ii) or (iii) obtain, then 'W_2' is *analogical*, loosely so in case (ii), strictly so in case (iii). Roughly then: the analogical is the indispensable non-literal, the metaphorical is the dispensable non-literal. The distinction, though useful, is crude because (a) criteria of dispensability, even when the purposes of utterances are reasonably clearly perceived, are vague; and (b) purposes of utterances vary—thus the (otherwise) metaphorical might be indispensable in poetry, and so take on

say in the way the story of Santa Claus is, being useful to get the children to bed on Christmas Eve and for sharpening the joy of their anticipation. For the use of a model in order to express something is quite different from the use of such a story. In the latter case there is quite a distinct sense of 'in order to': the story is told with the intention that some consequence may follow. But we do not use the screen-model in order that some consequence may follow: what consequence?—that we express worship? But using the model *is* expressing worship. Nor is it like a legal fiction, used to circumvent some difficulty in the law (where, for instance, it conflicts with common sense), for such a fiction is convenient, but the screen-model is neither convenient nor inconvenient. We cannot even say that it is a metaphorical way of putting the matter, for only where an expression can be suitably replaced by some other which is used literally is it employed metaphorically (see n. to p. 44); but here we cannot (so to speak) get outside our way of expressing the matter—and because we cannot get outside it it does not constitute a simple but imperfect diagram of the truth: it *is* the truth, if it is a true model.

However, this remark needs a special qualification.

XVII. THE DIVINE IS NEVERTHELESS INDESCRIBABLE

Surely, it will be said, our ways of describing the divine *are* imperfect. Is this not what religious writers continually emphasize? Is not Brahman that

> whence words return, together with the mind, without reaching It? [1]

Again, does not Śaṅkara say that the picture of the High God and omnipotent Creator (the *Īśvara*) is merely a useful way of portraying the divine for the satisfaction of the ordinary worshipper, but is not in reality fundamental? Thus he says:

> Hence there is no reason why certain texts should not teach, with a view to meditative worship, that Brahman has such and such a form. We thus avoid the conclusion that those Vedic passages which ascribe form to Brahman are devoid of sense.[2]

The object of worship, who rules the world, is only the lower

the guise of the analogical. But we usually know what is more metaphorical than what. e.g. 'He flew up the stairs' than 'He sped up the stairs'.

[1] *Taittirīya Upan.*, II.4.1.

[2] In his commentary on *Vedānta-Sūtras*, III.2.15.

Brahman: and since 'all this' is illusory, so the Creator too in highest truth is implicated in illusion. The worshipper, therefore, is still in the grip of ignorance (*avidyā*) and does not perceive the full truth about Brahman, which comes rather through mystical experience. So too in the *Kena Upaniṣad*:

> That which cannot be expressed by speech but that by which speech is expressed: know that this indeed, not what is adored here, is the true Brahman.[1]

That is, the Ātman or Self within is the true goal, to be attained through the mystic path: we must cease to concern ourselves with what worshippers here adore, the *Īśvara*.

These points raise two distinct issues. The first concerns the notions of indescribability, ineffability, etc., applied to the divine object of worship; the second springs from the conflict of two logical strands within the spiritual frame of language, and in particular within certain doctrinal schemes. For this latter issue is one which arises from the distinction between the logic of worship and that of mysticism; but since we have not arrived at the place where this divergence is made clear we shall leave the discussion of this second point until later. Suffice it to say at present that the inadequacy of the worshippers' picture of God in the eyes of the mystic is, briefly, a consequence of his preference for one type of spiritual activity over another.

As to the first issue raised, concerning the primary application of the notions of indescribability, etc., to the object of worship, two things may be said:

(*a*) The inadequacy of the words we use to 'describe' the divine springs from the lack of a limit to the amount of praise due to the divine. For in praising we are not primarily stating but expressing reverence and awe; and whereas the repetition and intensification of descriptive utterances serves no useful purpose (under normal circumstances) save, e.g., to dun facts into the obtuse or to make them plain to those who have not caught what has been said (and so on), repetition and intensification of expressive propositions can often help the expression. Thus it is that we often repeat ourselves when giving thanks or when admiring something. Similarly in saying 'Holy, holy, holy' we are not uttering two superfluous 'Holys'. So with regard to repetition: we are ever falling short of the *amount* of praise due to the divine; and in point of *intensity*

[1] I.5.

our praise is ever insufficiently expressive. So we cannot find enough words or the right words or enough behaviour or the right behaviour to worship God adequately.

(*b*) The humility before the holy which is directly expressed in ceremonial worship is supposed to be extended, in developed religions which integrate the spiritual and the moral life, to the whole of one's conduct. It is perhaps obscure as to what is to be counted as ceremonial worship: a man may be prevented from attending or performing the ordinary ritual, but the invocation of the deity would probably be counted in such circumstances, at any rate where a faith is not too formalized, as the equivalent. Thus there are two phases of the extension of the concept *worship* (*sacrifice*, etc.): first its extension beyond the formal ritual to informal invocation, private prayers, etc.; second, its extension to cover everyday actions performed in the right spirit.[1] As a consequence of this extension of worship to cover the moral life, shortcomings in the latter will exhibit lack of success in praise. Only the purified in heaven with eternity before them will be able properly to worship the Lord, and man, in his sinful state, will ever fall short.

For these reasons the glory of the divine is indescribable, inexpressible, etc., much in the sense in which we speak of 'indescribable grandeur/majesty/etc.' It is also true that God is not describable in another way—that is, that the propositions of worship are not descriptive.

It may, however, be objected that if it is impossible to describe fully the divine grandeur and to render the praise due, no sense attaches to the phrase 'Praise due'; for we cannot have a requirement to perform the impossible. And it would even seem that the duty cannot be stated, since that wherein we fall short cannot be stated. Is it then sensible to say that God is infinitely to be praised? However much we strive to magnify His name, we are bound to fall short; why then try to achieve the impossible? For the notion of *achievement* here becomes self-contradictory; and indeed the whole phrase 'adequate expression of our sense of the divine grandeur'. But though it is impossible to gain completeness in the task, it does not follow that nothing is achieved by continuing with it. Consequently, the injunction to praise God infinitely is merely the

[1] As in Paul's injunction, 'Do all to the glory of God' (I *Cor.*, X.31), and the hymn: 'Take my life and let it be/Consecrated, Lord to Thee./Take my moments and my days;/Let them flow in ceaseless praise' (*Hymn* 256, *Church of Scotland Hymnary*).

imperative never to cease. To leave it today is to do worse than otherwise (and to do it less intensely is to do worse than otherwise). And yet, although we can assign this sort of sense to the principle that God is infinitely to be praised (an interpretation enshrined, as was hinted above, in certain descriptions of heaven) it seems an unrealistic one. For not even the most spiritually inclined man would hold it to be our duty in this world to participate in ceremonial worship without interruption: but this objection is met by the extension of the concept *worship* alluded to above. Nevertheless, the difficulty of 'doing all to the glory of God' may give rise to a regret which is partly expressed in the propositon that God is indescribable. And indeed the expression of sinful inadequacy is part of the job of such propositions. This points to the fact that 'God is inconceivable', etc., do not merely indicate that the full amount of praise that is due cannot be given but serve also within the adoration, to intensify the praise (just so too 'I cannot tell you how grateful I am', etc.). We shall have occasion to return to this topic later.

XVIII. BRAHMAN IS NOT ONLY OUTSIDE ALL THIS BUT FAR

Given then that the divine is pictured as lying beyond or behind a unitary world, it is understandable that Brahman is outside all this. But further It is said to be far; and this latter assertion is illuminated by the former—for it indicates the gap between Brahman and the worshipper. But the distance of Brahman signalizes something more than Its being outside. For if the difference between the object of worship and the devotee is pictured spatially (in a manner found in such expressions as 'to exalt', 'pre-eminent', etc.), this difference is described as *distance*, not merely as separation by a screen. Another way in which the difference is expressed is by describing the divine as 'the Other'—a favourite expression of Otto's. Thus in the *Śvetāśvatara Upaniṣad*:

> When he sees the Other, the Lord who is worshipped, and His greatness, he is freed from sorrow.[1]

And also the same work (with reference to Rudra, here identified with the One God):

> He stands opposite creatures.[2]

[1] IV.7—the key word is *anyam*.
[2] III.2, *pratyāñ janān tiṣṭhati*. Otto's use of 'the Other' for mystical experience is however misleading.

We should be careful to distinguish the distance of the divine from its *remoteness*: for instance, the gods in Epicureanism can be said to be *remote*. Epicureanism does not properly count as a religion, at any rate as a worshipper's religion, because there is no adoration of the gods, and they are not numinous. By the same token, propositions about them are not spiritually expressive but detachedly descriptive. (Compare too the way in which Buddhist scriptures often speak of the gods: these appear merely as another species of animate beings in the universe and their abode is another part thereof—they can be likened to Martian supermen, and *lay* disciples at that.)

The vast value of the divine, in comparison with the wretchedness of the worshipper—for between the two is this great gulf fixed—has two aspects. First, the divine is an object of worship, and the worship is justified as being *due* simply ('One ought to worship the divine' is like 'One ought to believe that which is true'); and second, it is the *summum bonum*, the supreme practical end (and thus it is intelligible that men *seek* Brahman, God, etc.). We may describe these respectively as the mystery-value and salvation-value of the divine. It is principally the former that is expressed in saying that Brahman is far. And also, in accordance with another but similar spatial analogy, Brahman is the *highest* of beings and is situated in the highest world (which is in truth not a world).[1]

XIX. BRAHMAN IS, IN ONE ASPECT, PERSONAL

There was one further point, it will be remembered, the discussion of which was reserved until the conclusion of this preliminary sketch of the divine. It is this: that the Creator is spoken of as sentient—as possessing fore-knowledge, and dispositions such as love. Clearly these predicates are used analogically, for it is not to be supposed that when the Lord hears words of praise he hears them literally with ears, or distinctly, or from a certain distance (though we may wish to use all these words also analogically). Why then should the divine be spoken of thus at all?

We note that, as a preliminary point, Brahman, though usually referred to in the neuter, is in one aspect (as the *Īśvara* or Lord) anthropomorphic. And all Creator Gods are so too. Indeed it is a

[1] For a detailed account of 'height' analogies, see E. Bevan, *Symbolism and Belief*, pp. 28 ff.

mark of the worshipper's faith that the target is represented as having psychological attributes, however much they may be attenuated by the striving against crude and blasphemous anthropomorphism: the theist is held by a double tension here. Now one historical cause of this that readily springs to mind is that in early religious pseudo-science the forces of nature have minds ascribed to them; for final causation was the kind most easily understood, a point which makes the argument by analogy to the existence of other minds seem specially odd—that is to say, briefly, the attempt to allay the sceptical doubt whether other people possess minds, since we only see their bodies, by arguing by analogy from our own private experiences to the occurrence of similar experiences in other bodies. It would then be natural to describe the unleashing of a thunderstorm as an event like a fit of anger—and in this way, when we arrive at the picture of a unitary world behind which is hidden the Creator, final causation would naturally fit as the means of explaining the existence of the world. 'Final causation', be it noted, does not here necessarily involve the notion of *purpose* in the sense of *ulterior* purpose, but does involve the notion of *motive*. To explain a person's action as being due to anger does not imply that he had some ulterior purpose, e.g. the venting of his anger, to which the particular manifestations of anger stand as means—venting of anger is patently not an ulterior end. Thus there are different ways of describing the final causation of the world by a Lord: the Hindu view tends towards describing it as the sport of the Creator—he is playing a game, doodling perhaps, but exuberantly; while the Judaic faiths tend to describe God's actions as directed to an ulterior end.

On further scrutiny, however, a deeper reason for the ascription of a mind to the object of worship emerges. The argument for the existence of God from the contingency of the world, though hardly persuasive as a formal proof, for indeed formal proofs would seem inappropriate in this context and the desire for them, as though the spiritual domain were suffused with geometry, a typical consequence of failing to note divergences, nevertheless contains within itself something of importance. For it holds a kind of reasoning which becomes natural when we ask the question 'Why does anything exist at all?'. The question is, of course, odd. It asks for the explanation as to why *something* exists. Now whereas ordinary existential propositions allude to particular concepts and state that they have at least one instance ('There are flowers' is equivalent to 'The concept *flower* has instances'), the assertion 'Something exists' alludes to no particular concept. It could, however, be replaced by a disjunction of existential propositions thus: 'Something is P_1 or P_2 or . . . . P_n'—where we list all possible predicates. And as such it is indubitably true, for something is a printed page (this is), and this is enough to show the truth of the disjunction. But what sort of a question is it to ask why the disjunction is the case? On the face of it a sufficient answer would be to show why there are flowers (or what you will), and this would show why the disjunction is true. Yet there is an ambiguity about the question. Consider for example the questions (*a*) 'Why is a swan either black or white?' and (*b*) 'Tell me either why some swans are black or why others are white?' Showing why something exists by showing why there are flowers is like answering (*b*); showing why it is not the case that nothing exists is like answering (*a*). And indeed the question 'Why does anything exist at all?' is not aroused by any particular puzzlement over the explanation of some phenomenon or other, but by the shock of contemplating the possibility that nothing might exist: what Tillich calls 'the shock of non-being' (and: 'This word "is" hides the riddle of all riddles, the mystery that there is anything at all').[1] It *is* possible that there might have been nothing for such a state of affairs, though unimaginable, is not inconceivable—there are many true statements (in physics for example) which describe situations which cannot be visualized. To show that the proposition 'Nothing might have existed' is inconceivable it would be necessary to show that it is self-contradictory or otherwise logically malformed, and there seems no good reason to assert this. There are, it is true, some such propositions which are sometimes thought to be self-contradictory: e.g. 'I do not exist'; for their utterance exhibits the falsity of the supposition. And so too one could not sensibly say 'Nothing exists'. But of course 'I might not exist' (i.e. 'There might be no one of such-and-such a description') would not fall under this ban, and neither would 'Nothing might have existed'.

Yet the type of answer which we expect to the question (such an answer as 'God created the world') hardly mitigates the mystery and even in one way serves to increase it. For the sense of the radical contingency of things is strongly expressed by saying that the existence of the world flows from a choice made by the

[1] *Biblical Religion and the Search for Ultimate Reality*, p. 6; for the shock of non-being and the question, see p. 49 of the same work.

Creator. This then is one root of the claim that God has the power of choice, that is a will; and consequently in at least one respect the picture of God as sentient has an important function, in expressing the contingency of the world. And it is this expression which constitutes the allurement of the argument from contingency, which dresses up in formal guise the amazement that there is anything at all. Arriving at the conclusion that there is a Creator is hardly a long journey, for in asking the question at all we are already giving vent to something which is only completed by a certain type of answer. The reply, like the question, lies in the spiritual domain.

Hence God's necessity is religious also: it is (*a*) contrasted with the contingency of the world; (*b*) seen in the fact that one cannot go on to ask 'Why does the Creator exist?', a point nicely put by Yājñavalkya in the *Bṛhadāraṇyaka Upaniṣad* when Gargī tried to ask such a question:

> Indeed you are asking too many questions about a divinity about which we are not to ask too much. Do not, Gargī, question too much.[1]

And (*c*) God is held to be eternal, there being no time at which he will not exist (and has not existed), and is thus contrasted to things, which decompose after a time and so cease to exist;[2] hence propositions about the Creator are timeless, like necessary propositions.

We may note in passing—what will be touched on later—that pantheistic views tend to give a necessitarian picture of the origin of the world, as a determined emanation from the Godhead, etc. This goes with certain impersonalistic tendencies associated with that type of doctrinal scheme, the reasons for which will become apparent.[3]

Finally, it may be noted that the dread experience of the holy frequently occurs under the guise of an encounter with a person—

[1] III.6.1.

[2] See, e.g., Eusebius, *contra Marcellum*, I.i.19.

[3] But the *Upaniṣads* represent the transformation of Brahman whereby the visible world appears as due to a decision. E.g. *Chāndogya Upan.*, VI.2.3: 'It thought "May I be many, may I grow forth". It sent forth fire. That fire thought "May I be many, may I grow forth": . . etc.' And *Taittirīya Upan.*, II.7.1: 'He desired. Let me be many, let me be born.' Compare too *Bṛhadāraṇyaka Upan.*, I.4.3: the Supreme Self had no delight when alone and therefore creates a companion. But the creation represented as due to a decision arising directly out of a desire is less 'contingent' than one due to fiat.

as in Elijah's, Job's and Arjuna's confrontation with an awful manifestation of deity. There are also further reasons (connected with mysticism and with the moral life) why the divine is regarded as personal, and of these we shall speak later. Suffice it at present to remark that the sense of sin one has before the Almighty and the ascription to Him of numinous all-power together generate the principle that only the holy can remove sin (by grace) and make one's fear a clean fear. Thus the divine is represented as merciful, loving, etc. Of this too more anon.

XX. BRAHMAN IS FAR: A SUMMARY

Summing up briefly what has been said about the Creator so far: holiness is not a straightforward empirical property, for propositions about the divine express a humble reaction to the glories and mysteries in the world, which is directed at a divine target said to lie beyond the world, for thereby its dread mysteriousness is well delineated. This Power's nature is said to contain sentience, partly because the emergence of the world from the dark void seems chosen. And Brahman is not only beyond all this but far, for herein is signalized the great gulf fixed between the sinful worshipper and the pure and resplendent object of worship.

II

The Mystical Goal

I. BRAHMAN IS NEAR: BRAHMAN AND MYSTICAL ENDEAVOUR

But Brahman is not only outside all this and far: it is inside all this and near, smaller than a mustard seed. But why say this?

We need first to recall the main outlines of the doctrines about Brahman as given in one interpretation of the *Upaniṣads* which has been most influential—namely the non-dualism or monism of Śaṅkara.[1] Upaniṣadic mysticism takes the form (putting it succinctly) of seeking to realize the Self or Ātman; and the highest revelation of all is the insight that this Ātman is identical with Brahman, an insight summed up in the famous formula *Tat tvam asi*, 'That art thou'.[2] Thus that being which has conjured into existence the whole conglomeration of phenomena (a world which in highest truth is but illusion or *māyā*) is identical with the Self which is to be sought inwardly.

But this latter is not, as we shall see, the empirical self; or, more clearly, the Ātman is not a property or conjunction of properties of the individual; nor is it a mental image or construction out of them. It is something like the metaphysical subject; but that too might be misleading, for the point of the doctrine is not mainly philo-

[1] There is no doubt that Śaṅkara's interpretation of Upaniṣadic doctrines is strictly incorrect, for the cogent reason that the *Upaniṣads* present a heterogeneous collection of doctrines, so that no single systematic interpretation is possible. Further, certain points that he emphasized, e.g. the illusoriness of the world, do not appear at all prominently in the *Upaniṣads*, and some *Upaniṣads*, e.g. the *Śvetāśvatara*, *Īśa* and *Kaṭha*, are definitely more theistic than non-dualism is. Nevertheless, there was obviously a strong strain of monism running through the early *Upaniṣads*, and in any case the doctrine, as is stated above, is an influential one whether or not it represents accurately the views of teachers such as Yājñavalkya and Uddālaka.

[2] *Chāndogya Upan.*, VI.16.3.

sophical. Yet, as we have said, it is to be sought *within*, and other mystical quests are similarly interior.[1] In saying that the divine is to be sought within one is in fact recommending the mystical method, which gives such expressions as 'within' their peculiar meaning. Hence, in order to have a clearer view of the Ātman doctrine, it is best to glance at the whole field of mysticism.

II. WHAT IS MYSTICISM?

Determining what mysticism is involves little more than a piece of prudent legislation about the word—a task unfortunately necessitated by the looseness and disrepute into which such words as 'mystical' have fallen.[2] For we hear tell of 'Hitler's mystical belief in the superiority of the *Herrenvolk*', etc., and of the 'mystic influence of the stars', etc. Let us say that a mystical experience is one which is reported by a class of persons generally referred to as 'mystics'—such men as Eckhart, St. John of the Cross, Plotinus, the Buddha, Śaṅkara and so on. Such men are characterized by spirituality and asceticism and pursue a certain method. Thus we do not wish to call Hitler or astrologers mystics in this sense nor their doctrines mystical. We should note too that it is quite possible for someone to have feelings of joy and exaltation in a religious context without having any experience properly describable as mystical; and certainly mysticism is far from religious enthusiasm. For a most important characteristic, one which we may regard for the purposes of linguistic legislation as the defining characteristic, of the mystic is that he undertakes a certain sort of mystical discipline. The following are a few main points typically made by such men: that they have achieved unspeakable bliss; that this experience is timeless and other-worldly; that it is gained after a long course of self-mastery and meditation (referred to as 'the

[1] Thus Evelyn Underhill, having remarked that introversion is the characteristic mystic art, describes it as 'the whole of this process, this gathering up and turning "inwards" of the powers of the self, this gazing into the ground of the soul'. *Mysticism*, p. 303. And see generally *ibid.*, chs. vi and vii.

[2] Not only in our day has this group of words fallen into disrepute: in the Age of Enlightenment also. 'The word "mystic" was synonymous with "crazy dreamer". Kant called mysticism "Afterphilosophie", which means as much as "pseudo-philosophy" or "sham philosophy" '. (J. M. Clark, *The Great German Mystics*, p. 26.)

Path', 'the Way', etc.); that upon attaining it they acquire a new vision of the world, etc.[1]

III. THE MYSTICAL GOAL AND DOCTRINAL SCHEMES

These men have a goal which is largely defined by the rules and the presuppositions of the rules used to achieve it. Now since these latter are linked to, and in some cases constitute a central part of, the doctrinal schemes adhered to by the seekers; and since these schemes are often complex, being woven of different strands; it may for these reasons be useful for the purpose of uncovering the nature of mysticism to select the case of a doctrinal scheme built more or less purely round the mystic path. For the very fact which constitutes the power of a successfully complex scheme, its ability to unify different strands, can be obstructive when we wish to view these strands clearly. Thus a doctrinal scheme which recognizes a certain state as union with God or Brahman or etc. will inevitably force the investigator to broaden his field of enquiry beyond the range of mysticism: the concept *God* will not be given simply in the behaviour and experiences of the mystic and it will be necessary to show how the different aspects of the concept are united. This latter task is of course a most important one, but nevertheless not one to which we can confidently address ourselves until after the nature of mystical experience in isolation has been seen.

Thus if we investigate a largely mystical scheme we shall be able to see the side of Brāhmanist doctrines represented by the Ātman in separation from the other side whereon is found the adorable divine. Later, we shall attempt to show how the two sides are united, how Brahman is both far and near.

[1] There may be some objection to describing the mystical goal as one of *bliss*. For instance, it is sometimes said to be beyond bliss, since bliss implies enjoyment and if the mystic seeks enjoyment he will not find it. Also 'bliss', like similar words, has a tendency towards debasement in usage. Though other expressions might serve, such as 'peace' (see Prof. Shoson Miyamoto, *The Philosophical Basis of Peace in Buddhism*, Atti del VIII Congresso Internazionale di Storia delle Religioni, pp. 198–200), 'ecstasy' (E. Underhill, *Mysticism*, ch. viii), etc., 'bliss' has the advantage of being the common translation of the Sanskrit *ānanda*, frequently used of the mystical state (see, e.g., *Taittirīya Upan.*, II.8.1) and also used to describe an aspect of the nature of Brahman; and it is a reasonable word for the Pāli *sukha*, used in connection with nirvāṇa. Further, it is necessary here to give a somewhat schematic account of mystical bliss, in order that we may have a model of the mystical strand.

IV. THERAVĀDA BUDDHISM IS BUILT LARGELY ROUND THE MYSTICAL PATH

A doctrinal scheme suiting our purposes is to be found in Theravāda Buddhism, Mahāyāna and Tibetan Buddhism having assumed a rather different shape. For whereas in Brāhmanism we have such propositions as 'Brahman is all this', 'Brahman created all this', etc.; and in Christianity, 'God created the world', 'Men are the sons of God', etc.; in Theravāda no connection is maintained between propositions about the attainment of a certain condition (nirvāṇa) which is analogous to the State described as union with Allah, seeing Brahman, etc., and those of the form '— created the world', '— is the Supreme Ruler', etc. (we could not fill in with 'nirvāṇa' here). But it might be thought that so different are the concepts *Brahman-Ātman, God, Allah,* etc., on the one hand and *nirvāṇa* on the other, that it would be quite inappropriate to take Theravāda as a model of the mystical strand as it appears in other doctrinal schemes. And certainly, as has been said, concepts draw their substance from the *whole* of the schemes in which they appear and so one cannot claim too much for crude comparisons: each spiritual concept seems incurably particular. Just as in games the concept *goal* differs according to the rules of each game, so will a concept such as *God.* Nevertheless, some analogies can be drawn and a crude chemistry of doctrinal schemes can be constructed. By taking such a scheme as Theravāda or Sāṅkhya as a model of the mystical element without too much admixture and Stoicism, say, as a model of pantheism (or, more sharply, early Islām as a model of the worship strand), it may be possible to predict the type of scheme in which the two strands are interwoven. They do not of course remain unchanged in the combination, for one of the theoretical or formal virtues of a successfully complex doctrinal scheme is that it really *does* combine the elements—for if they remained the same this fusion would not be effected.

To show that there is at least some case for saying that the predominant element in Theravāda appears, albeit somewhat transmuted, in theistic faiths, the following list of propositions may well be scrutinized:

(*a*) 'The wise man . . . , seeing the point of this, should quickly clear the path leading to nirvāṇa.' [1]

(*b*) 'Those who are continually alert, who work at it day and night, who seek nirvāṇa—their delusions die away.' [2]

(*c*) 'The attainment of nirvāṇa, without clinging to the world, is the Supreme Good.' [3]

(*d*) 'Through his pure heart, exalted and upright, free from the obstacles, disinterested, the disciple of the Noble Ones who has attained full mastery sees nirvāṇa.' [4]

(*e*) 'It is impossible to tell the form, position, duration or measure of nirvāṇa.'[5]

In none of these would the substitution of 'God' for 'nirvāṇa' seem unnatural. With regard to (*a*) and (*b*), mystics commonly speak of the path to God. As for (*c*), God possesses supreme salvation-value and thus is the *summum bonum*. As to (*d*), we have already noted the analogical sense of 'see' in which we may be said to see God. Further, there is some sense in which it is appropriate to speak of experiencing God, as too about experiencing nirvāṇa. Finally God also is without form, position, duration or measure (*e*).

Consider too the usual epithets applied to nirvāṇa: *accuta*, 'immovable', 'everlasting'; *amata*, 'deathless'; *dhuva*, 'permanent'; *nicca*, 'constant'; *akutobhaya*, 'with nothing to fear from anywhere', 'fearless'; etc. These are predicates reminiscent of those that are applied to God.

On the other hand, worship and sacrifice—the activities which signalize the presence of the theistic strand—play no important part in the Hīnayāna. True, there remains the fear and reverence for *devas*, *nats*, etc., a survival from or infection by non-Buddhistic religion; but such cults are, so to speak, quite unofficial and in no

[1] *Dhammapada*, 289.

[2] *Ibid.*, 226.

[3] *Milindapanha*, II.i.5. This work, though not in the Pāli canon, is a beautiful and clear-thinking book, held in great reverence by Theravādins. It contains some traces of non-Theravādin tendencies, but these are direct extensions of existing doctrine rather than the introduction of new doctrines as in such 'high' Mahāyānist scriptures as the *Saddharmapuṇḍarīka*.

[4] *Ibid.*, IV.vii.16.

[5] *Ibid.*, IV.viii.64. It is easy enough to adduce parallels to the above quotations. It should be noticed that the common word for 'to experience' (nirvāṇa) is, in Pāli, *sacchikaroti*, Sanskrit *sākṣāt-kṛ-*, i.e. 'to realize, to make face to face'.

way connected doctrinally with the central tenets of Theravāda Buddhism (though Buddhism is tolerant in its own manner by allowing godlings as part of the furniture of the world—just as Westerners might include fairies in the universe without their having any central effect on religion). Further, there exists the veneration of relics, such as the Sacred Tooth at Kandy; but such practices tend to be explained away rationalistically, and again are perhaps mainly manifestations of the popular, lay religion (and here we see one reason for the tolerance of Buddhism, since the Hīnayāna is so very much founded on the mystical path to be pursued monastically that this breeds a certain laxity about the practices of the laity). Similarly, the popular worship, in Siam, of the Sommonokodom (Śramana Buddha) is often regarded as a concession to the ignorance of the laity who, unlike the monks, are incapable of penetrating to the heart of the Four Noble Truths and who content themselves with a lower form of religion. Hence, to sum up, we may say not too misleadingly that the Theravāda is built round the mystical path, even though there are extraneous manifestations of theism and polytheism. Consequently, it serves as a useful example of the mystical strand more or less in isolation. At the same time, as has been pointed out, there are a number of affinities between nirvāṇa and the deity of a complex scheme.

V. NIRVĀṆA IS THE ACHIEVEMENT OF A CERTAIN STATE

Literally, 'nirvāṇa' means 'waning away' (as of a flame) or 'cooling off',[1] and therefore suggests a connection with *taṇhā*, 'burning' or 'craving', which according to the Buddha's teaching is the cause of *dukkha*, 'suffering' or 'misery',[2] and is conducive to rebirth. Thus the Four Noble Truths declare (i) that all existence is sorrowful; (ii) that the cause of sorrow is craving; (iii) that there is a means of destroying this craving; (iv) and that the way to the destruction of craving is the Noble Eightfold Path. And with the

[1] The Pāli term is *nibbāna*, but I use 'nirvāṇa' as being more familiar to English readers. The latter, the Sanskrit expression, being one of a group meaning 'release', need not have a specifically Buddhist sense—for the Brāhmanist, nirvāṇa would be union with Brahman.

[2] *tanhā* = Skrt. *tṛṣṇā*; *dukkha* = Skrt. *duḥkha*.

destruction of craving, there will be no more rebirth, and one is thus freed from the ceaseless round of existence (*saṁsāra*). Thus there are four aspects of nirvāṇa which have to be noticed:

(*a*) Achieving the state of nirvāṇa involves destroying the fetters, depravities or intoxicating influences (*āsavas*) which implicate one in worldly existence; and thus involves the cultivation of good conduct, summed up in sections (iii) to (v) of the Eightfold Path as right speech, right activity and right livelihood.

(*b*) The destruction of the *āsavas* also involves spiritual training, summed up in sections (vi) and (vii) of the Path as right endeavour and right mindfulness (i.e. the struggle for self-mastery and continual watchfulness and self-awareness).

(*c*) These lead to mystical meditation (*samādhi*), summed up in section (viii) of the Path as right meditation.

(*d*) On death one attains to complete nirvāṇa, and there is no more rebirth.

We may thus refer to four achievements within the Eightfold Path: (*a*) the achievement of moral mastery; (*b*) the achievement of spiritual mastery; (*c*) the attainment of mystical bliss; (*d*) the arrival at death of one who has achieved the above and not fallen away (like the unfortunate Godhika who attained temporary release six times but fell away.)[1] It should be noted that spiritual mastery is held to bring knowledge or insight—insight into the truth of the Four Truths. Thus (*b*) and (*c*) are often referred to respectively as the emancipation of knowledge, and the emancipation of heart and mind.[2] The words 'nirvāṇa' and '*parinirvāṇa*' are sometimes used by Western scholars to distinguish (*c*) from (*d*), nirvāṇa being the attainment of bliss together with moral and spiritual mastery and *parinirvāṇa* being the attainment of death without falling-away. This distinction is convenient and shall be used here, even though it is strictly inaccurate, since '*parinirvāṇa*' (together with the perfect passive participle *parinibbuta* in Pāh) is used as much for (*c*) as (*d*) in the texts,[3] the only difference in Pāli being that *nibbāna* refers to the state and *parinibbāna* the

[1] *Saṁyutta Nik.*, i.109.

[2] *ceto*, see E. J. Thomas, *The History of Buddhist Thought*, p. 121.

[3] *pari-* is an achievement-prefix; a noun referring to a state is converted thereby into a noun meaning the achievement of that state. Thus *nibbāna*: *parinibbāna* :: 'tranquillity' :: 'tranquillization' :: 'luminousness' :: 'illumination'. See E. J. Thomas, *op. cit.*, p. 121, n. 4.

attaining of the state.[1] Thus *nirvāṇa* is, in our terminology, the state of one who has attained a short-term state or states of mystical bliss and insight, but it will also be used of the latter by itself, it being understood always that this is achieved in the setting of moral and spiritual mastery.[2] It should be noted with regard to (*d*), that some Western scholars have thought of *parinirvāṇa* as involving some special state after death, as signifying, that is, a sort of after-life; but this is a mistake generated by the desire to see greater similarities between Theravāda and Western religion than in fact obtain. But the question as to what happens to a saint upon death was declared by the Buddha to be one of the undetermined questions (*avyākatāni*): and 'What I have determined hold as determined, and what I have not determined hold as undetermined'.[3] He points out that to ask what happens to the *arahat* upon death is like asking where a flame goes when it goes out; no answer fits the case and so the question should not be asked.[4] But the doctrine of *parinirvāṇa* involves that the saint cannot be held to achieve it until he is dead (compare Solon's saying as used by Aristotle: 'Call no man happy while he yet lives' [5], with the rider that this achievement involves emancipation from rebirth). To say of a man that be has achieved *parinirvāṇa* is to make a spiritual judgment to which all his behaviour up until his death is relevant. Thus the issue discussed in the *Milindapañha* as to whether a saint (i.e. one who has achieved nirvāṇa) can do wrong is in part a logical question as to whether a wrong-doing person who claims to have achieved nirvāṇa can be counted as so having attained.

VI. NIRVĀṆA, LIKE OTHER MYSTICAL STATES, IS A GOAL

Like other mystical states as reported, e.g. by Western mystics and Ṣūfīs, nirvāṇa is a goal, as is shown by the universal references to the conduct leading to them as 'the Path', 'the Way', etc. And this path involves a method (in Buddhism, right meditation). John Cassian, for example, one of the earliest Christian writers

[1] And even here the distinction can become blurred, as also in such English words as 'success' which can be used both for the achievement and the state of one who is successful. See n. 2.

[2] It becomes quite natural for the point at which the state is achieved to be called nirvāṇa.

[3] *Majjhima Nik.*, i.427.

[4] *Ibid.*, i.483–8.

[5] Reported and interpreted in *Nicomachean Ethics*, 1100 a 11.

on mysticism, is insistent that mysticism involves method.[1] Again the whole concept of *yoga* (i.e. yoking) is one of controlled attainment.

Nevertheless, the goals achieved in different mystical endeavours are not in a sense the same goal. Someone who had correctly performed the injunctions laid down by the Buddha would be likely to exclaim: 'Now I have gained nirvāṇa', not 'Now I have seen God' or 'Now I am one with Brahman'. This is not accountable in the following simple ways: The Buddhist has never heard of Allah or Brahman—or: The Buddhist and the others are trying to say the same thing in different ways—or even: The Buddhist thinks he has achieved one thing when he has *really* attained another.

It is not simply a matter of not having heard of Allah, for even if he had and he were a Buddhist he would still express himself by reference to nirvāṇa. Nor is it a case of different ways of saying the same thing, for, on the contrary, the difference of language is one of the vitally important differences. It is indeed this which perhaps more than anything else distinguishes the achievement of the Buddhist monk from that of the Ṣūfī. For in many other ways there are similarities of behaviour: and the subtle divergencies are crystallized by the use of differing concepts. For, first, each is embedded in different doctrinal schemes. And second, they are partly precipitated out of the rules for attaining the goals represented by the concepts. In fact, in the case of nirvāṇa, the concept is in a very great degree bound up with the Eightfold Path (*Allah* and *union with Allah* are less tightly bound to a path, since another strand enters here too). Thus, it can hardly be said of one who has obeyed *these* rules that he has attained to the goal precipitated out of *those* rules, that the *nibbuta* has gained the peace of God. Nor that he thinks he has achieved one thing but has in fact achieved another. (Though there may be a missionary point in saying these things; but even so the real issue must be seen in the relative merits of doctrinal schemes.)

VII. THE ATTAINMENT OF THE GOAL AND ITS SETTING

From the foregoing it will be seen that it is absurd to entertain the possibility of stumbling, all unawares, on the mystic's bliss.

[1] *Confessions*, xiv.

For the latter is defined in large part by the procedure for getting there. Thus Plotinus' remark:

> It is pointless to say 'Look to God' without giving instruction on how to look,[1]

is a stronger one than that of St. Thomas à Kempis when he said:

> What will it avail thee to argue profoundly about the Trinity if thou be void of humility and therefore displeasing to the Trinity? [2]

In the first case, talk about the divine will be empty without 'unpacking' in terms of the Path; in the second, it will have content but no fruit. In the one case it will be pointless, in the other worse than pointless.

Thus propositions about the attainment of nirvāṇa need, for their verification, attention to their setting. Just as, in understanding 'He scored a goal' we must look to the setting of a game conducted according to certain rules; and in understanding 'He found the solution' we must look to a situation of search, so too with 'He attained nirvāṇa' we must attend to the setting. Even if a boy were kicking a football about by himself and then deftly shot it between the posts, we could only understand this as a goal on the supposition that he was pretending to play a game; even if someone while watching an opera were to cry 'I know the answer', we could only understand this oddly-situated solution by reference to another situation, some search that this Archimedes had been conducting. So too it would hardly make sense to speak of someone's realizing nirvāṇa unless certain conditions had previously been fulfilled, unless, so to speak, the stage had been set. Thus these conditions are not merely (or perhaps even) to be thought of as causal conditions, for unless they obtain it is *inappropriate* to say that nirvāṇa has been achieved. One must advance along the Eightfold Path. To verify the proposition 'He has attained nirvāṇa' one must consult the rules.

But it may be objected that there is a hint of an unjust comparison. For though it is true that concepts such as *goal*, *touch*, etc. (and others found in games-contexts), are precipitated by the rules, these rules are conventional, whereas the rules for realizing nirvāṇa constitute *advice* on how to succeed (like, not the rules of a game, but the rules for becoming proficient at it). Now in this case the goal is prior to the rules whereas in the other case this is

[1] *Enneads*, II.9.15. [2] *Imitatio Christi*, I.1.3.

not so. We set up the target and then seek how to hit it—the target arises neither out of our search on how to hit it nor out of conventions as to what will constitute a target. Did not the Buddha so often employ a medical analogy, suggesting that nirvāṇa was a cure and that the cure can be effected in a certain way?

There are two points here to be kept distinct. (*a*) What are the conditions under which we would count a change of character as ascribable to the attainment of nirvāṇa? (*b*) What are the causal conditions of such an attainment?

As for (*b*), it can be supposed that a certain pattern of life and direction of effort, as adumbrated in the Noble Eightfold Path, is likely to lead to liberation. Without delving too deeply into the foggy problem of what kind of causal connection is involved here we can at least make this modest claim. But we must nevertheless take account of one complication, namely that at least there must be some hope or intention of uprooting the misery-producing craving within us. But this 'must' is not simply causal in import, for otherwise, if there were no such hope or intention, it would not be unlikely but absurd to speak of an achievement. Thus one logically cannot attain to nirvāṇa by accident.

As for (*a*), since the goal is not capable of direct definition, and since it has to be indicated by the direction in which it lies, a necessary part of its description consists of the rules to be used in order to reach it; and therefore the behaviour expected of one who travels the Path must be referred to in considering the claim to have attained it. The correct pre-arrival behaviour is therefore one of the conditions which would have to be fulfilled before one could be said to have realized nirvāṇa. Over and above this, the nature of the goal is described within the framework of the doctrinal scheme under whose aegis the spiritual activity takes place, and this will to some extent affect the rules—for example, John Cassian pays some considerable attention to mystical *prayer*; but in a faith where prayer is not used because inapplicable —since there is no God—this part of the mystic's training will not appear.[1]

We may state the matter succinctly thus: The nature of the

[1] *Confessions* x, xi. But Cassian's description of such prayer is, it should be noted, rather different from that of ordinary prayer, being ineffable, expressed by groanings and sighs that cannot be uttered, etc. In some respects it is not far off rapture or bliss.

goal is revealed in the rules enjoined for its attainment, which are affected not merely by differing conceptions of the mystical journey, but also by differing features in the doctrinal schemes. Further, the attainer of the goal must intend to, in the sense that he deliberately submits to the enjoined rules, with the hope or intention of attaining the goal. The pre-arrival conditions which have to be fulfilled before the claim to have achieved nirvāṇa can be entertained are: the attainment of moral and spiritual mastery, as under stages (i) to (vii) of the Eightfold Path. Hence the claim is not a simple one to have had some particular experience or experiences: for the setting involved in the claim stretches well before the time of blissful rapture and the achievement is the achievement of a particular sort of goal.

VIII. A COROLLARY: HOW MISSIONARY UTTERANCES ABOUT NIRVĀṆA ARE TO BE INTERPRETED

It was said above[1] that, though in a way misleading, the missionary claim that one who has become *nibbuta* has really gained the peace of God (or etc.) may have some point, which can be explicated as follows: 'Our doctrinal scheme presents the truth about reality, whereas the Buddhist one is at least incomplete. Nevertheless, the Buddhist, in seeking what he calls nirvāṇa, is doing something not unlike what our mystics are doing, and so we can conveniently describe his achievement in our terms.' By so doing the missionary presses his belief, not necessarily in an unjustifiable way, upon his hearers, for indeed if his own faith is the true one, some account must be given of the deeper insights of other religions. But of course this account is in effect part of or a consequence of his own doctrine: it cannot be a statement of the other man's. Nor can it amount to saying that the other man has made a wrong diagnosis of his own pursuit, since his activities are *what it means* to take the Path to nirvāṇa. And at this level of complexity of concepts, it cannot be said that the Buddhist and the non-Buddhist merely use different words for the same thing, a situation which gives rise to the incurable particularity of spiritual concepts. Thus missionary translations will always tend to distort and, by the same token, even the impartial comparative study of religions is hazardous. For these reasons, it is best—as in the explication of the missionary point given above—

[1] See p. 62.

to trace back differences to the doctrinal scheme as a whole, using comparisons merely as a means of imperfect illumination.

IX. A QUALIFICATION: NIRVĀṆA A SPECIAL KIND OF GOAL

It is at this point convenient to mention a further complication to what has been depicted so far. The bliss is hoped for but not strictly intended. For in saying that bliss is the mystic's goal, we may well be confronted with the objection that spiritual teachers commonly impress upon their pupils that they are not to expect to gain such bliss. In Zen Buddhism this is particularly clearly (though paradoxically) insisted on: our target must be hit without aiming;[1] and we may compare the general Buddhist doctrine that we must fight free not merely from sensual desires, but also from *vibhavataṇhā*, the thirst for release from existence. How then can we call such bliss (and its consequent state of tranquillity) a goal? Maybe it is thus: we cannot be sure of attaining the goal, and so we should not expect to; but we can hope for it, and put ourselves upon the Path. For expectations of achievement militate against success. But this is not the whole story. For there is something even logically wrong about speaking of intending something which we are not sure is within our power (that is, reasonably certain it is such that we might be able to achieve). We cannot intend to realize nirvāṇa, but we can hope that setting ourselves on the Path may bear fruit. In this respect the hope of nirvāṇa is somewhat like the hope of happiness: we would gladly be happy, but it is not a practical aim which we can set ourselves.

X. THE BLISS OF NIRVĀṆA LIES WITHIN

It was said at the outset of the chapter that the mystical quest is interior. But there still remains some obscurity as to how 'within' and such expressions are used in such contexts. A consideration of this point will lead us on to see another aspect of the confirmation of a mystical claim (we have already adverted to the pre-arrival requirements, but these are obviously not the only ones).

First, some preliminary remarks about such feelings as bliss and

[1] See, passim, E. Herrigel's strikingly beautiful book, *Zen in the Art of Archery*. Also in characterizing the goal as (short-term) bliss rather than, say, serenity we slightly simplify matters, since the supreme state is sometimes said to be 'beyond bliss' (see later, pp. 98, 99).

joy. An experience of bliss is 'private' and cannot be shared, except in the way feelings are shared. That is: to feel bliss is not like seeing a table—two people can see the same table, but they cannot feel the same bliss, except in the sense that they both, under similar circumstances, feel bliss. The evidence that a man is feeling bliss or joy lies in his behaviour, including the utterances he makes, but not in the way we might infer that a man has seen something by observing his behaviour; for the feeling is revealed in the behaviour, not so the perception. Thus the utterances of the blissful are not reports of bliss, as though he were making a private eye-witness report. (Though there is a sense to 'reporting one's bliss' as when at t_2 a person reports that at t_1 he had a feeling of bliss: in so far as he is speaking of the feeling he is re-expressing his joy, like the man who smiles while reminiscing.)

That utterances of joy and bliss are not reports relying on introspection can be explained as follows:

Such a sentence as 'My joy is overwhelming' is used to express one's joy and is 'part of' one's behaviour. If it is untrue that one's joy is great, then such an utterance is insincere, not merely false. But what would be meant by saying it is *true or false* that one's joy is overwhelming? If that proposition can be true or false, why not say that one either describes or misdescribes, reports or misreports, a certain situation that obtains? There is, it may be added, no reason why a sentence should not be used in more ways than one at the same time. Why should this utterance not both be part of one's behaviour *and* a description of one's experience?

The picture we might have here would be something as follows: Being joyful is (i) behaving joyfully, and (ii) having a certain feeling. (i) is publicly observable, (ii) is not. So 'Ānanda is joyful' reports two facts, a behavioural fact and a feeling fact, and Ānanda's utterance is both part of the behavioural fact and a report of the feeling fact. But if there are two facts they should be separately statable (this remark is, of course, really about the nature of facts). Thus Ānanda might say: 'I have a certain sort of feeling, but by this I do not mean that I am behaving or even liable to behave in a particular way.' But if all reference to behaviour is cut out, he is for ever unable to explain what sort of feeling it is, since we define feelings by reference to behaviour. Thus we have to restate the distinction we tried to set out above in a different way: Being joyful is (i) being liable to behave joyfully and/or (ii) behaving joyfully.

For what we wished to point to was the distinction between manifested and unmanifested feelings. For though to use words like 'joyful' joyfully-behaving persons must be exhibited, and we place their feelings by reference to their behaviour, it often happens that Ānanda feels joyful without manifesting any signs thereof. But it would of course be absurd for Ānanda to believe himself joyful and yet deny that he would like to smile and/or etc., provided there is no reason for concealing his joy. The natural behaviour is replaced by another sort—and it is this replacement that is picturesquely referred to as 'masking his feelings'. When we wish to refer to such a concealed feeling, we construct a picture of the natural pattern of behaviour underlying the overt one. It is important to remember that behaviour is not here simply a matter of doing things which might be regarded as consequences of having feelings, for it includes most intimately the smiles and frowns which reveal the feelings; and in so far as behaviour *is* a consequence of having feelings it is also a consequence of these expressive smiles and frowns.

Since then (i) the experience is not localized like the smile, since first we define it in other ways than by the smile and second regard the behaviour as manifesting the feeling; (ii) it belongs to Ānanda in a way it belongs and could belong to no one else; and (iii) what we see, on the surface, and even under the surface, of the organism, is not always a good guide as to how Ānanda really feels; we therefore picturesquely say that the bliss or joy is 'inside' Ānanda. Thus too, the mystic, in hoping for nirvāṇa, looks for it within. There is, too, a further way in which the bliss is within, a reinforcement for the picture, since it is beyond the external world (not by looking around us do we find nirvāṇa): as to this notion of the 'external world' that bliss is internal to, a more detailed discussion follows later.[1] But to say that bliss is within is to use 'within' picturesquely, since in the ordinary sense it cannot, of course, be found inside the organism, as the heart or liver (though, incidentally, an additional reason for the placing of agitations like fear within is that one perceives changes literally inside, like the throbbing of the heart or the dryness of the throat).

When Ānanda says 'I am feeling joyful', this is true if he is feeling joyful. But also, in the way his smile expresses his joy, so does this utterance. The position would then seem to be that as a descriptive statement it is partly about itself as an expression of

[1] See pp. 81–104.

feeling. But a more economical account of the matter is this: the rules for this form of proposition are such that it may only appropriately be made when the corresponding non-egocentric proposition ('Ānanda is feeling joyful') is true. This is the snug epistemological fit required of such utterances; and where the requirement is not fulfilled the utterance constitutes pretence, insincerity or hypocrisy and in favourable circumstances tact and the like. The words help to provide an accurate registration of one's feelings, and the tests of the correctness of the registration lie in the behaviour; consequently a 'pure feeling' would not constitute evidence that one had had such a feeling. So when a mystic reports the attainment of a rapturous state; we can only confirm his claim by reference to his behaviour, both before and after the attainment, including his linguistic behaviour. Thus the *Milindapañha*:

> The king said: 'Venerable Nāgasena, does he who does not receive nirvāṇa know that it is blissful?'
>
> 'Yes, he does.'
>
> 'But how can he know this without receiving it?'
>
> 'Well, do those who have not had their hands and feet cut off know that it is a painful state to be in?'
>
> 'Yes, they do . . . from hearing the sound of lamentation that they make.'
>
> 'Similarly, Mahārāja, it is from hearing the words of those who have seen nirvāṇa that those who have not received it know that it is blissful.' [1]

XI. THE MYSTICAL BLISS IS INDESCRIBABLE

We have seen that utterances about bliss are expressive rather than descriptive: we can know but cannot say what such a feeling feels like. Perhaps this philosophical point is the one which is being made when it is said that the mystical experience is indescribable, unspeakable, ineffable, etc. (and such things are of course most frequently said). However, such an interpretation is a little unrealistic when we consider the function of such sentences as 'My grief is indescribable', 'My joy is indescribable' or 'The pain is indescribable'. To use such sentences is not to state that one is having a sort of experience which cannot (in principle) be described. Rather, it is only of a certain degree of pain that we say it is indescribable, namely a terrible pain, an intolerable one, an

[1] III.iv.8.

unspeakable one, an unutterable one. Such a one is not spoken of thus because it cannot be described (since this is true in a sense of all pains). Nor even because in some way it cannot be expressed. But somehow *words* cannot sufficiently express it. Even piling intensifiers upon intensifiers and saying 'It is a very, very, very intense pain' hardly helps: for the expressiveness depends not so much on the words used as on the way they are used and the behaviour in which they are embedded. (It might be replied: but this is so everywhere. Yet this is so only within broad limits, for in many cases, e.g. where information is being conveyed, there are very wide boundaries of behaviour within which one may range when uttering the proposition without altering its effect, whereas the limits in the case of expressive propositions are much narrower—as is witnessed by the 'paradoxical' effect of using joyous words in a gloomy manner. This, though, has to be distinguished from the use of cheerful words in adverse circumstances: a way of expressing an official front of optimism however fearful one may be in one's heart of hearts.) Thus to say that something is indescribably painful is to give a particularly strong expression of agony; and to say 'I can't tell you how terrible it is' both concedes and yet mitigates the failure in expression. For, though it superficially admits that the agony cannot be conveyed, it helps towards conveying it. Thus 'indescribable', 'ineffable', etc., are a special sort of intensifier. But there is, as we shall see, another aspect of their use to be noted.

In saying that bliss or rapture is indescribable, it is not being claimed that it is very curious and unfamiliar, in the sense that it is very very *hard* to describe it, so hard that one cannot, as a matter of fact, succeed—as if one were faced with an unknown animal shrouded in dense fog, and one could not tell whether it had a head or a tail or what colour or size it was. It would only be like this if there were some mental image which one had in attaining such a feeling of bliss. But first, mystics are often concerned to point out that they do *not* have any images or mental pictures when in rapture:

> The soul neither sees, hears nor understands while she is united to God.[1]

Thus, typically the mystic not only does not perceive his sur-

[1] St. Teresa *El Castillo Interior*, ch. i. See, re nirvāṇa, *Saṁyutta Nik.* iv.268; rapture as *animitta*, i.e. free from mental images.

roundings (does not, that is, have any 'external' perceptions), but does not have any mental images, and is not engaged in working out a problem, etc.: that is, is not even engaged in such thinking as does not involve visualizing anything, etc. (Though, as we shall see, there is at least one exception to this generalization, where a particular type of visualizing is used in meditation in a way which induces a trance.) The question as to what sort of mental images and visions religious people have is quite a different one, and has little direct relevance to mysticism.

We may therefore sum these points up thus: that the indescribability of mystical experience has two sides to it. First, the intensity of the bliss is such that it is best, albeit inadequately, expressed by saying that it is 'indescribable', 'ineffable', etc. Second, the mystical state does not involve having mental images or perceptions (and thus in the *Upaniṣads* is compared to dreamless sleep), and so there is nothing about it to describe (and thus it is unlike day-dreaming and visualization in general).

An effect of this situation is that, in considering a mystical claim, we are primarily concerned with seeing whether a mystic has had this special sort of experience in the right context: for though the mystic (if a theist) may describe his bliss as a seeing of God it is not in any ordinary sense a seeing nor even in any ordinary sense a vision (like a vision in a dream). It is not here to be treated as an albeit peculiar perceptual claim: the point at issue as between one who called his attainment a vision of God (or union with Allah, etc.) and one who called it the realization of nirvāṇa would be: how ought we to describe this achievement? Is it right to *call* this experience 'seeing God'? (And here there is a complex reference to a doctrinal scheme.) In the following chapter, certain reasons for identifying the mystical goal and the target of worship will be given.

XII. THE CLAIM AND POST-ATTAINMENT BEHAVIOUR

So far we have dealt briefly with the pre-conditions for the attainment of nirvāṇa and the type of experience marking the culmination of the Path. But also, of course, we must pay attention to what goes on afterwards. As Nāgasena, in the *Milindapañha*, declares (in answer to the question 'How is nirvāṇa to be recognized?'):

> It is to be recognized through freedom from distress, danger and fear, through peace, calm, bliss, joy, abundance, purity, coolness.[1]

These are the elements in the condition of one who has achieved nirvāṇa, and clearly the experience involves some great transformation of character. The *arahat* is unfathomable and deep. Now the existence of the dispositions listed above is prima facie inconsistent with certain sorts of conduct: for instance, violent and immoral actions. Thus one of the questions posed in the same work, viz. Can a saint do wrong? is largely a question about the criteria for applying the title 'saint': for one can rule out claims to have achieved nirvāṇa where conduct is inconsistent with the truth of the claim. One can say: by definition a saint cannot do wrong—this is not a question of fact. Nevertheless, there is a general fact which is most important when it comes to evaluating the Buddhist way of life, namely whether or not the Path does in fact lead to purity and holiness of conduct.

When, however, we wish to give an approximately full account of the dispositions to be expected of a saint, even though we avail ourselves of such a list as that given above, we remain in some difficulty; for one of the features of the situation, quite often adverted to in Buddhist writings, is that it is hard to understand the saint. He has crossed to the other shore. The deep impressiveness of such a one is out of the common run of human character, and so it is difficult for the ordinary man to comprehend the saint's springs of conduct:

> Whose pasture is emptiness,
> The signless and freedom—
> His track is as difficult to know
> As that of birds in the sky.[2]

Such a one is holy;[3] though this holiness is to be distinguished from that of the divine—the holy man is not necessarily or often an object of *worship*, though to him may be due respect and reverence. Indeed, in a theistic faith, attempts to worship such a man would usually be thought profoundly blasphemous; and in saying that the saint is holy the adherent would mean that he displays some of the sacred power of God, that his holiness is

[1] IV.viii.76.

[2] *Dhammapada*, 93, trans. I. B. Horner in *Buddhist Texts*, ed. E. Conze.

[3] It is common to refer to saints as (true) Brahmins in Buddhist writings (i.e. the priestly-caste concept is repudiated, but the notion of a holy person retained).

derivative. We can perhaps best understand so-called holiness of character by comparing it briefly with goodness.

A strict dividing line between holiness and goodness cannot, of course, be drawn: that is, we cannot mark off the merely-good by a sharp line from the good-and-holy (for it is a general feature of developed religions that the holy man is necessarily good; though sometimes a distinction between holy and sacred persons is retained—thus a priest may not be holy at all and can yet retain his status as a sacred person, one, that is, who is empowered to conduct rites, handle sacred objects, etc.). But though such a line cannot easily or at all be drawn, it is generally recognized that it is sufficient for the title of goodness that one should be moral and is kindly, forgiving, etc. He must keep to what he believes to be the moral rules (provided they do not differ too profoundly from our own: for if they do we are inclined to ascribe this to lack of moral perception either in him or in his society); and he must have certain valued dispositions. Quite a lot of people are good in this way, but few qualify for holiness. For to be holy such a man would also require to be exceptionally pure in conduct, possessing great power and depth of character, together with a certain otherworldliness. It is of course very difficult to explicate in words the first two criteria mentioned, though I think their import is not unclear. But otherworldliness is perhaps a controversial characteristic. But this can be said: it is exhibited in detachment from the affairs of the world, without involving indifference to the lot of fellow-creatures. Ordinary human interests are viewed *sub specie aeternitatis* and others feel that the holy man is absorbed in a different and deeper realm of interests. The beauty of these interests shines forth on his face and thus he becomes transfigured. Thus the shortest way to sum up the difference between mere goodness and holiness is by saying: holiness is a transfiguration of good conduct.

These remarks serve as some sort of delineation of holiness and otherworldliness, though it is better to find instances in the stories of the saints of the human race; for such examples are better than a mere general description—they give the *flavour* of holiness in the story of a man's life and conduct: and better still is it to meet one such, for the impact of his holiness will be recognized intuitively as different from the impression made by mere goodness (intuitively, but not by the operation of some strange faculty: I use 'intuition' in a rather ordinary sense, to cover cases where we can tell that something is the case without being able to formulate explicit reasons very effectively—as happens in a woman's 'intuition': she picks up important clues but cannot for one reason or another be explicit about them either because their precise importance is incommunicable or because she is genuinely unaware of what she has noticed).

It may further be remarked that the otherworldliness is intimately connected with the type of experience undergone by the saint. For this experience is unusual (to put it mildly) and quite different from any experience involving either external perception or imagination. It is therefore pictured as like the crossing over to another shore;[1] or as gaining the island beyond the ocean of *saṁsāra*; [2] or, less picturesquely, nirvāṇa is treated as a place.[3] The *arahat* has, as it were, attained a serene spot beyond the fluctuations of *saṁsāra*. The 'other world' here lies within.

XIII. WHY THE TRANSFIGURATION OF CONDUCT IS CALLED 'HOLINESS'

But why is a man of the sort we have described, whose conduct has become transfigured, called 'holy'? Was not our previous account of holiness only applicable to the divine? And is it not the property of man, when confronted by the divine, to be sinful, not holy?

One reply, with respect to those religions which possess an incarnate deity, is this: the holy man is one who in some measure succeeds in imitating the incarnate deity. But this only shifts the argument back a step, for it is the holiness of the God-man which makes him a candidate, so to speak, for Godhood: holiness, at least, seems to be a necessary condition of divinity, and the other relevant attributes, such as miracle-working, which the mortal man is not required to imitate, must go hand in hand with this purity and power of character to seem impressive. (Note that speaking of holiness as making a man a candidate for being counted divine is not intended to express any sort of adoptionist view—and if it were adoptionism it would be 'logical adoptionism', which would be quite unlike the usual adoptionist view, which gains its

[1] E.g. *Sutta-nipāta*, 322.

[2] E.g., *ibid.*, 1093–4 (*dīpa* means also 'terra firma', an appropriate sense here in that there is 'no beyond', i.e. no *saṁsāra* beyond).

[3] E.g. *Saṁyutta Nik.*, iii.143: nirvāṇa as the 'everlasting place' (*accutam padam*).

heretical flavour from being suffused with the picture of the Father waiting to adopt a suitable Son; whereas we are here merely concerned with the criteria for recognizing a possible Son of God, and our liberty to withold recognition in unsuitable cases, such as that of Simon Magus, does not involve believing that a recognized Son of God was not with the Father from the beginning.) Thus the question of the transcendently divine and the holiness of the individual is not answered by appeal to the *imitatio incarnati*.

Maybe the holy man is one who dwells on holy things, the man who worships and prays and does the works of the divine. Maybe somehow the divine is reflected in this manner of acting. This would be plausible, since it is common to count things and persons who have some strong connection with the divine, even in a monotheistic faith, as deriving holiness or sacredness therefrom: holiness and sacredness are commonly transmitted (sanctity conferred, for instance, on a shrine through a ritual conducted by a sacred priesthood). But such an account would not be of much assistance here, as yet at any rate, for we have been considering mystical experience in particular, in isolation from that which is worshipped. We would have no warrant for calling the experience holy save in so far as holiness is in evidence in the characters of those who have attained to it, though there may be some formal features of the experience which may assimilate it to the divine, and on these we shall touch shortly.

But it would seem that, with regard to the holy man's behaviour, there are some points about it which make the predicate applicable in a manner not too different from that in which it is ascribed to the divine (in particular to a this-worldly godling). For (i) the holy man is mysterious, since his line of conduct lies beyond the spiritual horizon of the ordinary man: it is so strange that it is surely to be wondered at; (ii) closely connected with this, he is apparently of another world, absorbed in something which is veiled off from human concerns; (iii) he is pure, free from ordinary weaknesses; and the sin seen in other men is in his case uprooted—this is the impression he gives to his fellow-mortals; (iv) he betrays great moral power, and this power is reminiscent of that displayed alarmingly by many instances of the numinous.[1] Such

[1] Thus the *guru* is often the recipient of *pūjā*, worship, and treated as a mortal god. And his powers are often portrayed physically: thus even the gods tremble at the ascetic since his *tapas* (austerity) is supposed to be able to create marvellous physical capacities—though the gods' fear has another

a man compels more than ordinary respect, but is worthy of the greatest reverence. Indeed, in a milieu where worship flourishes he may find himself looked upon as a god (for there is a continuum running from admiration up to worship).[1]

XIV. REALIZING NIRVĀṆA AND REALIZING THE ĀTMAN

In order then for us to be in a position to say that a man has attained nirvāṇa, he must have conformed beforehand to the moral and spiritual conditions mentioned previously; he must also as *nibbuta* be holy, a man transfigured. Further, we see the nature of his state by the manner in which he gives expression to his blissfulness, both in the words registering his inability to communicate the joy and those too which show that it cannot in a more usual sense be described. The tests, then, for checking a claim are fairly straightforward (even though they might involve discernment), and can stand as the type whereby we check on a mystical claim.

Thus the realization of the Ātman or Self is seen in like manner. But whereas Brahman lies screened from us by phenomena, the Ātman, it seems, is altogether more intimate:

> The thumb-size person, the inner self, is lodged always in the hearts of men. Him one should firmly draw out from the body, as the wind from the reed. Him one should know as the pure, the immortal, Him one should know as the pure, the immortal.[2]

The release that is obtained by penetration to the pure Ātman is interior, just as the bliss is within. And for this reason the Ātman is said to be near and within all this.

It is not of course suggested that the Ātman corresponds in any precise way to nirvāṇa. Indeed an important plank of Buddhist

side to it, for the ascetic way of life threatened the old cults. How often man's religious conflicts are portrayed as taking place in heaven!

[1] Even the Buddha, of course, came to be treated thus. Though the notion of a continuum seems appropriate, it does not exclude a *threshold* or *critical point*, as has been said.

[2] *Kaṭha Upan.*, II.3.17: the physical location of the Self within the space inside the heart and the ascription of tiny size to the Self are, of course, examples of the use of crude material models in unphilosophical discourse —but the materialistic edges of such language get rubbed off when *the Self* has to function in the appropriate sentences and through increased philosophical discrimination. The same remarks apply to the belief that the self is composed of different sheaths the one within the other, the outer sheaths representing the non-spiritual aspects of the self.

doctrine is the denial of a permanent Self, and this for two main reasons. First, early Buddhism was agnostic (as is modern Theravāda), whereas the hypostatization of the Self leads rather naturally, as we shall see, to some form of theism: it is already suggestive of an identification with Brahman. Second, even the belief in a true Self (opposed to the 'empirical' self) is in some danger of resulting in self-centredness and concern over immortality. The Buddha appears to have considered that metaphysical enquiries into such questions as whether there is a Creator distracting from the main job, to attain a cure for the suffering of the world: one does not, when struck by an arrow, stop to ask what was the name, etc., of the man who fired it. And he was very much alive to the debasement of religion liable to accompany concern over one's own future status (whether one is immortal, etc.). Thus his Middle Path includes only a moderate type of spiritual idealism: the external world is not unreal, but impermanent.[1] And therefore the goal is to be found not so much *behind* the stream of events or even, on the mystical picture, this side of it, but within it (though forming for the individual a limit to the *saṁsāra*, since on his death there will be no more rebirth). Nevertheless, nirvāṇa, though a verbal noun ('waning away'), does come in for some treatment as an ordinary substantive, being described as an immortal place,[2] etc., and in this respect has some resemblance to the Ātman. And it should of course be kept in mind that later developments in Buddhist doctrine, in the Mahāyāna, led to a position not at all unlike the Brahman-Ātman doctrine—and indeed it was a charge against Śaṅkara that he was a crypto-Buddhist.[3]

Yet there still remains the mystery that this Ātman is identified with Brahman. How is it possible that the strand of discourse about Brahman, expressive of a reaction to the mysteries of reality, is related to the language about the Ātman, expressive of inner mystical achievement? For not only are these strands closely related in some Upaniṣadic teachings, but, as it were, the

[1] See later, p. 101 ff.

[2] See, e.g. *Dhammapada*, 21.

[3] It will also, of course, be appreciated that the above outline of the nature of this-worldly nirvāṇa has been rather simple and by no means accounts for all the subtlety and variegation of the mystical techniques of the Theravāda: moreover the notion of mystical *insight* implicit in the attainment of nirvāṇa is not here considered, though this general topic is tackled later (see pp. 102, 135). But for the variegation and also the central type of mystical experience, see *Dīgha Nik.*, ii.290–313, esp. 313 (re the highest stages of meditation).

one is superimposed upon the other. And the claim that Ātman and Brahman are one is said to constitute the highest insight of Upaniṣadic religion. To the task of showing how such an identification becomes plausible we now turn.

III

Identification of the Numinous and the Mystical

I. IDENTIFICATION AND DOCTRINAL SCHEMES

We can begin to understand how the identification of Brahman with the Ātman is possible by reconsidering the nature of doctrinal schemes. For the language of these is not precise, a fact which is illustrated by the reluctance of theologians to draw definitory lines round concepts until some heresy renders a decision necessary. This lack of precision arises from at least two sources. (1) The language of expression needs, if it is to be commonly adopted in the form of doctrines and their attendant rituals, a certain looseness to accommodate the spiritual reactions of different individuals. It is seemingly for this reason that an over-dogmatic, precisely elaborated creed tends to appear merely as a list of strange articles of faith having little impact on the adherent. They are, so to speak, outside him and he finds difficulty in making them his own. (2) Perhaps more importantly, the type of precision which we might expect in science is not possible in the realm of the spirit since here it is the mysterious and half-understood that is spoken of. If a pretence of precision is made, then the wonder of religion is lost; and in the case of creeds where worship looms large, faith without wonder is robbed of its essence.[1]

This lack of precision enables doctrinal schemes to perform an important job which otherwise would be impossible. A religious creed claims to give the core of the truth about man's situation in the world, in such a way that one may see how one's life should

[1] It may be replied: Theravāda has very precisely worked out analyses of psychological states, etc., and classifications of the elements of experience, etc. The *Abhidhamma* (containing these) is highly scholastic, however, and much of it is not immediately relevant to the spiritual life.

be moulded; and this truth is claimed to be the highest truth, of far, far more vital importance than any other body of propositions. This overriding claim renders it desirable that a doctrinal scheme should in some sense be comprehensive. True, there is no need for it to present a detailed cosmology, for instance (though this has in some cases been done, not without evil effects—it requires both philosophical and religious insight to see what is and what is not relevant to religion); nor does it have to entail a detailed elaboration of social rules. But different aspects of religious and moral experience have to be accommodated, and it is certainly counted a grave defect in a doctrinal scheme if this is not effectively done. Thus, for example, the widening gulf between the legends clustering round the Homeric pantheon and the moral attitudes of enlightened Greek thought in the fifth and fourth centuries B.C. revealed a considerable deficiency in traditional religion. Hence, a profound doctrinal scheme may need to weld together differing elements in religious experience, different strands in spiritual discourse. It may fuse, for instance, the language of mysticism, born in the surroundings of certain practices, with that of worship, which springs seemingly from a different source. It should be noted, however, that this greater complexity in doctrine is bought at the expense of sacrificing a beautiful simplicity. Nevertheless, whether we should prefer the simplicity of Theravāda Buddhism or Islām (at different extremes) or the greater richness of Brāhmanism or Christianity need not now concern us—though it is interesting to notice the difficulty with which the simpler doctrines are preserved: for in Buddhism we see the luxuriant flowering of Mahāyāna, in which forms of theism serve to accommodate the worshipper within the framework of a largely mystical faith, and in Islām we observe the springing forth of Ṣūfī mysticism in a manner embarrassing to the adherents of a religion teaching profound submission to (not union with) a Supreme God. At any rate, the main point to bear in mind is this, that whatever the merits of a scheme which is spiritually comprehensive, the lack of precision in spiritual language makes this weaving together of diverse strands possible. How it is possible in detail will appear in some measure in the following discussion.

It should be added that the possibility of weaving together can be expressed differently: by saying that religion has its own criteria of identity, which obviously differ from our everyday ones. For instance, two persons, to be identical, normally cannot be in different places at the same time: it would count decisively against any claim that X and the brother of Y are the same person if it could be shown that at some time X was in York while the brother of Y was in New York. But on the other hand Christ was identical with His Father in Heaven while yet treading the earth; but our susceptibilities are less offended when we begin to free ourselves from the tendency to treat analogical expressions literally. It is a common feature of the religious mind to seek identifications, somewhat as elsewhere we like to classify. The term *upaniṣad* itself is first used to mean 'equivalence', and a main function of the writings is to formulate equivalences.[1] Ultimately it turned out that the Brahman-Ātman identification seemed the deepest and most persuasive.[2]

II. A WARNING ABOUT THE ENSUING DISCUSSION

Before we look at the similarities between the goal of mystical endeavour and the object of worship, it is necessary to repeat a warning. In dissecting a doctrinal scheme, we are hardly doing it full justice, since the genius of such a scheme lies precisely in the fact that it does succeed in weaving seamlessly together different strands. Consequently, the attempt to show, once these are taken apart, how they are put together again, is liable to give a false impression. Provided, however, it is remembered that the present enterprise is only a modest one, aimed merely at giving some inkling of the ways in which different aspects of doctrine hang together and provided also that it is realized that any other claim on behalf of this procedure would run counter to a tenet which has already been insisted upon, namely that it is only through the greatest religious insight, born of the activities which give life to doctrines, that anyone can discover new doctrines or show how old ones have been found—provided that these points are recalled, then the following discussion may not be too misleading. It may be remarked also, by way of warning, that although the manner in which different strands are woven together into an organic whole resembles in some degree the manner in which different aspects of a scene or an experience are brought together by an artist or poet, it

[1] See L. Renou, *Religions of Ancient India*, p. 18.

[2] It should be noted that, in addition to what is said hereafter, the Brahman-Ātman identification was made easier by a Vedic theory of the identity of wind (early materialistic conception of the controller of the universe) and breath (root meaning of *ātman*); see Renou, *op. cit.*, p. 26.

must not be thought that this quasi-aesthetic unification is of the same order of importance as that of poetry. For the claims of religion are, of course, much more solemn and profound, and if a comparison with the realm of aesthetics is not unnatural in view of the manner in which doctrines are brought together, it is nevertheless a distortion to append to this comparison an equating of values.[1]

III. SIMILARITIES BETWEEN BRAHMAN AND ĀTMAN UNDER THREE HEADS

The similarities between the Ātman and Brahman, between that which is realized in mystical experience and the reality behind phenomena, can be brought out under three main heads: first, by reference to certain formal characteristics of mystical experience; second, by reference to the type of doctrine associated with mysticism; and third, by reference to certain consequences of mystical attainment. We may study these in isolation from doctrinal complication by continued reference to nirvāṇa. Under the first head, there are three features to notice—the timelessness, imperceptibility and transcendence of nirvāṇa: the last of these connects directly with the second of the two above-mentioned heads.

IV. NIRVĀṆA IS TIMELESS

First, the experience of mystical bliss is timeless. Consider the two questions 'How long did you feel the pain?' and 'How long did you have this feeling of bliss?' To the former, a reply can be given; but it is doubtful whether the second can be answered (except where, for example, the word 'bliss' has a more debased meaning—where it is equivalent, say, to 'elation'). A mystic might say 'I must have been in that state for twenty minutes', judging, for instance, from what he has been told or from the new position of the clockhand. But the 'must' signalizes an inference—yet an inference not about his experience but about his state. And it is interesting to see how, with regard to the knowledge of the truth of this egocentric proposition, the mystic is in an under-privileged position. One may say that one has been in a state of ecstasy for

[1] I am here adverting to the difference in value *claimed*: one who disbelieves in religion would not perhaps regard it highly.

twenty minutes, but can it be said that one has had a feeling of bliss lasting twenty minutes? One cannot say this but not because it is over in a flash like a twinge of toothache or a stab of pain (here too it would be peculiar to talk of the twinge lasting twenty minutes). Yet surely, it may be replied, if you can date the beginning and the end of the state, you can clock the feeling? At any rate you can date the limits beyond which it cannot last? Can you not say that it lasted at most twenty minutes?—you can make this kind of remark about a pain. But you could not in any event notice how long it lasted.

For one notices how long a pain lasts by noticing how the time is passing and knowing that at earlier and later instants of time you feel as you do. But the mystic's trance is such that he is totally unaware of the passage of time, for he has no perceptions. This indeed is one of the ways of defining the state which he is in: thus in the *Upaniṣads* it is said that the highest mystic state is nearest to deep and dreamless sleep.[1] And the situation is not dissimilar in one respect to that in dreams also. The question 'How long do dreams *really* last?' arises because it is observed that people can describe dreams in which activities take place that seem to last over a long time, while the dreamer may have been asleep only a few minutes. But if someone says, in narrating a dream, 'I was playing the mandoline for hours' he is not contradicted by the contention that he was asleep for twenty minutes only. Similarly Vaughan is not contradicting himself when he writes 'I saw Eternity the other night' (from 'The World'). There is more than one way of talking about time. If one cannot notice how long the feeling lasts then it has no duration. The mystic bliss is such that the possibility of noticing its duration is by definition excluded.

Some might query the definition, on the ground that it is perhaps possible to have an experience similar in other respects to the mystic's, but wherein one is not cut off as it were from perceptions. Then there would be a sense to saying that a mystical experience can have duration. But (i) such a bliss is not discoverable; (ii) it would differ from the normal mystical experience in a very important respect, namely in not being timeless; and we should therefore have to decide whether the timelessness is of the essence of mystical

[1] See especially the *Māṇḍūkya Upaniṣad*, which deals with the four states of consciousness: waking, dreaming, dreamless sleep and *turīya* or spiritual consciousness.

bliss. And I think that committing ourselves to defining mystical experience in terms of the raptness of it is reasonable, since it is only from the language and behaviour of the mystics in the real world that we can judge how to use spiritual expressions in the mystical strand. And it is in accordance with established usage that a distinction is made between the perception-less raptness of the mystic and other types of elation.

Therefore we must strongly emphasize the difference between the case of the mystic and that of, say, the absorbed crossword-puzzle-solver. The latter does not happen to notice the passing of time, but the mystic could not notice it (unless, that is, he was not in a mystical trance). There is no sense in his case of speaking of his feeling bliss as having duration. So it is not surprising to read these words of Ruysbroek:

> For his coming consists, outside all time, in an Eternal Now . . . there is nothing else here but eternal rest, wrapped in the enjoyment of the immersion of love.[1]

And Tauler:

> A man who really and truly enters, feels as though he had been here through all eternity.[2]

And nirvāṇa too is said to be without duration.[3]

By describing the timelessness as a *formal* feature of the feeling of bliss I wish to point to the fact that it is not a property of the feeling, for feelings do not, strictly, have properties: not at any rate in the sense in which things dreamed of or imagined can have properties. Rather the timelessness arises out of the circumstances of the experience, as the difference of time-scale in dreams arises out of the circumstances.

It is now possible to consider the manner in which the timelessness of the mystic state gives it a similarity to the transcendent divine. For Brahman is timeless, since It lies beyond the changing phenomena which are, as it is said, *in* time. Brahman is thus 'outside time'—temporal references are inapplicable in propositions about Brahman. It might of course be complained that this is to confuse timelessness with eternity. For Brahman and God are commonly pictured as enduring eternally, lasting for ever, an infinite time: such that it is correct to say that God endures longer

[1] *De Ornatu Spiritualium Nuptiarum*, iii.4.
[2] *The Inner Way*, quoted in Underhill, *Mysticism*, p. 339.
[3] *Milindapañha*, IV.vii.6.

than any stretch of time you care to mention. However, the distinction is difficult to maintain, since it is clear from very brief reflection that the sense in which God endures is analogical. Further, this is not a distinction enshrined in mystical utterances, since their way of expressing the mysterious timelessness of the bliss includes, as we have seen, reference to the eternal. A further point about the achievement of such states as nirvāṇa where their eternity is assimilated to divine immortality is seen in their salvation-value. For the mystic, the attainment of these exalting experiences constitutes liberation or release, and this is in part akin to the notion of salvation in Christian doctrine. For by his achievement the mystic is liberated from the soiling sin (the *āsavas* in Buddhist terminology—the influences which contaminate us) and the distress of ordinary life; in gaining nirvāṇa the *arahat* throws off the fetters which have bound him to the fleeting and unsatisfactory world which still holds others fast. In throwing these off he has thrown off the fear of death; and it is partly for this reason that nirvāṇa is commonly described as *amata*, 'deathless'.[1] So too the Hindu mystic, in praying for release, asks that he be led from the mortal to the immortal. In the shining darkness of union with Brahman he has obtained a release from death, and has gained, even in this life, a kind of immortality.[2] For these two reasons the point at which he has arrived is not dissimilar to the mysterious Brahman beyond phenomena. He has arrived at

'The Unconditioned, . . . the Truth, the Other Shore, That which

[1] Compare Boehme's remarks about the New Birth that brings us here and now into that Eternal Life for which man has been made (*De Signatura Rerum*, viii.47); and for similar remarks by other mystics, see E. Underhill, *Mysticism*, pp. 122 ff. The notion of rebirth could not, of course, be used by Buddhist mystics (for them the conquest of death is also the conquest of birth: cp. *Kaṭha Upan.*, I.2.6, *Taittirīya Brāhmaṇa*, III.11.8, for the description of rebirth as redeath).

[2] Similarly *Kaṭha Upan.*, I.3.2: 'That bridge for sacrificers,/The imperishable highest Brahman,/For crossers to the fearless shore.' (As too nirvāṇa is often portrayed as the going to the other shore and as *akutobhaya* 'fearless'). This suggests a subtle nexus of ideas: if Brahman is set over against the worshipper as an Other it is an object of dread, but by transcending this separation, in the mystical state, one throws off this fear. Thus *Bṛhadāraṇyaka Upan.*, I.4.2, 'This one then thought to himself "Since there is nothing else than myself, what am I afraid of?" ' And for the contrast, see *Taittirīya Upan.*, II.7.1: 'For when one finds fearlessness as foundation in Him who is invisible, bodiless, ineffable, without support, then he has reached fearlessness. When, however, one makes in this One the smallest interval, then, for him, there is fear.'

is hard to see, the Ageless, the Eternal, That which transcends multiplicity, the Immortal, the Bliss, Safety, the Marvellous, the Sorrowless, the Troublefree, Purity, the Island, the Refuge. . . .' [1]

So much, then, for the first of the formal features whereby nirvāṇa and Brahman are assimilated.

V. NIRVĀṆA IS IMPERCEPTIBLE

Second, nirvāṇa, as well as being timeless, is said to be imperceptible.[2] As stated earlier, the bliss involved in the attainment of nirvāṇa does not include the visualization of anything or the having of any mental images. And when one is in such a state all perceptions are shut out—they just do not occur: and hence the importance of the concept of the Void, *Śūnyatā*, in Mahāyāna Buddhism. Thus in this condition one neither perceives anything nor imagines oneself as perceiving anything; and this is summed up in saying that nirvāṇa is imperceptible. For it is not by ordinary seeing that one sees nirvāṇa: the realization of the bliss of nirvāṇa is in no way an attainment made by careful observation of the world around us. So far is this from the truth that indeed the opposite is the case. We must positively turn away from the ordinary world of sense-experience if we are to gain a true insight into the higher truth, an insight which accrues upon the mystical experiences lying at the end of the Noble Eightfold Path. Therefore it is said that nirvāṇa is not to be perceived. So too no man, it is averred, shall see God and live; for God too is shielded from men's gaze. For although there are to be seen traces of God's handiwork in the natural world, they are not features of the world revealed by ordinary scrutiny; and moreover they are only traces and not parts, so to speak, of the surface of that which is divine. And so neither Brahman nor nirvāṇa can in an ordinary sense be seen. It is to be noted also that the desire to make the object of worship absolutely transcendent tends to bring it more into line with that which is found in mystical experience, since there will be a greater reluctance to ascribe to the divine even the analogical properties usually attributed to the Creator. But there is also a tension the other way, which we shall come to later.

As a corollary to the above point, that nirvāṇa and Brahman

[1] *Saṁyutta Nik.*, iv.360 ff., referred to in E. Conze, *Buddhist Meditation*, p. 108.

[2] *Milindapañha*, IV.vii.16. Nirvāṇa is also 'hard to see'; see below.

are both imperceptible, neither can be described in the way in which a garden or a man can be described; and their overtones of ineffability spring from similar sources. As God can never be praised sufficiently, nirvāṇa's joy can never be adequately conveyed. That which has supreme worship value is likened to that which has supreme salvation value. (Unite this to the principle that only the purely divine has the power of releasing us from sin, and the conclusion is not hard to see: though quite how it ought to be expressed is a matter for theologians, for as we shall have occasion to observe there are perils of blasphemy and heresy inherent in mysticism.)

VI. NIRVĀṆA IS TRANSCENDENT

Third, nirvāṇa is, in a non-monistic fashion, transcendent. By 'in a non-monistic fashion' I mean to indicate that nirvāṇa is not a unified principle like the Absolute or Brahman: that is, not in Theravāda, though in Mahāyāna the concept sometimes suffers a sea-change and is even identified (as for example by Aśvaghoṣa) with *Tathatā* or 'Suchness' (roughly equivalent to the Absolute). It is not a single entity like God—but for that matter it is not many things, and this is perhaps an important qualification. Nevertheless, to say 'There is one and only one nirvāṇa' would have a characteristically different flavour from 'There is one and only one God'. The former proposition would seem to be more like 'There is one and only one way of arranging flowers' or 'There is one and only one joy in this world'. Two who attain nirvāṇa attain the same thing in much the way in which two who sing the same song sing the same thing; though it is uncertain how this difference between propositions about nirvāṇa and propositions about God or Brahman is to be pressed, since there are clearly occasions upon which the concept *God* or *Brahman* does not operate like a simple substantive, that is like an expression used to refer to some determinate object as a member of a class of objects. For instance, it is said that God is Love; and this manner of putting it is not simply a succinct way of saying that the essential characteristic in the nature of God is love; further, it is repeatedly insisted that God is no ordinary entity, and even the sense in which He is a Person is analogical. Moreover, as we are wishing to point out, the bliss of nirvāṇa is in a special way transcendent, and herein a similarity is to be seen between nirvāṇa and Brahman.

Nirvāṇa's transcendence can be illustrated from the fact that it is said to be uncompounded, unlike ordinary objects. 'All compounded things', states the Buddhist principle, 'are impermanent'.[1] We have a picture of the world not unlike that given by Heraclitus, though more subtly elaborated, in which empirical objects, which are compounds out of elements, are in perpetual flux. It is perhaps difficult to see how this general affirmation about objects has any relevance to the spiritual life. Yet it is said that the perception of the truth of this principle is necessary to the acquirement of the *dhammacakkhu*, the 'eye for the truth', which is the sign of entrance upon *arhat*-ship.[2] Strange then that this doctrine should have such a spiritual impact.

But of course the important thing to notice is that whereas all *things* are compounded, nirvāṇa is not; and if perishability is a defect (and it is implied that it is), then the realization of the impermanence of empirical objects and indeed of mental states will involve a turning away from the world of ordinary sense-experience towards nirvāṇa. And we shall find, on extending our gaze a little further, that this type of doctrine is characteristically associated with mysticism. A more extreme version than that described above is found in the Idealism of Śaṅkara and Nāgārjuna. Similarly, there is something of this in Plato, where the supreme joy of the vision of the Good is set over against the unsatisfactoriness of preoccupation with the empirical world which is assigned a mere semi-reality. Indeed it is often by such contrasts in value that these teachers avoid vacuity in their assertions of the non-existence or unreality of the external world.

Consider, for instance, the claim that all things are impermanent. At first sight it seems like the supposition that all life is a dream; a supposition whose absurdity seems to be shown by the following argument:

If all life is a dream, then it is a dream containing (so to speak) what we now call dreams—in which case a new word is required for these latter. Call them *treams*: then all life, it is supposed, is a dream in which we sometimes tream. But this is not what we intended in the original supposition. For we wished to say that all life is a tream, and to this we are now driven. But the same

[1] Used tellingly by the Buddha at the approach of death: 'All compounded things are subject to decay: work out your own salvation with diligence' (*Dīgha Nik.*, ii.156).

[2] See *Dīgha Nik.*, i.86.

considerations reapply; so that we are perpetually unable to affirm that which we set out to say. So too, it seems, with 'All things are impermanent' and 'The external world is illusory'. We evacuate the distinctions of content by using one of the contraries universally. Yet these utterances, which thus take on this elusive metaphysical air, never to be caught it seems by confirmation or disconfirmation, being so overwhelmingly certain in their vacuity, are misunderstood if we once forget that in actual usage they are used to point to real contrasts.

For things, as well as being perceptible, extended in space and so forth, are also interesting and uninteresting, important and unimportant, etc. Viewed as being of interest (because they give occasion for pleasure or pain, because they are useful, beautiful, useless and ugly . . .), they constitute what may be called a realm of interests; and this realm is set over against another. Thus when it is said that the external world is unreal, this expresses among other things a value-judgment. 'Real', 'exists', etc., do not possess, in spiritual discourse, a merely ontological force, as might be expected. This is well brought out in Indian religious writings, where we find such uses of *sat* (commonly translated as 'real'—it is the present participle of the verb 'to be') as the following famous one:

> Lead me from the unreal to the real;
> Lead me from darkness into light;
> Lead me from the mortal to the immortal.[1]

And the evaluative force of *sat* is further made transparent by the following linguistic fact among others, that both masculine and feminine are used as substantives meaning respectively 'good man' and 'good woman'; the latter, for example, comes to mean 'good wife' (one who for instance throws herself on her husband's funeral pyre, committing *suttee*—the anglicized form of the feminine *satī*). Of these usages more will have to be said later; but for the moment it is sufficient to notice that the seemingly peculiar use of ontological words in religious discourse is not as logically malformed as might sometimes appear. Thus though it seems queer to speak of God as the *ens realissimum*—as though something could exist more intensely than something else (odd, because being is not like butter that it should be pure or impure or like heat that it should be intense or mild), yet this locution

[1] *Bṛhadāraṇyaka Upan.*, I.3.28.

begins to lose its bizarre flavour when we realize that these ontological words are evaluative. For goodness, unlike existence in the ordinary sense, admits of degrees of purity. The paradoxicality of the phrase 'Pure Being' begins to vanish. Thus the Ontological Argument, though useless as an argument, seems to point to the peculiar status of the notions of existence, reality and so on in the spiritual frame.

So it may be claimed that such assertions as 'All things are impermanent/unreal/etc.' are not simply statements of fact, even of 'metaphysical fact', but have a value force. And what is important to notice is this: that the value force is not dissipated by a lack of contrast, whereas this does seem to be the case if the assertions are interpreted in a purely epistemological sense. It is true that even the value force *could* be dissipated by lack of contrast, since the previous argument could apply here: for if all things are good, say, then what we now call *evil* would appear as 'not very good'; and this will acquire the same sense as 'evil'. But in fact, with regard to such propositions as 'All things are impermanent', all things do not constitute everything and so the propositions retain some life. But how can the paradox that all things do not constitute everything be sustained?

The following poem attributed to Śaṅkara may help to show how:

> Think truly, this life is but a dream.
> With mind fixed on truth one becomes free from attachment;
> To one freed from attachment, there is no delusion;
> Undeluded, the soul springs to clear light, free from all bondage.
>
> . . . .
>
> Give up this Māyā (i.e. *illusion*) -made world, gain true knowledge,
> And enter the path to Brahman.[1]

All things are illusory, that is to say, except Brahman. Brahman alone is truly real. Similarly the Buddhist's world-picture is of a flow of impermanent objects, but set against them is the true joy of nirvāṇa. All *things* are impermanent, but Brahman and nirvāṇa are not (in their different ways) things. Hence the perception of such a truth as that all things are impermanent or illusory is the first step in the upward path, since it turns one's interest towards the highest goal and away from mundane affairs, away from the world. Thus part of the force of such an assertion is that

[1] Quoted by J. Estlin Carpenter, *Theism in Medieval India*, p. 343, from R. W. Frazer, *A Literary History of India* (1898), p. 327 f.

none of the *ordinary* human interests, which are indissolubly attached to the world around us, is worth while as compared with the *extraordinary* goal which the mystic cherishes as the highest human state. The picture of the world as unreal or dreamlike or impermanent serves, so to speak, as an advertisement illustrating a spiritual slogan bidding us to adopt the mystic path. Thus nirvāṇa's transcendence consists in its being set apart from and above all impermanent objects which normally attract our interest and arouse in us, according to Buddhist doctrine, that burning thirst which can only be quenched by heeding the Buddha's prescriptions. But this transcendence, and the way it assimilates nirvāṇa to Brahman, can be clarified further by attending in some detail to the type of doctrine associated with mysticism.

For our remarks above are not enough explanation of why these propositions take the form of aspersions upon empirical objects and upon the external world. And moreover they might be misleading in suggesting that the external world is just what is out there. In the words of a famous examination question, what is the external world external to?

VII. DISTINCTION BETWEEN THE 'EXTERNAL' AND THE SPIRITUAL WORLD

One could briefly delineate the contrast between the so-called external world and the internal one by saying: The internal world is the direction in which the mystics travel; it is where they seek to place themselves. The external world is the world of ordinary experience. The internal world is within, but not within the mind —since there is hardly a proper distinction between what goes on inside the mind and what goes on outside. And in any case, even if such a distinction were made, there would be a temptation to place dreams and mental images within the interior region, and yet these are, as far as the mystic is concerned, part of the external world. His internal world is beyond even these.

Thus in Brāhmanical belief, the Ātman or Self is beyond even experiences such as dreaming, and deep and dreamless sleep was regarded as close to the highest mystical state, where the spiritual man realizes the Ātman. Nevertheless the attainment of Brahman involves some kind of experience, and the analogy of deep and dreamless sleep is defective in this respect. The Ātman is not beyond experience even if it is beyond perceptions and dreams and images. Indeed, if it *were* entirely beyond experience, there would be a strong case for declaring it to be an empty concept. This would be surprising, since it is a concept that has had considerable practical significance in many lives, and it certainly is not a merely philosophical one invented for logical or metaphysical reasons (to get out of some conceptual difficulty—this would make the charge more plausible). One can best, perhaps, illustrate the innerness of the Self under two heads: first, by attending to the procedures for realizing the Self, and second, by considering the type of experience involved.

As to procedure, it is useful to repeat that a certain degree of asceticism is necessary. The degree varies according to different prescriptions: for instance, the Buddha laid down a 'middle path' in this matter, extreme self-mortification being in his eyes as deleterious as indulgence.[1] Why such ascetic practices should be needed for the attainment of the goal is perhaps a question that hardly needs an answer, since it is a common brute fact that our natural inclinations, when indulged, run counter to the mystic path. Since the goal is unusual, it should not be surprising that common pursuits have to be sacrificed in the interest of its attainment. It being extremely difficult to renounce ordinary pursuits and pleasures, it is to be expected that a degree of moral heroism is needed to lead this kind of life. The asceticism is part training for success, part success itself. Whether the goal is worth it or not is hardly for the philosopher to answer, but the question is one that will have to be examined at a later stage when we come to scrutinize the justification of religious doctrines.

[1] Not merely was it that the Buddha found by experience that extreme self-mortification leads to repulsive consequences, but also his middle way was designed to weld together mystical salvation with moral conduct. For this reason those extremely self-mortifying ascetics with whom he at first consorted were condemned for concentrating exclusively on the attainment of the *jhānas* (mystical stages of meditation) (*Dīgha Nik.*, i.37 ff.). A further reason was that too consciously aiming at this higher form of self-enjoyment is self-stultifying. It is to be noted that the Buddha's blend of mysticism and world-renunciation on the one hand and moral action on the other was well served by the doctrine that all things are *anicca*, impermanent, since it confers on the world neither solidity nor evanescence: it is not an extreme idealism, but contains nevertheless a degree of idealism. However, the development of Mahāyāna theism, via idealistic monism, was in large measure due to the desire to have a religious basis for charity and good works towards others. For the pursuit of nirvāṇa, as in early and Theravāda Buddhism, still looked too egocentric. Hence too the evolution of the *Bodhisattva* concept: the Buddha-to-be renounces his own nirvāṇa in order to help others, by staying in the world, towards this goal.

Now if the rationale of this ascetic procedure is the destruction of most of our common interests or at least the destruction of attachment to these interests, this will ultimately involve the creation of a judgment that common interests and pursuits are nugatory and vapid. And this can be exhibited in the peculiar control of our perceptions used. Consider the following example.

I am sitting in a sun-lit garden. If I look round, even lazily, I shall find something which attracts or is liable to attract my attention. However, if it is borne in upon me that common interests are dangerous for my spiritual welfare, i.e. that to be interested in things which are ordinarily regarded as interesting whenever I come across them prevents my becoming tranquil and attaining a spiritual peace, I might wish to cultivate a spirit of detachment from my surroundings, whatever they might be. By way of practice, I may refuse to let my gaze wander round the garden but concentrate for the moment, say, on a patch of grass. This procedure, in so far as it confines my attention to one thing and an uninteresting object at that, conduces towards a destruction of ordinary agitations and towards a detachment from common interests. As a further exercise I might refuse to look at anything at all or listen to anything . . . and so on. The performance of this task indicates that spiritual welfare is not to be sought by attending to any perceptions or by attending to anything we might perceive. But furthermore it would be useless for me to refuse thus to attend to my environment if at the same time I am indulging in day-dreams—thinking of other and more delightful gardens, for instance; picturing Babylon perhaps. So not only must I reject the actual environment, but also all possible environments, thus:

(i) At t_1 in environment E_1 I must not attend to E_1.

(ii) The same holds at $t_{2 \ldots n}$ in $E_{2 \ldots n}$, provided I am meditating.

(iii) These rules seek to ensure that when at t_x I attend to E_x I should be in such a state that I could without difficulty refrain from attending to E_x.

Reflection upon (i) and (ii) generates the corollary that

(ii*a*) Whenever at t_1 I am meditating in E_1 I should not think of (imagine) $E_{2 \ldots n}$.

For it would be inconsistent to believe it wrong to attend to E_1 and all right at the same time to visualize $E_{2 \ldots n}$—as in a similar way it is inconsistent to think it morally wrong to perform an action and to delight in imagining oneself performing that action. Consequently, all possible environments, together with the particular environment in which meditation actually takes place, must be rejected. Thus all visualizations must be excluded, with one or two exceptions which we shall come to. For a visualization is imagining oneself seeing or hearing, etc., something, and this is to imagine oneself in an environment. So we may say, as a preliminary conclusion, that this control of perceptions consists in rejecting all possible environments. What is meant by 'rejecting' here is evident: it is achieving the state where the environments are no longer of interest to the one who meditates. As a result, even that which might seem the most exalted and spiritual kind of day-dreaming, the imagining oneself before the splendour and majesty of the Almighty in some heavenly city and the reflection on the joys of everlasting life, even this must be eschewed by the mystic. His state will that of one who neither wants to live nor to die.

Thus, if we may define the contrast between the external and the internal world in terms of experiences, then imaginings (which we look on sometimes as going on inside us, so to speak) are as much part of the external world as are perceptions, and together with them constitute the worldly realm. Therefore one who has gained inner peace and tranquillity will judge the external world to be vapid and nugatory. For a more detailed examination of the idealistic assertions of mystics and the place they have in the spiritual life, it is convenient to turn to an examination of Buddhist meditation. For the example we have been considering, of one who controls his perceptions while sitting in a garden, is not far removed from the actual practices of many Oriental mystics.

(It might perhaps be objected that choosing such examples is misleading and harmful, on the ground that the type of mysticism involved is not genuine mysticism, is not the best or highest mysticism; but my contention is that Buddhist mysticism of the sort described below can be counted *pure* mysticism; this however is not to say that it is the highest form, since it may be that the highest fruits of the spirit can only come forth under the auspices of a woven-together and complex doctrinal scheme such as is found in Christianity. But the present enterprise is to examine the anatomy of religious discourse, not to determine the best type of doctrinal scheme. It may also be remarked that there has been greater emphasis on mysticism in Oriental—and especially Indian

—religion than in the Judaic group, for various reasons, and this has resulted in the evolution of more formalized techniques of spiritual development than in the West.)

VIII. MYSTICAL IDEALISM ILLUSTRATED FROM BUDDHAGHOSA

A useful account of Theravādin meditation which throws some light on the nature of the idealistic propositions often asserted by mystics is given in Buddhaghosa's *Visuddhimagga* (*The Path of Purity*), a Pāli treatise written probably in the fourth century B.C.[1] The words 'idealistic propositions' are here used for those assertions which cast ontological aspersions upon the world, claims that is which make out that the external world is impermanent, unreal or illusory.

The type of meditation which Buddhaghosa describes leads, one may say, to nirvāṇa, although the rapture experienced is not nirvāṇa (see, e.g., *Dīgha Nik.* I.37 ff.). For it must be remembered that even though nirvāṇa is sometimes called the highest happiness or bliss, it is a long-term state a normal condition for the attainment of which is rapture or bliss (short-term state). The meditations described induce the short-term condition. Moreover, there is a transcendental claim involved in saying that someone has achieved nirvāṇa, viz. that he will not be reborn; but we may safely ignore this aspect of nirvāṇa in the present discussion. Further, the meditations cannot be undertaken fruitfully without the previous attainment of moral mastery. Finally, by way of qualification, there are certain other spiritual achievements following on the rapture, and so it would be a gross over-simplification

[1] See *Visuddhimagga*, ed. H. C. Warren, Harvard Oriental Series; *The Path of Purity*, I–III, translation by Pe Maung Tin, Pāli Text Society. Also for a compendious survey of the practices of Buddhist mystics, see E. Conze, *Buddhist Meditation*, and for a general account of Hīnayāna mysticism see F. Heiler, *Die Buddhistische Versenkung*. The *jhānas* (stages of meditation) which I deal with above are by no means, of course, the whole of Buddhist meditation; but it is not unreasonable to count them the core of Buddhist yoga. It is, moreover, not insignificant that the Buddha is said to have attained all the *jhānas* immediately before his decease, for whether or not the account is historically accurate it points unmistakably to the importance attached to the *jhānas*. The Pāli *jhāna* is equivalent to Sanskrit *dhyāna* 'meditation'. This was translated *ch'ān* in Chinese, whence the Japanese *zen*. But the account given by Buddhaghosa is of course specifically Hīnayānist and does not apply to the methods of the Chinese and Japanese Meditation Seers.

to count the *jhānas* as described by Buddhaghosa as the whole of the spiritual life. Unfortunately, not all accounts quite agree in detail as to the number and nature of the stages of meditation, but they do coincide substantially, and one can present the picture as given by Buddhaghosa as reasonably correct.

It is simplest to consider these stages as eightfold: four in the realm of form and four formless ones. What these phrases mean will presently appear. In the four *Jhānas* of the realm of form the meditator takes a suitable object such as a blue flower[1] and places it at a convenient distance so that he can sit and gaze at it without discomfort. He considers it simply as blue and of a certain shape, in isolation. He trains himself to concentrate on it, repeating to himself the formula 'Blue, blue' as an aid to this concentration. Further, he tries shutting his eyes and imagining the object until he has perfectly grasped it, i.e. he is able to concentrate on it at will, visualize it at will, and dismiss other sights and sounds. He is able at will to be in such a state that he does not see anything else, or imagine anything else, or think about anything else. This induces the First *Jhāna* of the realm of form. This involves 'applied and sustained concentration, rapture, bliss and collectedness of mind'.

> Aloof, then, from desires and from evil states, he enters into and stays in the First *Jhāna*, in which concentration is directed and sustained, and which arises from detachment and involves rapture and bliss.[2]

What does all this mean? The first point to notice is that 'form' (*rūpa*) is here used to mean something like *gestalt*: to speak of the form of a flower is to speak of what it looks like from a certain position. Moreover, we notice that the meditator must view the object merely as blue and of a certain shape. And therefore it would not be inappropriate to count the form in this sense as a sense-datum (for sense-data are sensed by putting ourselves in a peculiar frame of mind). The next step is to be able to visualize this sense-datum at will and to visualize nothing else. One must have this mental image and no other, though it still retains determinate size. But how is this possible? If it has a boundary, surely something must lie outside this boundary? If we visualize

[1] These selected objects of concentration are known as devices or *kasiṇa*: Buddhaghosa gives a list of ten considered especially suitable for the cultivation of trance.

[2] *Visuddhimagga*, IV.79: cp. *Vibhaṅga*, 245, and *Dīgha Nik.*, 1.73.

it of determinate shape, must we not also visualize its surroundings? Not necessarily, for the rest can be merely a gap, as in migraine, where one may fail to see part of an object even though the part is not covered by, say, a patch of blackness. This is merely a gap, but not a replacement, in one's visual field. And what is possible of one's visual field is also possible of an imagined visual field. Second, one must not visualize the object as at a distance: indeed, this is the way it becomes a visualized sense-datum. For otherwise it would be a visualized thing. More precisely, we should say: The patch of colour which is visualized must not be seen as if at a distance, as though one imagined oneself looking at it. And this is the way one 'loses oneself' in a sense-datum, for by the fact of its isolation and lack of distance one loses the feeling of being at a certain spot viewing something (a sense which leads to the unfortunate terminology which speaks of the 'subject' and 'object' in knowledge). Consequently, in so far as such a feeling constitutes a kind of self-awareness, then one is unaware of oneself, for such a feeling is absent. All the sensations (if any) which one may have when one is aware of where one is and what one is doing do not obtain: there is merely a gap. In this connection, it is important to notice that the request commonly made to imagine 'what it would be like to be in such a state' is grossly deceptive, for the demand suggests that one should imagine something, that is to visualize something, and that is to have a mental image of something: consequently the request to imagine—in this sense—such a state is, in so far as we are treating of the gap, self-defeating and so cannot be used in evidence.

However, it is important to realize that this gap in self-awareness is first-order: that is, to speak somewhat loosely, it is *within* the visualization. One might still be aware that one is visualizing: for instance, if interrupted one might give an account of what one had been doing. Thus there might be a second-order awareness of what one had been doing without a first-order visualization of oneself looking at a certain object, etc. Thus is seen what is meant by 'sustained concentration'. In the First *Jhāna* there is sustained concentration in the following sense: (i) one visualizes oneself as continually gazing; and (ii) there is a continued effort to do this, of which one is aware. This we call 'second-order awareness'.

In the Second *Jhāna* in the realm of form, which is entered on once the First has been mastered, there is, according to Buddhaghosa, neither applied nor sustained concentration, though rapture, bliss and collectedness of mind remain. By this, something as follows is meant: one reaches the stage where it is unnecessary to make any conscious effort in the visualization: the performance comes so naturally that one need not be aware of concentrating.[1] In the Third *Jhāna*, rapture is put away. One cannot always, as Buddhaghosa remarks,[2] distinguish between rapture and bliss. But here rapture seems to be like a thrill of pleasure, the thrill in this case which accompanies the achievement of an aim: whereas bliss is more like enjoyment. Buddhaghosa remarks that rapture is a cognitive state,[3] while bliss comes under the heading of feeling. The justification for this classification lies in the fact that rapture is consequent upon the recognition that one has *achieved* something, whereas bliss does not accrue upon such a recognition, because the bliss is the pleasantness of the achievement which in some measure justifies aiming at it, while the rapture is in a sense parasitical—the joy involved in realizing a success which counts as a success because it is blissful. Thus rapture is a second-order good, while bliss is first-order: if there were no bliss, rapture would be irrational. Now since the latter involve awareness of achievement and is a short-term agitation, it is regarded as gross. The Third *Jhāna* arises when one loses the sense of achievement and the thrill. One enjoys a tranquil bliss and collectedness of mind. The Fourth *Jhāna* is somewhat paradoxical, for one wishes to aim at it in order to put away the bliss, on the ground that this is to some extent enjoyable and so to some extent (albeit a minor extent) gross. Thus the justification of the attempt to attain the fourth stage seems to be such that there could be no first-order motive for doing so.[4] The aim is absolute tranquillity and collected-

[1] Hence it is *ajjhatta*, 'interior', 'personal', or better, 'spontaneous'.

[2] IV.94.

[3] IV.100.

[4] It is to be noted that this feature of the situation is one which helps us to understand the application of the concept *grace* within the mystical strand. For the idea that one can achieve the mystical goal by one's own efforts has to be considerably qualified, as in the present instance, or it becomes dangerous and stultifies the effort. Thus, though the Buddha's last words were an exhortation to effort, it is also said (e.g. in *Milindapañha*, IV.7.13) that though the Blessed One gave hundreds of reasons for entering on the path towards the realization of nirvāṇa, he never gave a cause out of which nirvāṇa could be said to be produced (this point is, of course, connected with the thesis that nirvāṇa is uncompounded). Again, there is a rudimentary doctrine of grace (*prasāda*) in the *Kaṭha Upanisad*: 'Only by the man whom He chooses is He comprehended' (I.2.23); and cp. *Śvetāśvatara Upan.*, VI.21. And in general, consider the way in which yoga, as a technique for liberation, became theistic. On the other hand, it must be remem-

ness of mind, yet one cannot appeal, by way of showing the propriety of the pursuit to its intrinsic pleasantness. But we must remember at this point the central tenet of Buddhism that pain or suffering (*dukkha*) must be uprooted. By passing beyond the stage of any enjoyment, one averts disappointment at the cessation of the *Jhāna*.[1]

However, these four *Jhānas* in the realm of form are not the highest, since they all involve concentration upon a sense-datum and this has a tenuous link with other sense-data and with the world round about—in short with the external world. It is to be independent of that world that constitutes a major part of the rationale of this mystical discipline. There are, then, four higher stages of meditation which are called formless (*āruppa*), and to these we now proceed. These are dubbed 'formless' because they do not involve concentration upon a form or gestalt. Since their formal characteristics, as involving applied and sustained concentration, rapture, bliss and so forth, are the same as those of the stages of the realm of form there is no need to describe them further. Rather I shall direct attention to the repeated formulas used, which correspond to the formula 'Blue, blue' mentioned above as being employed in the first four *Jhānas*, and which are of considerable interest to us in the present enquiry since they represent an important use of sentences expressing idealistic propositions.

The formula in the first four *Jhānas* had the function, it will be recalled, of aiding concentration: for the repetition of 'Blue blue' helps one to retain the image and to prevent others from being inadvertently entertained. But the formulas of the next four stages which we are about to consider, though they perform the same kind of task, are altogether more subtle.

In the first *Jhāna* (in the formless realm), one

> thinking 'It is all infinite space' enters into and stays in the sphere of infinite space.[2]

bered that the primary use for doctrines of grace is in theistic contexts; and with this cp. the protest against the importation of the concept into mysticism expressed clearly by Suzuki (*Essays in Zen Buddhism*, ii.84): 'Ecstasy is a bad word for the neutral state of consciousness, because it suggests passivity, not active concentration.'

[1] To avert, for instance, a disappointment commonly called by Western mystics by such titles as 'the dark night of the soul' 'in which the self which thought itself so spiritual, so firmly established upon the supersensual plane, is forced to turn back, to leave the Light' (E. Underhill, *Mysticism*, p. 388).

[2] *Visuddhimagga*, X.12: cp. *Vibhaṅga*, 245, *Dīgha Nik.*, ii.112.

By repeating this formula one is helped to concentrate upon no visualized sense-datum whatsoever. Nevertheless, there is some sense in which infinite space is visualized. Perhaps we may describe the matter thus: one visualizes oneself as involved in space, but without regarding this space as bounded in any way. Surely, though, it may be objected, this space must be coloured in some fashion? Would it not, for instance, have to be imagined as black like the lightless night or blue like the morning sky? How can a thing be visualized without giving it a colour? But if we give 'visualize' an extended sense, some way out of the difficulty is to be found. There is unfortunately no English verb which does for hearing, smelling and so forth what 'visualizing' does for seeing—doubtless because humans happen to be better at seeing and at imagining sights than they are at hearing and at imagining sounds (and so on). Yet imagining sounds, smells and so forth could all be suitably covered by the verb 'to visualize' provided its sense were extended appropriately to fill these gaps and thereby to serve in a generic capacity, including within it the different species of imaginings. On this usage, one could be said to visualize muscular sensations (though of course in the extended sense such questions as 'What does that which you visualize look like?' will no longer be guaranteed a meaning, for 'What does that sound look like?' has no sense). Now if we are allowed to speak thus—a permission granted, so to speak, by the fact that it is possible to recall smells and muscular sensations, then one may visualize space as in itself without any properties (not containing objects, patches of colour and so forth), but yet possessing the quasi-characteristic of being able to be gone through in any direction. Thus the formula guides us to a picture of a sense-propertyless world, a universe of possible muscular sensations and no more. When we achieve this capacity to visualize infinite space, we have reached the first stage of the formless realm. But it is sufficiently close to the *Jhānas* of the realm of form to be no great advance, since the external world is regarded as (though void) extended and to that extent 'objective'.

The Second *Jhāna* has for its formula 'It is all infinite consciousness'. As Buddhaghosa comments,[1] the meditator herein attends to consciousness which touches or diffuses through space as infinite. The interpretation of this is difficult, but perhaps a clue has been afforded by our remarks above. No longer is space regarded

[1] *Visuddhimagga*, X.27: cp. *Vibhaṅga*, 245, *Dīgha Nik.*, ii.112.

as lying around one and such that one may journey through it, but simply as a construction out of possible sensations related in a certain way to each other. One drops the notion of extension derived from our ordinary experience and interprets such extension as space thus visualized possesses as the possibility of a series of muscular sensations.

In the Third *Jhāna*, the formula is 'There is nothing'.[1] One must repeat these words in order to attain the frame of mind where even the possibility of muscular sensations is ruled out: the world is seen as a blank, so to speak; and we cannot even talk of visualization, not even in the extended sense. It is difficult to explain what is meant by saying that the world is seen as a blank. In any case what does 'There is nothing' mean? We must note that part at least of the function of the formula is to guide the imagination in such a manner that nothing is visualized, and in particular that the previous picture of the world as constituted by a series of sensations is washed away. Tenuous as the world is thus, it is not tenuous enough. The final stage, the Fourth *Jhāna*, is arrived at when the effort to replace the previous picture by a blank is no longer felt, and where the smoothness of this imaginative operation is such that there is no awareness of strain in concentration or rapture at achievement: so that one is neither aware that one is picturing anything nor aware that one is refraining from so doing. It is therefore called the stage of 'neither perception nor non-perception'.

So much for the brief description and explication of the eight *Jhānas*, the central stages of Buddhist meditation. It will be seen that the formulas of the Formlesss *Jhānas* fall within the family of idealistic propositions; and perhaps our appreciation of the force of such utterances is sharpened by observing one milieu in which they occur naturally. For it is a notorious fact that idealistic propositions have, as has been seen, a surface vacuity which arises from their insusceptibility to refutation; and yet Dr. Johnson's action does at the same time have a certain persuasiveness about it. Part of this persuasiveness comes of course from the way in which it illustrates graphically the extent to which idealistic utterances involve the employment of language in a bizarre

[1] *Visuddhimagga*, X.36. Cp. *Vibhaṅga*, 245, *Dīgha Nik.*, ii.112. And compare Eckhart: 'All things are a mere nothing; I do not say that they are slight or that they are anything, but that they are a mere nothing' (quoted in J. M Clark, *The Great German Mystics*, p. 21).

manner. But this is perhaps not the only cause of the persuasiveness of the demonstration. For it is a kind of counter-ritual wherein one way of viewing the world is met with a forcible performance which epitomizes another, more practical and down-to-earth, attitude. And it certainly throws into relief the oddness of idealism as applied to everyday affairs. On the other hand, it can be replied that to object to mystical idealism in this way indicates a misunderstanding—one which can only be dispelled by attending to the circumstances in which idealistic utterances are relevant and important.

From the above examples drawn from Buddhist meditation we see that propositions which in other circumstances might seem alarming and even lunatic do at any rate serve to guide the imagination of him who meditates. We may ascribe to them a function which is, so to speak, an engineering one: for by the repetition of the formulas a certain state of mind is induced. Yet it would be dangerous to stress this utilitarian role overmuch; for these utterances do not always act merely as instruments to help the mystic in his strange pursuit, but also are held to express in some systems spiritual truths. Thus, for example, the proposition that the phenomenal world is illusory expresses a belief which is central to Śaṅkara's non-dualism. In one respect, therefore, there is an analogy between these utterances and the propositions enshrining moral rules. For the forcible utterance of the latter helps to induce a mode of behaviour which is in accordance with the rules, while the perception of the correctness of the rules comes with obedience to them. Thus the seemingly nugatory reply to the question why something is wrong by saying simply 'Because it is wrong' is not as pointless as at first appears. So too in the case of idealistic utterances we see that the use of the formulas helps in the first instance to guide the mystic along his path and secondly serves to express a view of the world the point of which becomes apparent with spiritual mastery. However, it only causes confusion to consider these pronouncements outside their mystical context: to regard them, for example, as somewhat theoretical descriptions of the metaphysical state of affairs. This is a temptation which arises from the common fact that such utterances appear in the systems of certain philosophers. When, however, we consider the peculiar nature of idealistic propositions and the strange disproportion between philosophers' readiness to reject, for instance, Zeno's conclusions (though based on the most subtle argumentation) and to accept idealism, we are drawn to think that idealism must have an intrinsic attractiveness little related to the strength of the philosophical premisses on which it has been allegedly based. And this would not be surprising in view of the manner in which it expresses a mystical view of the world.

We have seen, in attending to the procedures used in gaining spiritual mastery, that what is to be cut out is not merely perception of the world but also imagination of that world. Thus the spiritual state has a peculiarly intimate 'innerness'. It is to be noted that this innerness of the mystical goal accounts in part for, and is expressed by, psycho-physical dualism. In Western philosophy and religion such a dualism received a powerful initial impulse from the Orphic thesis that the body is a prison or tomb for the soul, which has to be purified through ascetic practices, etc. It is not fortuitous, in view of Plato's spiritual tendencies (the ultimate aim: a vision of the Good), that he should have imported this dualistic Orphic picture into his philosophical scheme.[1] Largely for this reason, Platonism appealed to the more mystically inclined Christians, notably St. Augustine. And, as has been remarked, 'a similar view of the relation of soul to body finds popular expression in a great deal of Christian ascetic literature'.[2]

In India, psycho-physical dualism is a common characteristic of all orthodox systems: even the non-theistic Sāṅkhya system recognizes the spirit-matter distinction. It is the denial of the Self which makes Buddhism seem so unorthodox, but it should be noted that though the Buddha denied that there is any persisting Self underlying experiences, he did nevertheless cleave to the essential dualism of the mystical path, by describing nirvāṇa in a manner which set it sharply apart from ordinary states: briefly, orthodox Hinduism propounds a substance-substance dualism, Buddhism a state-state dualism. What is set apart in the one is a permanent substance; and what is set apart from the common flux of experience in the other is an immortal state.

We see then that the distinction between the interior world of the spiritual life and that other world which must be rejected does not correspond to the common philosophical distinction between the external and internal worlds. For the state of one who is lost in rapt meditation is, as we have observed in the example from

[1] For a general account of Plato's mysticism, see A. J. Festugière, *Contemplation et Vie Contemplative selon Platon*.

[2] F. C. Copleston, *Aquinas*, p. 151.

the *Visuddhimagga,* devoid even of mental pictures: while according to the philosophical distinction mental images would fall within the mental world, not within the external world. Another important difference between the two contrasts is that while the philosophical one can only be explained with some difficulty and in such a manner as to raise hard problems, the mystical contrast is explicable by reference to different ways of life, that is with reference to different modes of behaviour. For it is easy enough to see what the mystic means by saying that he has to turn inward: he behaves in a manner which is detached from ordinary interests and the state that he seeks is not one of observing what lies about him. The traces of his condition lie, assuredly, in the so-called external world, for it is his behaviour that reveals the glory within that he has achieved; but this glory is a state which even if it lies beyond bliss in some descriptions, yet is of the same order. Thus we can explain the inner spiritual world by pointing to the way in which certain states are to be attained.

IX. MYSTICAL PROPOSITIONS AND BRAHMAN-ĀTMAN

We may say, then, for brevity's sake that the contrast between the inner spiritual life and the external world is a distinction between different activities. One of these activities, mystical discipline, leads to a state of blissful detachment which accrues upon certain experiences; and these form the basis upon which is constructed the concept of the Ātman or Self. Thus this latter concept is not like certain metaphysical ones which lie quite beyond experience, though this impression is frequently given because the mystical state is different from all *ordinary* experiences. Consequently, the shorthand whereby it is described as transcendent and beyond sense-experience is easily misunderstood. However, it is not only because the mystical goal is described as different from all ordinary perceptions and so forth that this mistake springs, but also because the overwhelming impact of the bliss or insight calls for a strong and even violent expression of the difference between this and all other experiences. Part of this expression occurs in the form of the picture adverted to above, the picture of the world as impermanent or illusory. But though the world is illusory, the Ātman is not; in the Ātman reality and immortality are to be found. In a similar sense nirvāṇa too is transcendent.[1]

[1] It will, however, be obvious that there are considerable divergencies

Yet the Ātman is not primarily figured as lying beyond the world. It is near and within all this; and we begin to see why. It is near because realization of the Ātman is to be understood in the setting of a mystical path at the end of which lie experiences given expression in the behaviour of the mystic. In an analogical sense of *within*, the sense in which a feeling may be said to be within somebody, the bliss of the Ātman is to be found within us. It is therefore, nearer than hands or breathing. Also it is within the world in a special way; for the world encloses the mystic as a kind of mirage and he turns away from these appearances about him, cutting himself off, as it were, from ordinary perceptions. His salvation is to be found, so to say, this side of the phenomenal world. Therefore, the Ātman is said to be near.

Now it will readily be seen that an extreme idealism dovetails well with the Brahman doctrine. For in the latter we have this picture: that beyond phenomena lies a mysterious and supremely holy Reality. In the mystical picture of the world as unreal we also have the picture of Reality as lying outside phenomena. The world is, as it were, a screen, and what lies outside that screen, whether that side or this, is the truly Real. Thus the mystical doctrines of spiritual transcendence and worldly illusion assimilate the Ātman even closer to that immortal being which lies shrouded behind the shifting events of this illusory world. And it will be remembered

between the Ātman and nirvāṇa; more particularly we may ask: Why is it that though idealistic formulas are used even in Theravādin meditation, Theravādin doctrines are less idealistic than the formulas? I think the answer is to be found under two heads: (i) yogic methods were developed before the founding of Buddhism, and were retained, together with the formulas, in the new religion, even though they were likely to lead to an extreme idealism (as in Mahāyāna) which was apparently rejected by the Buddha himself; (ii) the Buddha was agnostic about a genuinely transcendent Reality; now, as we shall see, extreme idealism (world as illusion) fits in smoothly with and tends towards a doctrine of a divinity beyond the world, Succinctly: only a moderate idealism (world as impermanent) is likely to serve as doctrinal expression for a religion centred on the mystical path and rejecting worship. Further, the Buddha's middle path between extreme asceticism and indulgence is partly due to his desire to incorporate a strong moral element in his doctrines: an illusory world is one, seemingly, where moral effort is nugatory (that is, where efforts to help others, etc., seem less important: there is, of course, in every mystical religion great emphasis on personal effort towards liberation—not here the reliance on grace). Hence, too, another reason why the traditional *jhānas* should not be simply identified with nirvāṇa: for the formulas do not themselves express properly the central insight of Buddhism—so that the final culmination of Buddhist mysticism is detachment from the world seen as impermanent (see *Visuddhimagga*, XXII.65).

that both Ātman and Brahman are not (in an ordinary way) to be seen and that they both are timeless and deathless. There seems to be the glimmering of a similar pattern in each.

X. THE CONSEQUENCES OF ACHIEVEMENT AND BRAHMAN-ĀTMAN

We come now to the third main ground of identification, namely that which is revealed in the consequences of mystical attainment. (i) It is a feature of the mystic who has attained release that his character displays wonderful power: indeed this power is sometimes portrayed as physical and miraculous, e.g. the *iddhis* of the Buddhist saint. Good actions seem to flow naturally out of the newly acquired tranquillity: for which reason there is no great danger in the doctrine that the enlightened ones are beyond good and evil—meaning roughly that they do not need to concern themselves about the rightness and wrongness of actions. Hence, the mystic seems to have gained a release from the commoner bonds of sin; and the source of his purity of character appears to be the (possibly divine) experience. This dovetails with the conception of God as capable of freeing us from sin; and if alone capable, He is found within. Moreover, the overwhelming nature of the experience in itself gives it a power perchance divine. The *summum bonum* has its mystery-value also.

(ii) The mystic path involves self-abnegation, the sacrifice of ordinary interests and pleasures. This self-negation has an affinity to the self-abasement of the worshipper who, in adoring intensely, becomes well aware not merely of a glorious ideal but also of the contemptible sinfulness of himself. This despising of his 'lower nature' is, then, not too different from the self-denying attitude of the mystic. The two ways may here coalesce and with them the concepts thrown up by them.

XI. THE IDENTIFICATION OF BRAHMAN AND ĀTMAN

For all these reasons—the timelessness, imperceptibility and transcendence of each, the convergence of mystical and theistic doctrines, the power displayed by both—the Ātman and Brahman are identified, are said mysteriously to be one; and this is the highest *upsaniṣad* of all. The creation of the phenomenal world through the magic of Brahman (figured in popular presentation as the sporting of the Lord or *Īśvara*, the personal manifestation of Brahman) is seen anew as the illusion cast over the Self by wrong perception of the world (*avidyā* or ignorance); and the sacred rites used to invoke the Creator are turned to new uses as preparations for and expressions of the mystical path.[1] Not only does the sacred sound OM serve to express the mystery of worship but to prepare the mind for its initiation into the highest mystical knowledge: it signalizes both the indescribability of the mysterious and also the ineffability of bliss. This superimposition of the two concepts is what justifies and explains the paradox with which we began.

For Brahman is seen as far and beyond all this, because of Its exalted stature as an object of worship and of sacrificial ritual and because of Its position, appropriate to Its mysteriousness, behind phenomena. While as the Ātman It is near and within all this, because of its being connected with the experience of intimate liberation gained at the end of the mystic path and because of its lying apart from, yet this side of, the phenomenal world. The identification of Brahman with the Ātman serves, then, as a prominent example of the kind of weaving together of different strands of discourse in a doctrinal scheme.

We have of course here mainly considered the similarities that would give some kind of backing to the identification. Certain of the divergencies are also important, as we shall later observe. But for the moment it is sufficient to see the manner in which superficially different strands are closely woven together.

Brahman is both far and near.

[1] See, for instance, *Maitrī Upan.*, VI.35.

IV

Incarnation

I. A THIRD STRAND IN THE SPIRITUAL FRAME OF DISCOURSE

THERE is a further important strand in spiritual discourse which we have not yet touched on: if we may call the two that have been discussed the *mystical* and the *numinous* strands respectively, then the name for the third will be the *incarnation* strand. For it is a feature of many religions that certain humans or certain beings of human appearance are held to be divine. In the major religions we have such examples as these: Christ the incarnate Creator, Kṛṣṇa the appearance of God (as portrayed in the *Bhagavadgītā*), the Buddha in certain forms of Mahāyāna—as described for instance in the *Lotus Sūtra*. Now clearly, if the claim is made that some human is identical with or the manifestation of God, its confirmation must be of a somewhat different sort from that found in the other two strands. For belief in a Creator is backed, at least to some extent, by appeal to features of the world around us; and mystical claims find at least some of their confirmation in the behaviour of holy men and the experience therein expressed. But it is not simply in these ways that a claim as to the divinity of someone appearing in the world is to be justified. Further, it is clear that if someone is to be identified with God, with a Being who dwells in another world, belief in the divinity of the one who is incarnated presupposes belief in the existence of such a God in another world. This is, for instance, brought out in the Hindu concept of the *avatāra*, 'descent': for this implies that the descending Deity has his proper abode beyond the manifested world.

However, it might be replied that there are cases of the ascription of divinity where there is no identification with a Creator or with any Being beyond the stars: as for example in the deification of Roman Emperors and in the claims of Father Divine. Moreover, it may be said, there is little need to speak here of another strand of discourse since we observe a continuum between reverence and worship: the gap between the revered *guru* and the Man-God is merely one of degree. If enough adoration and worship is directed towards a human being he acquires the status of a god: holy man to god stands as hill to mountain. There are not two strands of discourse, one about hills and another about mountains; so too there are not two strands of religious discourse, one about holy men and another about fleshly gods.

While I do not deny the force of these objections, there do seem to me to be reasons why the notion of an incarnate God will best be treated separately and why discourse about such a Being should count as of a different strand. First, the behaviour of the holy man is important in the mystical strand in a somewhat different manner from the way such behaviour is important in the incarnation strand. For in mysticism and in mystical doctrines we are concerned with the experience and with its relation to general doctrines about the world; but in the incarnation strand we are interested in the behaviour of the God-Man because it directly displays divine properties. Again, more importantly, though it seems true to say that the status of a saint differs from that of an incarnate God largely in degree, yet the grounds for believing that a certain individual is a manifestation of God are of rather a distinct nature. And this will, I hope, become apparent as we proceed.

II. INCARNATE DEITIES, SAINTS AND PROPHETS

Since it seems to be the case that one who is a candidate (so to speak[1]) for divinity must possess holiness in a pre-eminent degree it would perhaps be reasonable to consider the lesser cases of holiness first and work up to that intense holiness as we proceed. For the lesser instances of human holiness are perhaps more easily

[1] I do not wish to speak irreverently by using this terminology: though I think that excessive fear of being blasphemous has often obscured this and other issues. In calling someone a candidate, I am speaking of logical candidature, for it is obviously the case that a person to be properly considered divine must fulfil certain conditions—thus unless Jesus is sinless he cannot be God. To some people this may sound like saying that we are sitting in judgment on Christ and this is blasphemous. But here there is confusion: it is a truism that it is we who judge Jesus to be divine or non-divine, but this of course assigns us no superiority whatsoever (it is we who judge Him to be so vastly *better* than we are). But if we are to judge there must be criteria for judgment, and hence the language of candidature.

understood. It is therefore appropriate to examine first the nature of saints and prophets. For these in their different ways represent elements which appear in the God-Man. It should also be mentioned that in what follows I have my eye mainly fixed upon the Christian doctrine of Incarnation, though in the subsequent chapter I shall have remarks to make about other similar doctrines. The case for confining my attention largely to this instance of incarnation doctrines is that it is in a way a specially simple example; and moreover it is in Christianity above all that vital emphasis is placed on this element of spiritual doctrine.

It has already been remarked that the holy man is characterized by four features which assimilate him in some measure to the divine. These are: his mysteriousness, his purity, his other-worldliness and his moral power. Nevertheless, this similarity between the two is hardly emphasized in faiths which contain in large measure the atmosphere of worship. For in the high theistic faiths it is thought overweening and presumptuous to consider oneself or any other man divine, since the appropriate reaction to the numinous is one of abasement. True there may be no great harm in counting certain persons as in some degree numinous; but though they may be marvelled at they are not accorded the supreme honour of worship: their powers and their mysteriousness are ascribed to God, not to them. God may be seen in them but they themselves are not divine. For one cannot, as I have said, even think of another as divine, for that other one is human and so like oneself. Hence the revering of another one as divine is like to lead to vicarious pride, a blasphemous pride in humanity. Or looking at it from above rather than below: it is gross idolatry to debase the currency of divinity and to worship anything other than the One True God. To this is due the intensity with which the enemies of Christianity among Muslims and Jews attack the doctrine that Jesus is God: it appears as a violent blasphemy and a return to polytheism. It therefore seems to be a spiritual revolution to entertain the belief that God (the Creator and single object of profound adoration) is identical with a human being who ought otherwise to share our abasement before the holy. As a sign of this, the holiness of the saint is consistently underplayed in faiths where worship is vital, though it should be noted in religions where there is greater emphasis on mysticism and hence upon union with the divine (an emphasis which serves to bring the divine closer to us, so to speak, and therefore seemingly to a less exalted position) there is much less repugnance towards ascribing eminent status to the saint. And we see moreover that in such a faith the number of incarnations tends to be proliferated (thus in Hinduism there are many, and Mahāyāna Buddhism multiplies its Buddhas and Bodhisattvas), Christianity, on the other hand, inheriting as it does a strong measure of the numinous strand from Judaism, is concerned to stress the uniqueness of the incarnation; for although in this doctrine it crosses the border into a realm which the unitarian Jews and Muslims cannot enter, it does so only with the greatest reserve and precaution. In insisting on the uniqueness of Christ and by conferring on Him the attributes reserved otherwise only for the Creator, it is comparatively severe upon the saints who adorn the Church's history. Thus their holiness hardly entitles them to a higher religious status than that accorded to ordinary men. It is true that canonization and the belief that saints can intercede on our behalf in another world do set them a little apart from the ordinary sinner; but nevertheless the likeness that a saint may have to the divine is regarded simply as a sign of divine grace: a shadowy reflection, so to speak, of the glories of the divine Creator. And this despite the fact that imitation is made easier in a creed which includes the doctrine of incarnation, since it enriches the possibilities of assimilation. Not only are there the analogical similarities in respect of mysteriousness, purity, etc., but also there are literal similarities between the lives of the saints and that of the Man who is identified with God. A man, for instance, may be crucified for his faith.

However, there is one power which the saint does not normally possess (it is not, that is, a condition for sainthood), but which is of some considerable importance for the ascription of divinity (and this apart from the difference in degree of purity and so forth that constitutes a gap between the divine and the merely holy man). This is a power which is displayed in some degree by the prophet: the power, that is, either verbally or by conduct, to institute new doctrines or at least a new way of regarding old doctrines. These innovations of spiritual doctrines, usually depicted—as a result of religious conservatism, the causes of which we shall later consider—as a deepening of what has gone before, issue from *prophets*; and these are normally expected to be saintly. For it seems that a prerequisite of spiritual insight is spirituality. This does not necessarily imply, however, that throughout a man's life he should be good, etc., or even that obedience to divine and moral laws should have been manifest before the institution of spiritual reforms. But it assuredly seems that unless some such holiness is manifested, unless there is depth and purity of character, there is real doubt as to the genuineness of the new preaching. It is not to be thought that this is only an external condition imposed upon the teacher; for if we attend to the manner in which doctrines are intimately connected with such practices as worship and mystical discipline it will become clear that there can be no real understanding of the force of religious propositions unless one has trained oneself in the practices mentioned. And if there is no real understanding there can presumably be no invention or discovery. This is one of the reasons why the truths of religion are not attained by simple cogitation or observation; and in this respect they bear more resemblance to moral insights than to plain descriptive judgments. Hence also there is no direct way of describing the way in which spiritual innovations come about; at best we can give inklings and hints of the reasons impelling the prophet. This is part cause of the difficulty of depicting religious language. For at certain points one can merely repeat doctrines when one is trying to show what they are like. Herein, however, lies the advantage of tackling the matter from the standpoint of the comparative study of religions; for the repetition is hereby given a wider scope (as happens in criticism: we see what the composer is meaning by paying attention to his other pieces).

However, neither the saint nor the prophet is divine, though saintliness and spiritual insight would appearto be necessary conditions of being an incarnate God. What more is required to be the latter?

First, we must repeat a point already made: the God-Man should possess holiness of character and spiritual insight in a pre-eminent degree. For there are, as we have said, already traces of divinity in the prophet and saint. But these must be transformed in the case of the divine human; though precisely how depends on the nature of the initial doctrinal scheme within the framework of which divinity is ascribed. For example, whereas the conception of the Creator in the Judaeo-Christian tradition is so exalted that only the most luminous life could for a moment be considered as displaying intrinsic divinity, the untidiness of Greek religion allowed the ascription of divinity to Hellenistic monarchs upon very lax conditions. Again, the Brahman-Ātman doctrine, whereby the individual enshrines the eternal principle of the universe, is easily suited to a proliferation of incarnations, since these can be defended as signifying instances where the underlying Self shines out in a conspicuous manner. This brings us to a principle which should be borne in mind in what follows, namely that the conditions for ascription of divinity will be much stricter where only one incarnation is allowed than elsewhere. And there is a second principle already adumbrated: that the conditions will also be stricter in monotheism than polytheism and, correspondingly, stricter in monotheism than pantheism or monism. As I am mainly concerned here with the strictest case (strict on two counts, by virtue of the two above-mentioned principles), the remarks below will not suit all cases.

So far then we may say: to be a logical candidate for divinity a man should possess holiness and spiritual insight to an intense degree.

III. THE DIVINE MAN AS A LIMITING CASE OF PURITY

There are two traits an incarnate God in a strictly theistic faith ought to possess, sinlessness and the power to save. The former is the limiting case of purity of character we might expect to find in a saint, but merits separate consideration. Since the gap between God and man is the gulf fixed between the holy and the sinful, then one who is to be identified with the All-Holy should be free from sin. However, this condition is one which looks at first sight to be theoretically impossible in an inhabitant of this world. For the wonder and purity of the divine seems to depend upon a contrast with the unsatisfactory nature of the world of creatures. Thus in so far as such a being shared attributes with humans, he would be, even if his moral character were stainless, still in the position of a worshipper. It would therefore be hard to maintain that he was identical with the object of worship. There are, however, two points to be made in this connection.

(i) The difficulty about identification with the object of worship is one which, as we shall see, arises also in the case of mystical experience in theistic religions; and of this we shall need to treat later. However, this much can now be said: this is not an isolated religious difficulty.

(ii) The cosmic situation is treated, in the doctrinal schemes containing in large measure the numinous strand, as in a sense contingent. We have already had occasion to remark that the picture of the world itself as contingent is closely bound up with the conception that its existence depends upon a free act of God's Will. Again the gap separating God and His worshipper is described as due to the fall of primeval man. Finally (and most relevantly here), the incarnation is depicted as contingent in a similar way; and not only the original act whereby God becomes man, but throughout the divine man's career, he is shown as rejecting the power and majesty which be his even in this life in virtue of His being identical with God. He is therefore presented as being contingently a creature separate from the glory that lies beyond the world. This serves to mitigate in some degree the difficulty aforementioned, since the divine man is thereby regarded as being dispositionally identical with the object of worship, though choosing in actual practice to separate Himself from God, and thus to aquire the status which fallen man possesses. In a faith of more mystical flavour, however, where appearances are viewed as unreal, the contrast between man and the object of worship is presented as a necessary part of the scheme of things. For it is as an appearance, that is as one still moving within the ambit of the illusory world, that the individual is contrasted with the divine; and this world is necessarily separated from its source. This feeling of the necessity of cosmic facts is expressed with some force by Plotinus in his *Against the Gnostics*, who fell, so he thought, into the error of picturing the spiritual situation as somehow accidental, since it depended on divine fiat. In the numinous strand there is great predilection for the story-form; not so in the mystical. Hence, in such idealistic doctrinal schemes we find it common, where there is some event similar to the Incarnation, to describe the manifestation of the divine as merely an appearance, on a par in many respects with other events in the phenomenal world; an appearance to guide men back to the true path, but not something expressing the core of the faith—eternal truth cannot, on such a view, depend on the accidents of history. We therefore see that the violent contrast between worshipper and object of worship in faiths where the numinous strand is important has the at first sight paradoxical effect of making a *genuine* incarnation easier: the factors which make for sharp expression of man's dependence on God also serve to mitigate the difficulty of identifying a man with God (provided, that is, this man is not every man); though on the other hand mystical faiths will find it simpler to accommodate the *appearance* of divinities in this world.

This much is seen, then, that the divine man, even if he does not sin, must, to share the humility which men must display before the divine Creator, acquire the puny stature of a creature. Consequently he is, in one sense of 'unholy', unholy; his sinlessness extends, however, throughout his moral life. In this he possesses a formal similarity to the divine. Further, evidence of extraordinary powers (for example, to heal) are taken as intimations of the all-power or omnipotence which He has chosen to reject. Again, the luminous display of spiritual wisdom seems to be a sign of the omniscience which, too, is rejected. These signs are similar in status to the traces of divine majesty which are seen in the world. What lies 'behind' is hidden, but there are glimpses, so to speak, through the concealing veil. And these can be signs that the finiteness of the divine Being, a finiteness which he shares with all other creatures, is only half the story. Contingently, the God-Man is unholy though sinless; but ultimately He is also numinous, like the strange Power behind the universe; His unholiness is merely his chosen humility.

We may note that the claim that some human being is morally sinless is, provided we are agreed on the moral criteria, an empirical one. Consequently, historical investigation, which is of less relevance to the confirmation of propositions about the Creator, becomes highly important in this peculiar case. And here again we observe the extraordinarily complicated status possessed by religious propositions: for they are backed by such a variety of evidence. Therefore no simple analysis of religious claims, as though they were homogeneous, will succeed.

IV. THE DIVINE MAN HAS THE POWER TO SAVE

A second main trait which ought to be possessed by the God-Man is the power to save. Now we have already said something which is relevant in this connection: for words sometimes have the power to save, when, that is, they are spiritual instructions. Thus the teaching of the master, wherein is displayed his wisdom, contributes in some measure to his ability to free sinners from the yoke. This aspect of the teacher's power is almost exclusively insisted on in Mahāyāna Buddhism where the quasi-divine status of the Buddha is described largely in the setting of his ability to lead us out of our present ills by his saving advice.[1] Not without point is

[1] See, e.g., *Saddharmapuṇḍarīka*, ch. ii–iv.

the story of how the high god Brahmā comes to the Buddha to persuade him to preach.[1] Nevertheless, even in the case of Gotama, whose words are not only of such vital moment within the faith but are also set out with great clarity, the story of his life is of great moment to the believer in that therein is seen the evidence of his enlightenment and all the actions and words which throw light on that great event.[2]

But the power to save is not simply the healing property of preaching. In a fully fledged doctrine of incarnation there must be something more than luminous words. It is not merely the Sermon on the Mount which makes Christ a Saviour—and indeed it might even be said that such teaching is of comparatively little importance in this respect. His dying on the Cross as a living sacrifice is much more central here.

But first of all, we must consider what the power to save in this sort of way amounts to: then we can go on to see how it is that a particular human being can have ascribed to him this divine prerogative. For whereas it is rather easy to see how teaching can save, in the sense that it leads to an effort on the part of men to liberate themselves from their spiritual deficiencies, it is difficult to understand how the actions of an individual can effect salvation.

It should be noted that the power to save belongs to the divine (or so it is commonly held); and this in two main ways. (*a*) Knowledge of God is held to bring release, and this is intelligible when we are dealing with mystical knowledge. For that knowledge which

[1] *Jātaka Nidāna Kathā*, pp. 81–2.

[2] There is, be it noted, something of a split in Mahāyāna Buddhism between the two powers to save, i.e. the power to save through preaching and the power to save by mysterious means. The historical Buddha is usually represented as the giver of saving doctrines (as in the *Lotus* parables of the fire, the errant son and the rain-cloud), while the popular evolution of the doctrine of largely unhistorical Bodhisattvas contains as a central notion that the Bodhisattvas, through renouncing nirvāna till others are saved and by transferring to lesser beings the merits they have acquired, can lead them to final peace. Thus the concept of mysterious saving-power was developed independently of doctrines about the historical Gotama. In Hīnayāna, of course, neither Bodhisattvas nor unhistorical Buddhas such as the six predecessors of Gotama (*Dīgha Nik.*, ii.2 ff.) have any great doctrinal significance: salvation comes through one's own efforts; guidance comes, when the Buddha has passed away, from the teaching (*dhamma*) (*Mahāparinibbāna-Sutta*, VI.1)—it does not come from prayer, nor does salvation accrue through grace to those who call upon the name of a Saviour such as Avalokiteśvara. Such modes of salvation are characteristic of the numinous strand, which emphasizes our subordination to and dependence upon the object of worship.

is said to be yielded by union with the divine, that is by mystical experience within the context of a theistic faith, will be part of the dispositions in virtue of which the mystic, after a certain point, is to be described as liberated. Further, the unfortunate situation of men is often expressed as the search to discover the 'meaning' of life, to penetrate to the heart of the mystery of existence, etc.; and it would not therefore be surprising if knowledge of God (in whatever sense appropriate—a point we shall need to dwell on later) should bring release from the spiritual travail of those who are in this condition.

(*b*) On the other hand, the divine is supposed also to bring salvation in a more direct manner. This is *a priori* likely in view of the following two facts: first, the divine is holy; and second, man's need to be saved arises from his lack of holiness. Thus one would expect the source of salvation to lie in that which is divine; and this indeed is the picture which is commonly presented. Consequently, in a faith which emphasizes the immense exaltedness of the object of worship, the power to save will be regarded as belonging exclusively to God. Hence, if this power does belong thus to God, it would not be unreasonable to look for the exercise of this power in One who is identified with God. However, what form would such a demonstration take?

The reason why man needs salvation is because he is sinful and inadequate; thus his attaining liberation from these defects will bring him to resemble God more—for they are what create the gap between worshipper and worshipped. Yet his abasement is said to be such that this, in the normal course of events, is impossible; only God could help man up towards divinity. And what needs wiping out is the blemish acquired in man's original separation from God, pictured historically in the Judaic faiths—not as implicitly flowing from the cosmic situation. Given the principle that sin needs expiating, it follows that God will need to perform the expiation. And herein lies the heart of the Christian doctrine that by the sacrifice on the Cross man is raised up again from his fallen position.

At the same time it is obvious that the events in the life of Christ do not have a simple causal efficacy in bringing about a certain spiritual state of affairs: for example, the Resurrection is regarded as important because it shows in some manner the new possibilities of salvation, and the fact that rising from the dead is an astonishing and improbable event is hardly significant except in its context as being a *sign* of something. It is not like a surprising achievement such as the stopping of a landslide, which has immediate and important causal effects. Instead, the results brought about by a Saviour are more akin to legal effects; they are also of the same general nature as non-divine instances of expiation. These in turn are not unlike certain performances which are quite frequent and well-known in ordinary human intercourse. To these we now turn.

V. EXPIATION IS SIMILAR TO CERTAIN SOCIAL GESTURES

As our first example we take the expression of gratitude. A performs some important service for B—saving his child from drowning, for instance. B, apart from expressing his unspeakable gratitude in the usual manner, will doubtless desire to do something more; and this may take the form of doing something on A's behalf. This act will not simply be a service, but a service in a certain context, namely the context of B's being deeply indebted to A. Thus the action will take on the character of being a *gesture*, symbolizing B's gratitude (similarly a gift becomes a *token*). Inasmuch as we can speak of there being an *effect* of the action, it is something as follows: though it does not wipe out B's debt, it serves as a pledge that the debt would be paid off. For the importance of *doing* something for A, rather than just going through the performance of uttering words of gratitude, lies in this, that it demonstrates B's willingness to act on A's behalf, should the opportunity for a really major service arise. Thus to some extent, the effect of the gesture is to mitigate the unbalance between A and B.

But A may be owed something by B not only in the case where he has performed a service for B, but also where B has performed a disservice to A. Here is a position where B, to right the situation, must proffer apologies. Again, these can either be verbal or enshrined in an act; and the latter occurs in the context of indebtedness and serves as a pledge of good intentions. We note that in both cases exactly matching recompense is not required for the act to be counted as setting matters straight: what is needed is a recognition that intentions are good and hence that the disequilibrium is in a sense accidental, accidental because the opportunity of a major and equal service has not arisen (though there is a difficulty here analogous to the perplexity we have in matching a good against an evil in moral decisions; what positive service will wipe out a disservice?). Thus the intentions expressed in the gesture are of overriding importance; it would normally be thought churlish and uncharitable to refuse to forgive one whose intentions were shown to be transparently good and who had thus gone through a real change of heart. The reason why words expressive of contrition or gratitude are often deemed insufficient is no doubt the fact that words do not display intentions as clearly as deeds—it is easy enough in many cases to say one is sorry, less to make a genuine sacrifice in making it up to the other party. So a symbolic deed is better than a mere verbal gesture. (Though the qualification may be entered that sometimes a verbal gesture, involving for instance sharp loss of pride, may be harder than the giving of a token; but what is said above seems to be generally true and rests on the same grounds as justify the proverb that deeds speak louder than words.) And the effect of a gesture is to adjust the personal situation which had been thrown into disequilibrium. It is sometimes, however, the case that the indebted party still feels serious qualms; and this is usually expressed by saying that one wishes one could *show* how deep the gratitude (or etc.) is. Thus is displayed dissatisfaction with the gesture, which can only be allayed for the moment by the other party's accepting the gesture as sufficient.

Thus too with the expiation of sins, which constitutes an attempt to right a situation which has gone amiss. But, as has been remarked, if the gap between God and man is violently stressed, the possibility of anything like appropriate expiation seems to vanish. Anything that may be done will be hopelessly inadequate and the only relief seems to be the trust that God is merciful. Not for nothing, in the austerely unitarian creed of Islām, is it so repeatedly emphasized that Allah is merciful: this the adherents must take on faith. Where is man to look for the gesture that will right the situation?

We may note in passing that the conception that an unequal situation may be adjusted by a gesture and not merely by words—which in their expressive uses ever remain suspect because of men's remarkable capacity for insincerity—is important in the rituals of sacrifice. These supplement in a weighty manner the usual ceremonies of worship, since by giving up something as an offering a concrete gesture of expiation is performed. True, tokens can often degenerate into bribes, but this is not in accord with the deeper and more solemn significance of sacrifice. Yet in view of the immense disequilibrium between the worshipper and the divine, even these gestures, together with the living of a sacrificial life (an extension of the concept *sacrifice* characteristic of the religious permeation of morals), appear insufficient.

It may then be said that a unitarian faith creates a certain need for the doctrine of atonement (though this doctrine is bought at the expense of doctrinal simplicity; and it must be insisted that though there may be pressure towards such a doctrine in monotheism, this is not to say that there is an absolute necessity for it). A suffering Saviour performs the function of being an adequate sacrifice to expiate the sins of mankind. In this way, the situation is adjusted and, for the faithful, there is bright evidence of God's mercy.

However, the sacrifice is in a double way a gesture. For the act of expiation itself is a gesture in the manner described above; but also the Saviour is held to expiate *vicariously* the sins of others. This notion of taking on sins itself needs explanation.

VI. VICARIOUS EXPIATION IS A COMMUNAL GESTURE

As has already been said, the accepting of responsibility vicariously is also in the nature of a gesture. One form of this may be called a *communal* gesture, which depends for its efficacy upon the recognition that members of a certain community have a solidarity one with another.

To illustrate the point we may consider the following instance. The military commander of a garrison of occupying troops demands hostages for some crime committed in the territory under his control and certain citizens volunteer as hostages. There are two aspects of this case of interest to us here.

(i) The occupying power does not demand any kind of hostage, but specifies that citizens of the occupied country must serve as such. (If a commander were to ask for volunteers from his own troops he would be thought odd; perhaps odd in a good way if his intent were the unusual one of insisting upon the solidarity of the human race.) The requirement that hostages must come from citizens of the occupied nation shows this, that the death of compatriots is thought to be a cause of special sorrow. This implies that there is a feeling of solidarity between members of this parcular group, and that therefore the infliction of punishment upon one member of the group is the punishment of all. Similarly, the insult of one member of such a group would count as a gesture against all. Thus we may say briefly that the possibility of communal gestures is grounded on the sense of solidarity felt by the members of a group.

(ii) The volunteering of certain members of the group, in the above example, indicates that there are occasions when a person can freely choose to represent the group. One thereby performs a gesture on behalf of the community. In such a situation, then, there is something akin to the vicarious expiation of sin.

For, first, the human race forms a community, in the eyes of a universal religion, whose members have or ought to have a sense of solidarity. And second, the suffering of the Saviour is a voluntary gesture of expiation. Were this not so, Jesus would be considered merely a scapegoat, a blood sacrifice (of a barbaric sort) exacted by God from mankind. But the sense in which Christ is a sacrifice is clearly different from the sense that Isaac might have been one: for Isaac is a sacrifice for his father to make, not one who sacrifices himself. Hence the picture sometimes drawn, that God was cruel to allow Jesus to be sacrificed, is misleading; for what God allowed was Christ to sacrifice Himself. What role would the Father be playing in preventing Him from doing this?

The sacrifice of the divine human being in a way which expiates humanity's sins has two sides to it, first as a gesture analogous to the proper expression of remorse and second as a communal gesture.

For the first aspect, what is required is this: that the action should be of a certain sort; and this condition is held to be fulfilled if the Saviour suffers extraordinarily—a condition already made easier of fulfilment by the very fact that the Saviour is supposed to be divine, for then the infliction of torment and humiliation upon Him will seem so much the more momentous and outrageous than would the torturing of any human being (though one may wonder in passing whether this point, so often employed in sermons, is quite just, since it militates against the second condition, which we come to presently). For the second aspect, what is needed is this: that the action should be that of one who is identified with the group; and this condition is held to be fulfilled in the case of a Saviour by the fact that He is a member of the human race. For then He can serve as the representative of humanity, and so expiate the sin which divides man from God. By performing a colossal communal gesture, the situation, so long awry, is adjusted; there is atonement.

We note then that the actions of the divine Saviour do not necessarily have any important causal effect, even though their occurrence is momentous. For at least some of them are important as gestures; and gestures have effects which are akin, as has been said, rather to legal than causal effects, in which the religious situation is readjusted from a previous state of grave unbalance. It may also be remarked parenthetically that this notion of a *gesture* will prove important in the analysis of moral actions viewed *sub specie religionis*. Of this we treat more fully later.

However, it would be somewhat misleading to suppose that the extent to which the Saviour's actions are significant is exhausted by this description. There are other ways in which the events in the life of a divine human may take on special meaning. For clearly the sense in which Christ's death upon the Cross is a gesture differs from the way in which His rising from the dead is thought to be significant. Briefly: in the one case the action is a symbol, in the other a sign. For the sacrifice of the Saviour performs the function of righting a situation which is in a sense wrong (wrong, that is, because it cannot but be a matter of regret that man is inadequate before the object of worship; not wrong, in this respect, that humility before the Creator is the appropriate reaction). And it is apt enough to call gestures which adjust moral relations symbolic actions. On the other hand, the Resurrection of Christ has a different sort of significance: it is a sign both of Christ's divinity and that death has been defeated (in a special sense of 'defeat'). Whereas the sacrifice on the Cross constitutes the expiation of the sin of mankind, the Resurrection does not constitute the defeat of death but serves rather to show that death is in fact mastered. Whereas the one is a performance, the other is a demonstration. The one does, the other shows.

Again there are other events in the divine life which have an even more complicated status. For instance, the institution of the sacrament of Holy Communion. The institution itself is an act, though not a symbolic act (more like the handing over of a city's keys than the hauling down of a flag); but the rite instituted is commemorative of a symbolic act (Christ's sacrifice). We note too that the institution of rites which themselves have something of a saving effect is a part of the Saviour's power to save. It shows too the rather complicated status of the concept of *saving*, since although the gesture of the divine human is held to be in itself sufficient expiation for the sins of mankind, yet it does not follow that every person is thereby automatically freed from his burden. Potentially, he is saved if he calls on His Saviour, if he avails himself of the means of grace, etc. Thus the individual worshipper acquires a right which he may exercise, though the exercise is limited by certain conditions. Or briefly, what he gains is hope.

These remarks, perhaps, help to make clearer what is involved in the notion that a divine human has the power to save. Not only does he possess the spiritual wisdom and authority which will help men to understand religious truth and be better able to release themselves from their religious shortcomings, but also he has a status in his own person such that a gesture on his part will right a situation hitherto out of joint. However, this latter status can only be somewhat dogmatically established. For whereas the holiness and purity of the divine man are evident from his conduct (albeit that one has to have, so to speak, an eye for these characteristics—as too with beauty, for the criteria cannot be tidily described so that rules of thumb could be laid down beforehand which would be sufficient to guide anyone of common sense to a correct judgment); and whereas too the spiritual wisdom of the teacher is recognizable from pondering his words and behaviour; his status as a Saviour has, up to a point, to be taken on trust. Up to a point, but not entirely, as we shall see.

VII. EVIDENCE ABOUT THE SAVIOUR'S STATUS

On the assumption that a certain person has the status of Saviour, it may be that the events of his life will fall into place, and so the dogma will acquire some persuasiveness; but because of the subtlety of the evidence they will only acquire this persuasive significance once his position as a Saviour has been acknowledged. Thus although the divine man will possess the power to save, this power will not be one of the initial criteria for recognizing him as divine, but will be seen as involved in the claim that he is divine.

Thus the criteria for conferring the title of divinity, which we may call the criteria of *divination* (to use a term of Otto's), are of two different types: first, those which are evident before faith, such as the possession of holiness; and second, those which become evident after faith, such as those which show him to be a Saviour. In respect of the latter, the particular courses of action adopted by the divine man will have to be viewed in close connection with the doctrinal scheme in which belief in his divinity appears. By consequence, since there may be certain general points relevant to divination, such as the principle that sin is expiated by sacrifice, the distinction between the two types is not rigid. Nevertheless it is a useful one in pointing to the way that a divinatory claim is, since it is eventually to be backed by appeal to after-faith evidence, very closely bound up with the particularities of history. For whereas the saintliness or holiness of an individual is such as to be capable of display in a variety of epochs, the manifestation of divinity is much more severely limited (one presumes). And tremendously so, of course, where the principle of the uniqueness of a Saviour is maintained. Thus the transfiguration of conduct into holiness would retain its flavour, so to speak, in a quite different life; but an alteration of the circumstances of a Saviour's career might impart a quite different atmosphere to it—and we might not be so sure that the new pattern is the right one for a Saviour. So historical investigations will be of vital import for the establishment of the divinatory claim; though by themselves they would be by no means sufficient, since the ultimate divinatory judgment is somewhat analogous to an aesthetic one. Not, however, to a simple aesthetic judgment, such as that a piece of music is good—but rather to an elaborate opinion, such as that the works of some composer possess a certain characteristic. It being then discovered that one of the key examples cited is not after all by this composer, the judgment may fall to the ground. Thus though the opinion may require insight as well as attention to the facts, the facts nevertheless constitute the material upon which the judgment is formed. Similarly with a divinatory judgment.

As to the insight needed: the pattern of events in the Saviour's life may be such as to provide clear cross-references to previous events and thus fall into a wider historical pattern. For if one and only one is the Saviour, it immediately seems apposite to ask: Why at this point in history? Why under the aegis of that doctrinal scheme?

Thus we may contrast the situation with respect to the divinatory judgment with that obtaining in the other two strands discussed. In the numinous strand, claims are to be confirmed by reference to the features of existence found wonderful and mysterious; in the mystical strand, claims are to be confirmed by reference to the words and behaviour of the mystic; while in the incarnation strand, the divinatory judgment rests upon a much more elaborate structure of evidence concerning the career of the incarnate deity: historical evidence to form the material basis of a quasi-aesthetic judgment.

VIII. DIVINATION AND WEAVING TOGETHER

It was remarked at the outset of this discussion that the notion of incarnation presupposes the existence of a deity in another world. As a natural consequence, the establishment of the divinatory claim is very largely bound up with showing how the propositions about a holy Teacher are to be woven together with those about an object of worship (a weaving together analogous to that described earlier in connection with the numinous and mystical strands), and it is worth while, by way of concluding this present outline of the third strand, appending a summary of the modes in which this is done. It will serve to recapitulate what has gone before.

(i) The incarnate deity has formal resemblance to the object of worship, since he has an analogical similarity in respect of purity and holiness. And it should be noted here that the capacity to work miracles is seen as a sign of that dread and holy power that is ascribed to the numinous: the marvellous works of the incarnate deity are intimations of omnipotence.

(ii) His teaching displays a power to save which brings him close to God, on the principle that the holy constitutes a source of salvation. God reveals himself not merely in the world but in words. And in this the Teacher displays intimations of ominiscience.[1]

(iii) His life includes some gesture or gestures which have the effect of bringing salvation to mankind: and for this to happen he must either be God's very special instrument or God himself.

(iv) A foreshadowing of the weaving-together may occur in the form of Messianic prophecies; and the Saviour's life may be seen to fall into the right type of pattern, so that there are continual cross-references between his life and earlier images and predictions. (We may observe: Isaiah's picture of the Suffering Servant is pregnant with the principle that man can be saved only by God

[1] As Śaṅkara remarks: the omniscience of Brahman 'follows from its being a source of scripture' (Comm. on *Vedānta-Sutras*, I.i.3), cp. the kind of omniscience attributed to Gotama.

Himself becoming man and sacrificing Himself; and a fulfilment of this is seen in the life of the Saviour.)

We may note that the first two characteristics may be possessed, albeit in less luminous and impressive fashion, by the non-divine saint or prophet.

Finally, it should be remembered that once the weaving together is done (so to speak: the tenses are 'as if'), the incarnate deity will be viewed as possessing attributes proper to the numinous strand, though showing that He does in fact possess these will not be possible, beyond pointing to the features of His character and life which justify the weaving together of the two strands. And conversely, the properties of the object of worship will take on a new appearance once God and God-Man are identified. Jesus acquires the characteristics of the Divine Creator and sits at the right hand of God in heaven; while through the figure of Christ we see that God is Love.

V

Priorities among Doctrines

I. THREE ELEMENTS IN THE JUSTIFICATION OF DOCTRINES

So far three elements in the justification of religious doctrines have been noticed. For, in the first instance, attention has been drawn to the bases upon which propositions in the different strands rest: for example, the reactions of awe which lie behind propositions about the Creator. Second, attention has been directed to certain quasi-theoretical or *formal* considerations operative in the formation of doctrines: for example, the requirement of simplicity whereby a monotheistic or monistic doctrinal scheme has a formal advantage over polytheistic ones, and again, the requirement that a divine entity must be concealed. Perhaps we can also place in this category the somewhat lower-level principles that can be appealed to, such as the principle that sin is to be expiated by sacrifice. Third, we have seen that the weaving together of doctrines allows of their being justified by appeals to analogies and similarities, as when the timelessness of a mystical experience helps to cement propositions about the Ātman to those about Brahman. These elements can be named respectively *basic*, *formal* and *organic* justifications. There is, however, another type of consideration not easily separable from formal justification, but which in any event it is convenient to treat separately

II. PRIORITY DECISIONS AS BETWEEN STRANDS

This other element in the justification of doctrines may be called the making of *priority decisions* as between strands (and we may call the justification of one doctrinal scheme as against another by appeal to priorities a *preferential* justification: we then have four sorts—basic, formal, organic and preferential). It is useful to deal with priority decisions separately for two reasons: first, it is at least a peculiar type of formal justification; and second, such a treatment will help to illustrate by a number of examples the manner in which different doctrinal schemes are produced by varying the strength, so to speak, of the basic ingredients.

A limiting case of a priority decision is where one strand does not appear at all and where there appears only one. Such a case would be that of Theravāda Buddhism, which is agnostic as to the existence of a Creator and in which rites of worship play no important role. Moreover, the high status accorded to the Buddha does not involve the ascription to him of divinity (where we draw the line between reverence and worship is a matter depending on taste and insight); his rank as Enlightened One is much on a par with Mohammed's status as prophet: though deeply respected as givers of truth, neither is a god.[1] As a consequence of this more or less exclusive insistence on the mystical strand, the insistence that salvation consists in the mystical release of nirvāṇa, the life of Southern Buddhism centres on the monastery, for it is precisely those who have given up ordinary interests in the pursuit of the mystical goal who constitute the core of the religious community. Though it is said in the later part of the *Milindapãnha*[2] that the ordinary householder can in this life achieve nirvāṇa (that is, he would not have to await rebirth), this assertion is merely a sign of the stresses threatening the usual doctrine. These stresses are well summed up in the question asked in the same work as to whether the Buddha is equally compassionate to all, since it appears that only the few can achieve liberation in this life; and ultimately it was such questions that led to the transformation of Buddhism manifested in Mahāyāna, where we arrive (in some sects, such as the Pure Land School and the Nichirenite Sect) at the other extreme: salvation is open to all even in this life, if they but call upon the name of Amida Buddha.[3] This points to one type of consideration which can be important in determining priority decisions. For religion, in its higher forms, aims at being available to all men, directly or ultimately; and so it might be

[1] For which reason the Western names given to these religions, 'Buddhism' and 'Mohammedanism', are not apt, since they suggest a parallel with the name 'Christianity', as though Mohammedans, for example, are devotees of the Prophet in the way Christians are devotees of Christ: adherents of Islām therefore object to the Western name.

[2] VI.2.

[3] Salvation means here assurance of rebirth in Amida's Paradise (the Pure Land): nirvāṇa stays in the doctrinal framework by being the ultimate goal attainable in the Pure Land, where conditions for its attainment are most favourable.

counted a defect in a doctrinal scheme if it concentrates exclusively upon the mystical goal, for mysticism is undoubtedly for the few, not the many. On the other hand, it happens that the doctrine of successive rebirth, common to all Indian post-Vedic religions, considerably mitigates the exclusiveness of Hīnayāna Buddhism, since the ordinary householder who does not give up the world may by good conduct assure himself of a higher position in another life, from which he can embark on the arduous monastic journey towards nirvāṇa.

At the other extreme from the mystical faiths such as Buddhism and Jainism (and the Sāṅkhya version of orthodox Hinduism), we find the rigid monotheism of Judaism and Islām. It is interesting that the latter displays the opposite tendency from that of Buddhism. For the religion, in origin firmly monotheistic, was brought to a severe crisis with the appearance of the Ṣūfī movement, which stressed, not the practice of worship which plays so central a part in the life of the ordinary Muslim, but the attainment of a spiritual vision along the disciplined path of the ascetic. Why this should produce a crisis will be examined shortly in some detail. But at any rate the fact of the crisis is sufficient indication that this strand of religious propositions was not already woven into Islamic doctrine and that the characteristics of the scheme as presented by the Prophet (or at least as understood by his followers) are those to be expected of one which has as its basis the propositions of worship: the daily prayers prescribed are basically expressions of awe and prostration before Allah, and the religious ideal is surely not retreat from the world but the playing of a forceful moral part in it.

We note in passing that the monotheistic faiths which stress the numinous strand involve a view of the world which finds its sophisticated expression in a type of 'philosophical' realism. For though the world is held to be a contingent creation which conceals Something of greater wonder and mystery, it is also the work of God and a splendid work. Hence, a radical denial of its reality not only constitutes a slighting of the Creator, but also helps to undermine the evidence, in the shape of traces of glory in the world and in life, upon which faith has its basis. We should recall, of course, the peculiar role in spiritual discourse of such concepts as 'reality' and 'existence'. A consequence of this 'realism' is the emphasis laid, in such schemes, upon the importance of works as well as faith; for men ought to play their part in the real world;

they do not withdraw from it as they would from a mirage. (It should perhaps be said, to prevent misunderstanding, that there are two kinds of works which can be contrasted to faith: namely, ascetic and moral works—to give them brief titles. The Buddhist mystic does not rely on faith because the mystical goal is to be achieved by strenuous spiritual effort: ascetic works are necessary for release. The theist goes beyond faith and beyond ascetic quietism, for his submission to the Will of the Almighty leads to works in the world—charity, the help of those in distress, conscientious performance of his duty, and so forth; moral works, though not perhaps necessary to salvation, are a sign of it: they flow from faith. In the above remarks on 'realism' I am of course concerned with *moral* works, which is what the word 'works' customarily refers to in the Christian contrast between faith and works.) Thus the active part played by the adherent of Islām, with the strong insistence on obeying God's commands and the supremely exalted position accorded to Allah, signified in the forceful accusations of dire blasphemy against those who for one reason or another seek to present a different picture of the Divine, serve to show the extent to which Islām is concentrated on the numinous strand. As a further result of this, the role of Mohammed himself is carefully defined, so that the shadowy line between reverence and worshipped is never overstepped; and the example of Christianity is held up constantly as a dread warning against misinterpreting the position of the Prophet and lapsing into polytheism (for of course, in Muslim eyes, Christians are polytheistic; and the Trinity doctrine is looked on as an unsatisfactory attempt to conceal this).

It is not therefore surprising that the Ṣūfī movement, by bringing man up to and close to God, should have caused grave difficulties. An understanding of how these arise affords us an insight into the gap which remains between the numinous and the mystical strands, even when we have recognized the analogies which allow of doctrinal interweaving and which present some organic justification for this combining of the strands. For the resemblances are never so close that it would be absurd to deny that the strands are inextricably involved in each other: and this is another way of saying that they *are* different strands.

III. CONFLICT BETWEEN THE NUMINOUS AND THE MYSTICAL STRANDS

The chief problem which accrues upon the juxtaposition of the numinous and mystical strands, the coalescence of worship and mysticism, can be explained as follows. First, a great gap divides man from the divine. Second, mystical experience is often described as union with the divine. And these facts generate a situation where the mystic's utterances will appear blasphemous. For it seems he will be putting himself on the level of God. But something obscure about the matter remains, namely why the experience should so frequently be described as *union* with God (identification with Brahman, etc.).

Here we revert to what was said about mystical bliss. It was emphasized that, almost as a matter of logic, this bliss is not a perception. True, mystics speak of seeing Brahman and God, but, as has been remarked, this is an analogical use, arising partly from the fact that the achievement of this state is in some sense an illumination. Hereafter, everything will be viewed differently. Despite this, what is felt is not an object, since there is no publicly observable entity which two mystics might conceivably perceive simultaneously. It is not therefore like the case of a man observing something, such that it is reasonable to make a distinction between the seer and the seen. Thus there are not (in any ordinary sense) two entities, the mystic and the object of his vision. As a consequence, his experience, in so far as is described as experience of God, will most likely be thought of as union with the divine. And 'experience of God' will function in some respects rather like 'experience of bliss'. It is in this way that the mystic is driven to describe (doctrinally) his experience in a manner which on other grounds he might wish to avoid. And indeed mystical utterances are sometimes alarming. Thus, for instance, al-Jīlānī:

> I plunge into the sea of God's knowledge, and I have seen Him with my eyes. I am the living evidence of God's existence.[1]

Here he seems on the brink of blasphemy. And even more violent is al-Hallāj's famous cry, 'I am the Real.' Similarly, the language of deification among Christian mystics, though more controlled, is nevertheless rather strong:

> Some may ask what it is like to be a partaker of the Divine Nature . . . ? Answer: he who is imbued with or illuminated by the

[1] See I. Goldziher, *Mohammedanische Studien*, ii, p. 289.

Eternal or Divine Light and inflamed and consumed with Eternal or Divine Love, he is a deified man and a partaker of the Divine Nature.[1]

Again, Eckhart writes:

> If I am to know God directly, I must become completely He and He I: so that this He and this I become and are one I.[2]

This contrasts sharply with the other sentiment, that it is *hybris* for any man to seek to be among the gods: that it is 'a sin to regard any creature as Viṣṇu'. Devendranath Tagore has summed up the conflict succinctly:

> What we want is to worship God. If the worshipper and the object of worship become one, how can there be any worship? [3]

Thus there is at least considerable tension between the two strands of language when they come together. We have already sketched briefly the way in which this conflict can be resolved, but it is interesting to look at the different results so achieved, depending on the assignment of priorities.

IV. DIFFERENCES BETWEEN MYSTICAL AND NUMINOUS THEOLOGY

It should first be noticed that the two strands produce characteristically different types of theology (in the case of Hīnayāna Buddhism, we do not find theology, of course, except in a very limited way; but I am speaking now of doctrinal schemes which do include the concept *God* or an analogue). We have already had occasion to remark that idealistic propositions are characteristically associated with mysticism, whereas numinous theologies tend to be moderately realistic. There is another difference, represented by the distinction between positive and negative theology, the latter being more in the style of the mystical, the former in that of the numinous strand.

Negative theology may be described as being largely *ontological*, in that the use of ontological and allied expressions is common. Thus words such as 'reality', 'being', 'unity', etc., are often used to characterize that which the mystic discovers, attains to, etc.

[1] *Theologia Germanica*, xli, quoted in Underhill, *Mysticism*, p. 418.
[2] *Mystische Schriften*, p. 122, quoted in Underhill, p. 420.
[3] *Autobiography*, p. 72.

Consider the following examples, where ontological expressions are naturally used:

I am sure that if a soul knew the very least of all that Being means, it would never turn away from it.[1]

For I saw and knew the Being of all Beings, the Byss and the Abyss.[2]

And here is a death in fruition, and a meeting and dying into the nudity of Pure Being.[3]

Again:

Satori is the perception of Reality itself, so to speak.[4]

Lead me from the unreal to the real, Lead me from darkness to light, Lead me from death to immortality.[5]

And as a doctrinal corollary: these ontological predicates will be held by the mystically inclined to those which aptly describe the divine. Thus, Brahman, according to Śaṅkara, has two aspects, with and without attributes (*saguṇam* and *nirguṇam*): the impersonal Absolute and the personal Lord (*Īśvara*). But the latter picture of the divine as Creator and Lord is infected with illusion: in highest truth Brahman is without attributes. It is *neti neti* (not this, not that).[6]

[1] Eckhart's *Mystische Scriften*, p. 137, quoted in Underhill, *Mysticism*, p. 93.

[2] Boehme, *Collected Works*, English Trans. (1764–81), vol. I, p. xv.

[3] Ruysbroeck, *De Ornatu Spiritualium Nuptiarum*, iii.4.

[4] D. T. Suzuki, *Introduction to Zen Buddhism*, p. 93.

[5] *Bṛhadāraṇyaka Upan.*, I.3.38.

[6] Compare the Kabbalistic doctrine that the *En Sof* (the Boundless, i.e. the Supreme Being) has 'neither will, intention, desire, thought, language, nor action, as these properties imply limit and belong to finite things' (Ginsburg, *The Kabbalah*, p. 146; quoted in F. H. Smith, *The Elements of Comparative Theology*, p. 122). Compare too the impersonal character of the Tao, the stark descriptions of Reality in Mādhyamika doctrine and the Vijñānavādin school of Mahāyāna. Again, for a contrast which closely follows that of Śaṅkara: 'In the *Insam'l Kāmil* (of Jīlī) we find the same contrast as in the Vedanta system between Being with attributes, i.e. God, and Being which would not be absolute unless stripped of all its qualities. Divinity (*Ilāhiyya*)—the domain of Allah—is the highest *manifestation* of the essence' (R. A. Nicholson, *Studies in Islamic Mysticism*, p. 97). Jīlī calls the simple essence, apart from all qualities and relations, 'the dark mist' (*al- 'Amā*) (*op. cit.*, p. 84), a phrase which is most suggestive of the origin of the doctrine in mystical experience. A modern theologian who betrays the same tendency to use mystical and ontological language is Tillich—a reaction, we may say, to the numinous-based theology of Karl Barth. It should be noted that impersonal ontological doctrines, though justifiable ultimately from the spiritual point of view in terms of mystical experience in which they find their real basis, are also thrown up by metaphysical speculation: of this strange conspiracy between philosophy and mysticism we shall speak more anon.

We have already remarked that these ontological expressions have an unusual use in spiritual contexts, that is that they serve, among other things, to express value judgments. But to say this alone would be to fail to get their full flavour and their full force. To do so one must attend to two further points: (i) the way in which mystical experience is held to yield an important kind of knowledge; and (ii) the ineffability of the experience and its relation to the use of these expressions.

V. THE KNOWLEDGE YIELDED BY MYSTICAL ATTAINMENT

The knowledge claimed to accrue upon mystical experience is often contrasted with other types of knowledge in two main respects: first, in its far higher value; and second, in its direct or intuitive character.

As to (i), it is, of course, difficult to find a yardstick wherewith to measure the relative worth of pieces of information or fields of enquiry. However, the persuasiveness of the first distinction rests to a large extent on the correctness of the second. For clearly, mystical knowledge, with its ineffability, is hardly likely to fulfil the condition required of an important field of scientific enquiry—namely its strategic position among other similar enquiries. And in general it would, of course, be extremely doubtful whether spiritual achievements would have anything directly to do with scientific investigations (indirectly, perhaps, in as much as certain dispositions such as humility which are fostered by a religious attitude would prove of use in scientific and other pursuits). Thus it cannot be the case that mystical knowledge is much more important than types of scientific knowledge as judged on the same scale. Consequently, the claim that mystical knowledge is supreme involves what we may call *jumping scales.* This is harmless, provided it is understood what is going on. It is, on the other hand, dangerous for those who are off their philosophical guard, and results in the ascription of miraculous theoretical powers to the mystic, which he must repudiate and which are quite foreign to his insights.

Thus, as we have said, the plausibility of the exalted claims made on behalf of mystical knowledge rests on the making of a distinction between this kind of knowledge and other sorts. For if no such distinction is made, then it can hardly be given a high place on an inappropriate scale. However, the distinction that is sometimes drawn, by saying that mystical knowledge is intuitive and not discursive, is by itself inadequate. Nevertheless, by describing the contrast by reference to language, its fundamental appositeness becomes apparent. Thus: there are certain claims to knowledge which are such that the items of knowledge can be expressed in a description. For example, if I know how high a mountain is, it is entailed that I can say; for if I cannot say, this is overriding evidence that I do not know (here allowance is made for odd cases such as this: I cannot say at the moment, but still maintain that I know—and rightly—because given some reflection, or the consultation of a notebook, I shall be able to say).[1] On the other hand, some claims are different, for it is not entailed that I can say. Thus I can know what something sounds like even if I cannot say what it sounds like. Such a claim can be backed because under the appropriate circumstances I can recognize the sound which I claim to know. Mystical knowledge is to be placed under this second heading: it is a form of knowing what something is like. One knows Brahman, to quote the *Bhagavadgītā*, 'just as one feels one's own grief and woe'.[2] Nevertheless, though silence is an appropriate and solemn way of expressing the knowledge gained, the situation is complicated by the fact already adverted to, namely that the insight so gained leads to the expression of a new attitude to the world which is figured in the picture of the world as unreal or impermanent, etc. Thus St. Gregory remarks:

> The subsequent effect of the divine vision on the soul is noticed, not merely in detachment from the world and contempt for it, but in the experience of being above it and that it is a passing show.[3]

Consequently, though the experience itself yields immediate knowledge which is ineffable, it has the effect of promoting attitudes which can in some measure be expressed. It is to be noted, however, that even with these the advancing of reasons on behalf of the claims is difficult, since one can only see the truth of idealistic propositions such as that the world is unreal through the experience; what has to be said is something of this sort: 'Pass along this way and then you will see the truth of what I say.'

Further, what distinguishes the ineffable mystical knowledge from its analogues such as knowing what happiness is really like or what the sound of a flute is like is seen in the path towards the

[1] See Wittgenstein, *Philosophical Investigations*, p. 78.
[2] ix.2.
[3] *Ep.*, i.5.

goal. It is the strange setting in which mystical claims occur that give them their peculiar flavour. It is therefore necessary to remind ourselves that the sense in which mystical claims to knowledge are said to be of far more importance than other claims to knowledge is scale-jumping: that the knowledge gained by spiritual practices is of far greater *general* value than other branches of knowledge. Here the word 'general' has the force of signalizing that the claim jumps scales; and that the compared values lie on a super-scale. But, it may be asked, is it not illegitimate to employ such a super-scale? It is intelligible if someone says that this picture is better than that one; but senseless to ask if the portrait of Rembrandt's second wife is better or worse than Babe Ruth's displays of baseball skill. However, there is a kind of super-scale which makes sense of the mystical claim, which can be described crudely as one on which activities, etc., are ranged in order of practical value: the mystical knowledge so valued is ranked high because it touches the whole of our lives. It is certainly not supreme in the way some may say that physics is supreme, in that it will ultimately provide the theoretical framework within which chemistry, biology, neuro-physiology and so on will fall. Rather, the claim as to the supremacy of mystical knowledge is based upon the different premiss, that it provides the most vital kind of know-how, since it generates the principles upon which the best pattern of life can be fashioned.

This point may be illustrated from the role which *vidyā* or knowledge plays in the *Upaniṣads*. As Edgerton remarked:

> Oldenburg's figure of a Vedic philosopher seeking 'to unfold a picture of things as they are, out of the pure joy of perceiving and understanding', is more than 'rare', as he calls it. Such an individual never existed, either in the Vedic period or in later India, as far as our records show.[1]

He goes on to say that the later systems of philosophy are all supposed to be practical means of attaining *mukti* or *mokṣa*. He is perhaps overstating a good case here, since, though the ultimate concern of most or all Indian philosophers may have been release, there is ample display of logical acumen and the desire to tackle logical and epistemological problems. Nevertheless, he points to some significant facts: that the word *vidyā* ('knowledge') in Classical Sanskrit commonly means 'magic', and that there are only two

[1] *The Upanisads: What do they seek, and why?* J.A.D.S., 49, pp. 97–121.

passages in the *Upaniṣads* where the fruits of knowledge are not stated.[1] But it is not to be thought that the attention paid to the fruits of knowledge is merely utilitarian mean-mindedness; it is appropriate just because spiritual knowledge is of this sort, as a background and guide to salvation. The authors of the *Upaniṣads* are reflecting the nature of the case. Unfortunately, and this has been a consistent feature of religious history, attention to the fruits can soon relapse into magic, as the use of *vidyā* in post-*Upaniṣadic* writings shows. But the mystical claim is not to be construed as a magical one—for the hall-mark of the magical is to boast of doing the startling by inappropriate means, and mystics do not, in their clearer moments, lay claim to technical or scientific knowledge of a superior kind. The fact that their knowledge is superior to the knowledge gained in physics does not entail that it is a superior form of scientific knowledge. One cannot, by settling down to ascetic practices and to meditation, gain information about the universe which would be available to the scientist only after long and arduous investigation (so too one cannot by philosophical cogitation arrive at a special theory of the cosmos which will supersede empirical enquiries). But it *does* claim to provide a picture of the religious situation, together with advice on how to live, such that one may have a guide to salvation. In this sense, it is practical knowledge. For convenience we may describe it under two heads: first, the knowledge *of* (Brahman, etc.); and second, the idealistic and other propositions generated by the experience —this is the mystical knowledge *that*. (In addition, there is the knowledge *how*: how to gain blessedness, through mystical discipline.)

About the mystical knowledge *that*: why use the term 'knowledge' here? It is worth while here appending some remarks on this, since it might strike some as hardly to be called *knowledge*, differing as it does from standard examples. The reasons for using the term are threefold:

(i) it is based upon experience which is held to be sufficient to establish the truth of the idealistic propositions beyond doubt, whereas in at least some uses of the contrasted 'belief' a belief is still awaiting confirmation in experience. The claim to knowledge can be backed autobiographically, as in more mundane cases one says 'I *know*, because I was there', etc.

(ii) The experience produces a feeling of certitude, which

[1] *Bṛhadāraṇyaka Upan.*, V.2.1, *Chāndogya Upan.*, VI.8.

renders inappropriate such expressions as 'belief' or 'opinion', suggesting as they do some hesitation.

(iii) The experience is often described as illumination (etc.); and seems to be like realizing something: one realizes the truth, perhaps, of the idealistic propositions. But one cannot be said to have realized the truth of P and not to know that P.

VI. ONTOLOGICAL TERMS AS DEVOID OF DESCRIPTIVE CONTENT

Bearing in mind, then, the importance which is held to pertain to the insight which the mystic calls knowledge, we may now turn to the second main consideration which is relevant to the use of ontological terms in spiritual discourse. It has already been said that the bliss attained is indescribable, though this ineffability is qualified by the remarks that can be made about the formal features of the experience and by the fact that the consequent attitudes (about the unreality or impermanence of the world) can themselves be expressed in words. Yet the mystical bliss is itself such that the best grammar for speaking it is silence. So too Śaṅkara remarks: 'This Ātman is silent.'[1]

Yet how is this reconcilable with the fact that ontological expressions are sometimes used to make claims about the experiences? For example, with the assertion that herein somehow we come into contact with Pure Being?

The reconciliation arises out of points already mentioned. For (i) ontological expressions are devoid of descriptive content. Moreover, the uses of these words in mystical contexts is such that they do not occur in descriptive combinations. Thus while 'human being' is a descriptive combination ('being' here functioning merely as a grammatical place-filler), 'Pure Being' is insured, so to speak, against the possibility of its describing. For 'Being' is an ontological place-filler, and 'pure' is itself contentless, being what may conveniently be termed an intensifier (like 'very', 'supreme', etc.). Similarly with such combinations as 'Ultimate Reality'.

(ii) Ontological words have an important value use. Nor is it difficult to see why this should be so. For (*a*) many nouns have functional criteria of application—e.g. 'table', 'ford', 'teamster': we apply the terms to the entities because they perform functions. Consequently, ontological expressions used to qualify these will

[1] Comm. on *Vedānta-Sūtras*, III.2.10.

take on an appraising air, since the failure of some object which is a candidate for being called a table to fulfil the required functions will be counted a defect. Thus it is understandable that the ontological expressions should have an extended use here, to signalize that the entity fulfils the functions well (e.g. 'This is a *real* watch!'; 'He is a *real* artist', etc.). And (*b*), in general the ascription of a noun-word to an object enshrines a number of expectations, and if it turns out that the object does not live up to its nominal reputation this will usually be to some extent uncomfortable. Thus in general it will be untoward if an 'X' does not turn out to be a real or genuine X after all. For these two reasons, words like 'real', 'genuine', etc., will take on a valuational air, while expressions like 'unreal', 'illusory', etc., will be used to disvalue. It is not, therefore, as we have said, hard to see why ontological words should acquire some of the properties of straight value words such as 'good'.

And so it is not surprising that they should be used to give expression to the ineffable. For the latter is, as we have pointed out, rightly so-called in as much as it is (in the strict sense) indescribable; but it is not rightly so-called in that it may nevertheless be expressed, albeit inadequately, in virtue of its having value, as joy and bliss and pain have value. Thus the two points we have drawn attention to find here their fulfilment, for ontological words are without descriptive content on the one hand, and on the other they have a valuational use.

Furthermore, the two aspects of ontological words are given greater expressive power for dealing with the knowledge gained in mystical endeavour. In virtue of their connection with the ascription of nouns (and some other elements of a sentence), they are quite closely related to expressions which are used to appraise the status of propositions as a whole, that is to such words as 'true' and 'false' (which we shall call 'truth-value words'). That this relation is fairly close is illustrated by the way ontological words are sometimes used truth-value-wise and conversely (genuine claims and true friends, etc.). And it is *a priori* likely since ontological expressions are used to show that a predicate applies, and this is equivalent to claiming that the proposition containing the predicate is true. (In any case, the distinction between word or phrase and sentence, together with the parallel distinction between concept and proposition, is vague.) This relation between ontological and truth-value words allows of the divine's being called Truth Itself, and it is this Truth also that we come to know in mystical experience. This is, so to speak, the quintessence of the world, its Ground. And because this is the highest knowledge, as judged on the practical super-scale, so also the assertions are about That which transcends the perceptible and the describable, not about this appearance or that, but about the Reality beyond. Thus the value assigned by the use of the ontological expressions is far more intense than the mild value often ascribed in ordinary contexts. 'He is a real artist!'—to say this exhibits enthusiasm, sure enough; but it is not possessed of the depth and solemnity of spiritual utterance. To speak of knowledge of the Truth, of the Being of Beings—in these ways the dark goal of mysticism is invested with its due transcendence. Here lies, not knowledge, but the highest knowledge, not reality but Reality.

Yet these remarks as to why such words find a mystical use can be misleading in so far as they might have the effect of detracting from the solemnity and force which they should have in such contexts. To correct this error, all that can be done, unfortunately, is to repeat that indeed these words are highly charged; and of course it is no easy task to show how much power they do have—for this we need another context and even supplying one artificially by quoting will not succeed. Suffice it then to repeat in general terms the warning that the present discussion is only designed to give some brief indications of why ontological and other such expressions find a fruitful use in spiritual discourse, even though such indications may tend to obscure the force and liveliness that these words in fact possess.

VII. ONTOLOGICAL EXPRESSIONS PROVIDE THE MATERIAL FOR NEGATIVE THEOLOGY

These concepts, then, provide the raw material for mystical theology, which is in its general characteristics more negative and impersonal than the theology of the numinous strand pure and simple. Yet it might seem surprising that there should be a *theology* here at all. Indeed it is surprising in this respect, that there are mystical religions which are devoid of theology in the proper sense; but of course it is not surprising in view of the weaving together of which we have spoken. And we find that, from the theological angle, some peculiar properties of ontological words help to reinforce the connection held to be established between worship and mysticism. Consider, for example, these points. First, 'being' has a mysteriously ambiguous status, between a concrete and an abstract noun; and so serves well to name the transcendent object, since (*a*) though the divine is spoken of substantivally, it is also to be distinguished from mere objects (or persons) of this world, and (*b*) the mystical experience of God is accommodated, for 'being' has some of the features of 'bliss' (neither works like 'mountain'). Second, the opportunity is created for suggestive ways of speaking: God as the Ground of all being, the Pure Being on which all finite beings are dependent. There is another point we shall come to later, namely that the ascription of extreme numinous transcendence to God leads to the denial of anthropomorphisms as being blasphemous; and here there is a convergence of the two theologies.

It might be thought that such jugglings with odd items of language is precisely what nowadays we are trying to get away from—that indeed the most significant philosophical advances in recent years have been made because the genesis of useless metaphysics has been recognized as due to misuses of language. Is it not important, for instance, to see the linguistic fallacy upon which the Ontological Argument rests? Now, it would seem, these absurd modes of parlance are being smuggled back in through a back door.

There are two points to be made in reply. First, it is perfectly true that the oddities of language afford no ground for metaphysical speculation; the failure, for instance, to perceive that the same grammatical form may conceal differences of logical structure has sometimes led to widespread metaphysical conclusions, and it is distressing that such trivial causes should have such resounding effects. But secondly, and on the other hand, the salutary assault upon facile and unsound metaphysics can be too destructive; it may blind us to the fact that there is an inner compulsiveness about certain ways of speaking and thinking which has its roots in religious discourse, and that an indiscriminate attack upon these odd ways of using language may leave those who are under bombardment dissatisfied. One might coin the aphorism: philosophical theories are decayed doctrines—an aphorism which, though misleading in that philosophical theories have various and often unrelated purposes, yet points to the important truth that often the philosophical mistake lies not so much in the language of the conclusion as in the mode of arriving at it. Thus, for example, we have argued that a form of idealism expresses well a view of the world which is produced by the discipline and experience of the mystics; and this idealism is intelligible and appropriate within its own context. But it can sometimes become almost unintelligible, and certainly a little bizarre, when it appears in the environment of academic debate and metaphysical argumentation. For, first, its force and vitality are lost in such surroundings, and second, the arguments which are used to back it appear so unimpressive. Similarly, the Ontological Argument, which is designed to show no less than that there is a God, depends upon a piece of argumentation which, were we not so enamoured of the conclusion, would appear trivial. When we further reflect that such arguments often enshrine odd analyses or uses of language, we are tempted into supposing that what the premisses are alleged to show is also absurd. But here we go too far: for the fault lies, as we have said, not so much in the way the so-called conclusions are expressed as in the manner in which they are arrived at. It may be strange to speak of God, but it is not absurd, even if some of the arguments used to demonstrate God's existence are absurd. The modes of reasoning are inappropriate; and indeed it is in this discrimination of different ways of arguing that the modern critique of language finds its principal success.

Yet all that has been said here might seem to be beside the point, in that previously it was remarked that the peculiar ontological concepts such as *Being* provided suggestive ways of speaking (of God as the Source of all being, etc.); and this would appear to be an implicit defence of ontological methods of philosophical argument—that is, of those metaphysical moves which are sometimes subsumed under the title of 'ontology'.

But here it is necessary to distinguish between a defence of a certain kind of *argument* and a defence of a *way of speaking*. An argument is such that the premisses guarantee the truth of or establish the probability of the conclusion, and it seems in no wise plausible to maintain that ontological argumentation succeeds in doing this, at least in any obvious manner. The situation is much more complicated than either the supporters or opponents of such intellectual manœuvres customarily think. For much ontology can only be understood properly within the religious context, and therefore the bases upon which such broad conclusions rest will be religious ones, of the sort we have attempted earlier to describe. Nevertheless, the new ways afforded by the peculiar character of ontological terms serves further to cement the relationships already established between different strands by what we have called 'organic justification'. Thus ontological ways of speaking are a mode of embroidering upon organic justification. But the extent to which this is allowable must be tightly controlled by reference to the experiences, etc., which the modes of parlance are designed to describe; unless this is done the way will be left open for the wildest speculations. Thus, the ways of speaking will not be correctly described as arguments, but rather, first, as means of illuminating what is already in principle established, and second, as means of expressing a religious position. This latter phrase may well appear obscure; but with it we return to the main topic of this chapter, namely the elucidation of priority decisions as between strands of religious discourse. For the kind of religious position which the use of ontological ways of speaking will express is such as to show the view adopted with regard to the relative importance of the different strands. So let us now illustrate this point.

We can begin with a contrast drawn by Evelyn Underhill:

> The metaphysical mystic, for whom the Absolute is impersonal and transcendent, describes his final attainment of the Absolute as *deification* . . . The mystic for whom intimate and personal communion has been the mode under which he best apprehended Reality speaks of the consummation of this communion, its perfect and permanent form, as the *Spiritual Marriage* of his soul with God.[1]

It is a commonplace that the negative ontological theology of mystics such as Eckhart and Śaṅkara is impersonal: the divine is not described as having psychological attributes (will, love, etc.): why then should there be another sort of mystic who talks of 'intimate and personal communion', of 'Spiritual Marriage'? Evelyn Underhill does not seem to have seen the reason for the distinction she has drawn, and I think this is largely because she is working within a theistic framework. The limiting case of impersonal mystic is one like the Buddhist whose doctrinal scheme hardly contains the numinous strand at all. But where, as in Brāhmanism, we have a weaving together of the numinous and the mystical (with strong emphasis on the latter) the language of deification seems appropriate, since there is no distinction between subject and object in the experience. But this, of course, seems blasphemous to theists, and theistic mystics who, as well as paying homage to the Almighty, connect their worship up with their

[1] *Mysticism*, p. 415.

mystical effort (via devotions, for example) speak of their attainment of God more circumspectly. Marriage serves as a good illustration, since in the sexual act there is a feeling of union, and yet there still remain two persons. Further, as Yājñavalkya says in the *Bṛhadāraṇyaka Upaniṣad*:

> As a man when embracing his dear wife knows nothing without or within, so the person when in the embrace of the Self knows nothing without or within.[1]

Thus the marriage analogy serves to retain the subject-object (worshipper-divine) distinction while also portraying the raptness of the soul. Similarly theistic mystics tend to lay more emphasis on the analogy of *seeing* (also implying subject-object contrast); e.g. Philo commenting on *Deuteronomy*, xxxii.39 remarks:

> What He says is 'See that I AM', that is 'Behold my subsistence.'[2]

Being a theist he does not wish to say that we can behold God's essence, but only His existence, as we see the sun's light, though unable to gaze on the sun itself: this is an interesting use of an ontological term in a subsidiary position.

Succinctly: all mystics tend to use impersonal language, but the more numinously inclined mystics within a theistic tradition effect a compromise. The numinous strand will thus remain doctrinally predominant in their way of speaking, and their goal will be described in terms of Spiritual Marriage, etc.: contact with the Divine, not deification. The impersonal mystics on the other hand will favour ontological discourse as representing the truth about the divine, and the numinous discourse as ultimately unsatisfactory (even though perhaps a partial aspect of the truth).

A tidy illustration of the ontological doctrinal description of the divine by a mystically inclined theologian is given by the division of the divine attributes in order of importance made by the Ṣūfī mystic Jīlī:

(i) attributes of the Essence, e.g.: One, Eternal, Real;
(ii) of Beauty, e.g.: Forgiving, Knowing, Guiding Aright;
(iii) of Majesty, e.g.: Almighty, Avenging;
(iv) of Perfection, e.g.: Exalted, Wise, First and Last, Outward and Inward.[3]

We note that the qualities commonly associated with the numinous

[1] IV.3.21.
[2] *On the Posterity of Cain*, 167.
[3] R. A. Nicholson, *Studies in Islamic Mysticism*, p. 100.

object of worship fall centrally in division (iii) above, while the ontological and similar predicates fall under (i). Thus all three examples in (i) are descriptively empty, save in as much as 'Eternal' reflects the timelessness which is a formal characteristic of the mystical experience. Division (ii) represents a transition between (i) and (iii), in accordance with the common devolutionary method of mystical theologians. In Jīlī also we find the contrast seen in Śaṅkara, between the Being with attributes, that is God, and Being which would not be Absolute unless it were stripped of all its qualities.[1] The first step, then, in the devolution is the manifestation of the God with attributes, the Creator who is immediately responsible for the existence of the world and who is the object of worship. This devolution signalizes a decision as to priority. For the picture of God as almighty and providential, as ruling the phenomenal world, is only partial. Behind and beyond this manifestation there is the bare Essence, Absolute Being.

However, Jīlī does not go so far as Śaṅkara in the direction of idealism, for the phenomenal world is no illusion, but exists as the self-revelation or other self of the Absolute. Thus the priority of mysticism in Jīlī is not as sharply expressed as in Śaṅkara (this is, of course, not surprising, in that Jīlī comes under the aegis of a monotheistic faith). Śaṅkara with his extreme doctrine of illusion puts the mystical strand in the forefront of his theological picture: for the lower Brahman, the creative *Īśvara*, is, like the world, infected with illusion. The picture of the *Īśvara* is satisfactory for the purpose of worship, but not the ultimate truth. We can point to another double-aspect doctrine in Eckhart, who makes a distinction between Deus and Deitas—the former possessing the marks commonly given to the Almighty, the latter being incomprehensible and inexpressible.[2]

But it should be noted that there is a way of combining the mystical and numinous strands doctrinally which manages, up to a point, to preserve a balance. Evelyn Underhill, commenting on the theory of emanations (as opposed to that of immanence), remarks:

> The Absolute Godhead is conceived as removed by a vast distance from the material world of sense; the last or lowest of that system of dependent worlds or states which, generated by or emanating from

[1] *Op. cit.*, p. 97.
[2] See Rudolf Otto's fine comparison of Saṅkara and Eckhart in *Mysticism East and West.*

> the Unity or Central Sun, becomes less in spirituality and splendour, greater in multiplicity, the further they recede from their source. That Source—the Great Countenance of the Godhead—can never, say the Kabalists—be discerned by man.[1]

The point of this sort of doctrine is this: it succeeds in conflating three elements of religious thought which reflect spiritual experience, namely (i) mystical psycho-physical dualism, (ii) numinous dualism, and (iii) the ontological description of the Godhead. As for (i): the dualism coalesces with numinous dualism (the great gulf fixed between man and God) in two main respects. First, the ordinary self is regarded with contempt; but in contrast with doctrines of immanence, there is no emphasis laid on the notion of an underlying Self (God as immanent within us), and therefore the mystical Something for which we strive is far from us, not, as Ruysbroeck says, 'in the most secret part of the spirit'. Hence the path is described as a long pilgrimage; and this idea fits in with the conception of a great gulf fixed between man and God. Second, the contempt with which such a mystic views himself and this sinful world matches the abasement felt before the divine. As for (ii) and (iii): the numinous strand possesses a certain tension, since the personal and creative attributes assigned therein to God are liable (since they rely on analogies between man and God) to appear anthropomorphic and thus blasphemous. God, however, is indescribably beyond the praise we lavish; and by widening the great gulf further we are led to speechless prostration before the divine which accords with the ontological language of the emanationist mystic. Absolute Being is even further removed from man than the anthorpomorphic God. Thus there is an alliance here between mystical and numinous ineffability. In this way, a mystic can do justice to the numinous strand, though there still remain unorthodoxies, viz. (*a*) emanationism has an atmosphere of necessity rather than contingency, which is not in harmony with the more usual numinous account of creation; (*b*) the exaltation of the Godhead also involves, in this doctrine, the demotion of the empirical world; it is partly because the world is regarded as so much infected with sinfulness that the gradual emanations from the Godhead are postulated (the Godhead does not in this way have to come into direct contact, so to speak, with the base material world in which the mystic lives), and this low value assigned to the empirical cosmos is out of accord with the realism of the numinous

[1] *Mysticism*, p. 97.

strand. There the works of God, as well as being signs of His majesty, are a bountiful expression of His love.[1]

VIII. NEGATIVE THEOLOGY IN SECOND PLACE: THE BHAGAVADGĪTĀ AND RĀMĀNUJA

An interesting example of a priority decision the other way, with the numinous strand predominant and the mystical in a somewhat inferior position, is provided by the doctrines of the *Bhagavadgītā*.[2] The importance of the numinous strand therein can be gauged from three facts:

(i) There is the truly awful theophany of Kṛṣṇa in the Eleventh Reading; Arjuna is struck dumb with amazement: his hair stands on end.

> Thou devourest greedily all the worlds on every side with flaming mouths; filling the whole universe with brightness, thy splendours glow terribly, O Viṣṇu.[3]

(ii) There is the paramount emphasis upon *bhakti* (loving adoration):

> Abandoning all duties, come for refuge to me alone. I will free thee from all sins; do not grieve.[4]

[1] One might elaborate on this point: the realism of the purely numinous doctrinal scheme is moderate, i.e. though there is something beyond the real world of higher value, the glory of the Creator is reflected in His works. Again the idealism of the purely mystical strand is moderate, as in the doctrine that all things are impermanent. In a numinous doctrine which is permeated with mysticism (like the above example), the coalescence of the two strands (with the numinous nevertheless remaining stronger than it does in the *Brahman-Ātman* conflation) involves, if not idealism with regard to the external world, at least a loss of value in the external world. On the mystical side, this is expressed by saying that the world is far from God's spirituality; on the numinous side by saying that the lowest world in the devolution from the Godhead is of little splendour. The world is real, but of little value, and in this way there is a compromise between the moderate idealism of mysticism and the moderate realism of the numinous strand. It may be mentioned that the tendencies towards idealism in emanationism clash even more strongly with orthodox Christianity, since the realism of the numinous strand is there reinforced by an important Christological consideration, viz. that Christ is equally man and God so that the empirical world is sanctified; and idealism leads to docetism (compare the docetic doctrines about the Buddha in idealistic Mahāyāna: if the phenomenal world is unreal, the historical Buddha is but an appearance).

[2] Needless to say, there are different interpretations of the work. Śaṅkara, for instance, interprets it in an Advaita sense. However, despite apparent inconsistencies within the work, due largely to the mingling of concepts from different systems, the remarks made below appear to be a correct account.

[3] xi.30.

[4] xviii.66.

Whereas the early *Upaniṣads* lay their greatest stress upon *jñāna* (knowledge, i.e. mystical knowledge), and a lesser emphasis upon *śraddhā* (faith), the new scripture brings to the forefront adoration of and reliance upon the Deity.

(iii) A considerable extension is given to the concept of *yoga*. Heretofore the latter concept was confined to the mental and physical discipline required for attaining the mystical goal: yoga, that is, was a spiritual technique. In a sense, it appeared in isolation from the moral life, for the cultivation of the technique involved withdrawal from ordinary activities, from the works of the world. For, it was held, concern with works kept one tied to *saṁsāra*, the round of rebirth and the flux of phenomena. It was breaking out of this cycle that constituted liberation. However, in the *Bhagavadgītā*, the concept is widely extended, so that the performance of works in a spirit of devotion and detachment counts as yoga. By rejecting the fruits of action one is more truly workless than the Sāṅkhya adept who withdraws from the works of caste and religion (who withdraws, that is, from the ordinary social and religious duties by becoming a hermit).

All this represents, of course, a departure from much of the Upaniṣadic teaching, with its main stress laid upon the attaining of union with Brahman through mystical endeavour. A new and more personal account is given of the Deity. The old Vedic gods had lost their power and had become secondary, but now something of their spirit is renewed: Viṣṇu appears as the One God who on occasion descends to earth for the recall of men to the true path; and He is given a higher place than the monistic Brahman of the *Upaniṣads* who had before then usurped the place of the Vedic deities.

An illustration of the priority of the personal over the impersonal is given at the end of the Fourteenth Reading:

> He who serves me with unswerving devotion (*bhakti-yoga*) becomes, by going beyond the strands (*guṇas*), fit to become Brahman. For I am the foundation of Brahman, the changeless and immortal, of the everlasting law, and of absolute bliss.[1]

Thus God upholds Brahman, even as He also upholds the world. A clue to this point is to be seen in the strange verse:

> Of the forms arising in all wombs . . . the great Brahman is the womb, I the father that gives the seed.[2]

[1] xiv.26–7.

[2] xiv.4.

Here Brahman is, oddly enough, identified with the Unmanifest substrate of matter, the *avyaktam* of the Sāṇkhya system, as the matrix out of which Viṣṇu creates the manifested world. At first this might seem a strangely materialistic account of the Brahman of the *Upaniṣads*. But it must be remembered that the *Bhagavadgītā* welds together concepts of different origins—those of Sāṇkhya-Yoga, those of the *Upaniṣads*, together with the personalistic notions implicit in Vaiṣṇavism. This welding together is perhaps not always successful; but in the present instance, the way is left open for two cross-references. First, the image of the womb fits in with the description of God as the Supreme Male. Second, and more relevantly for our purpose, the lower *avyaktam* that provides the substrate for the world is reflected in a higher *avyaktam*, a higher Unmanifest, corresponding to the *avyaktam uttamam* of the *Upaniṣads*:[1] that Unmanifest, Concealed Being that is the Highest Reality. But in the *Bhagavadgītā*,

> though this higher *avyakta* is regarded as the highest essence of God, yet, together with the lower *avyakta* and the selves, it is upheld in the super-personality of God.[2]

Thus, although realizing Brahman is gaining contact with God, God is more than Brahman:

> Though the Brahman is again and again referred to as the highest abode and the ultimate realization, the absolute essence, yet God in His super-personality transcends even Brahman, in the sense that Brahman, however great it may be, is only a constitutive essence in the complex personality of God.[3]

Thus the way is open for a doctrine of both transcendence and immanence. God dwells in all men and can be reached for within:

> He will not rejoice at gaining what is pleasant, nor will he be vexed at gaining what is unpleasant: with stable mind, unbewildered, he knows Brahman and abides in Brahman.[4]

On the other hand, beyond this imperishable Brahman is the Supreme Person:

> Since I am beyond the perishable and beyond the imperishable also, in the world and in the Veda I am proclaimed the Supreme Person (*puruṣottama*).[5]

And so those who attain Brahman are described in a special way,

[1] See, e.g., *Kaṭha Upan.*, II.3.7–8.
[2] Dasgupta, *History of Indian Philosophy*, ii.476.
[3] *Op. cit.*, ii.524. [4] v.20. [5] xv.18.

in which the ontological expression is placed in a subordinate position:

> Many are they who, purified by the austerity of knowledge, have come into my Being (*madbhāvam*).[1]

Though the ascetically purified become Brahman, they do not become God: they enter into Him and He is their refuge, but He is more than His abode:

> Though he always performs all duties, making Me his refuge, it is by My grace that he attains the eternal immutable region.[2]

And even there he recognizes something beyond that region, for

> Becoming Brahman . . . he acquires supreme devotion to Me.[3]

This, then, represents a priority of the numinous over the mystical, albeit a narrow priority—in that though God is seen as the supremely adorable beyond even the bliss and eternity of the mystical goal, yet the mystical path is ultimately the way to God. Yet the emphasis, for the many, is on faith and devotion: 'Come for refuge to me alone': service to God through the selfless performance of works, both social and religious, itself counts as yoga; and through God's grace we can be set upon the path to final liberation.[4]

A second illustration of a numinous-preponderating interwoven doctrinal scheme is to be found in Rāmānuja. His system is known as 'Qualified Non-Dualism' (Śaṅkara's being straight non-dualism); and the important qualification is this: that both the world and souls are real—whereas according to Śaṅkara there is only one real entity: Brahman-Ātman. Now though Rāmānuja's doctrine is counted a form of non-dualism, on the ground that both souls and the world exist in and through Brahman, this non-dualism is largely a concession to those ways of speaking in the Scriptures which seemed to justify Śaṅkara's rather extreme view. For instance: though Rāmānuja stuck to the scriptural descriptions of Brahman as the truly real, this, he held, did not imply that the world is unreal, since the world is in some places described as the body of Brahman. All this is Brahman. Nevertheless, Rāmānuja drew a fairly sharp line between the world and God, and this is brought out in his somewhat Pickwickian analysis of the concept

[1] iv.10. [2] xviii.56. [3] xviii.54.

[4] Compare the way in which *nirvāṇa* is still described as the ultimate goal (possibly in another world) in theistic Mahāyāna.

body: it is that which is completely subordinated to the soul, which is capable of completely controlling and supporting it for its own ends. Anything, therefore, which is both an instrument of, and supported by, another entity counts as the latter's body. It will be seen, then, that Rāmānuja is enabled in this way both to retain the scriptural accounts of the world as the body of Brahman with a doctrine of the dependence of the world upon the *Īśvara*, its Creator.[1] Similarly, the relation between God and individual souls is ambiguously stated. Though they are in a sense parts of Brahman, it is again in a modified sense: in the sense in which the radiance emitted by a luminous body is part of it. Both world and souls are modes (*prakāras*) of Brahman, and this term covers up Rāmānuja's forced ambiguity. Even when the liberated soul is with the Divine, it is no absorption therein: the iron does not become the magnet which attracts it.[2] But, it may be enquired, why should Rāmānuja wish to preserve a distinction between soul and God, and between the world and God?

Perhaps because of this: the worshipper is a dualist, for he conceives himself as separated from the veiled object of worship. It is in accord with the spirit of the numinous strand that there should be such a dualism. And we see Rāmānuja's dualism reflected in his emphasis on *bhakti*. The way to God starts through worship and devotion; and then, through God's Grace (a vital aspect of Rāmānuja's doctrine), we may be led to a vision of God.[3] And his dualism is also reflected in the way he speaks of God's nature: not only is the *Īśvara* comprised of the three qualities often quoted as summing up His nature, viz. being, consciousness and bliss (*saccidānanda*), but He is much more fully describable: as

> the Lord of all, whose nature is antagonistic to all evil, whose purposes come true, who possesses infinite auspicious qualities such as knowledge, blessedness and so on; all-knowing, all-powerful, supreme in causation, from whom the creation, subsistence, and dissolution of this world proceed.[4]

[1] Not, however, Creator in the Christian sense: Rāmānuja is, roughly, an emanationist.

[2] SBE, xlviii, p. 156.

[3] We may bear in mind what was said earlier, viz. that the use of 'vision' effects a compromise, since the word implies a dualism in the mystical experience. Carpenter writes: 'The character of *vision* is again and again emphasized in the word *pratyakṣatā*, "before-the-eye-ness"' (*Theism in Medieval India*, p. 402, n. 3).

[4] SBE, xlviii, p. 156. I quote Carpenter's correction to Thibaut—see *Theism in Medieval India*, p. 396 and n.1.

And, inasmuch as He is the inner controller of all things, so also the operation of the law of *Karma* is part of His activity: His nature includes therefore not only the intelligence which guides the world but also impartial justice in distributing rewards and punishments. This picture then, of a Supreme Lord, worthy of devotion, good, just, omniscient, omnipotent, purposeful, creative and blissful, is quite far removed from the impersonal Absolute of Śaṅkara. There is no distinction between the Higher and Lower Brahman; and what for Śaṅkara would characterize the Lower Brahman is held by Rāmānuja to characterize Brahman.

At the same time Rāmānuja is by no means unmystical; the Divine is not merely ruler of the universe, but also the Inner Ruler (*antaryāmin*), who cooperates with us in our efforts by the operation of Grace. And when our hearts are pure we can then live in communion with God, and share the divine bliss. But this is never the full union with Brahman as conceived by Śaṅkara.[1]

We see similar tendencies in theistic Buddhism—to exalt the numinous at the expense of the mystical strand. This is perhaps the more surprising in Buddhism than in Hinduism, since Buddhism was in origin (and still is, in the Theravāda) an almost purely mystical religion; and it comes as something of a shock that such sects as the Pure Land School and the Nichirenites should count as Buddhists at all. The basic notion in the Pure Land doctrine is that salvation comes through calling upon Amida Buddha and by worshipping him; and for the faithful there is the hope that upon death they will be reborn in his Paradise, the Pure Land of the West. This seems at first quite out of accord with orthodox Buddhism, but it nevertheless is accommodated to orthodoxy by describing the Pure Land as a place where conditions are especially favourable for the realization of nirvāṇa—so that theoretically the mystical goal is still the ultimate one, while the other world of glory in which one may be reborn counts, from the point of view of orthodoxy, merely as another segment of the universe. And this 'life after death' that looks so much like that immortality promised to the faithful in monotheistic religions such as Christianity and Islām is, from the point of view of orthodoxy, merely another existence in the cycle

[1] Hence Rāmānuja has to interpret '*Tat tvam asi*' (*Chāndogya Upan.*, VI.8.7) thus: *That* is God having the universe as his body: *thou* is God having the individual soul as his body. Again, he has to interpret *Muṇḍaka Upan.*, III.2.8, as meaning that the soul attains identity of nature, not numerical identity with God.

of rebirth. And it would not therefore be surprising both that this should remain within the fold of world Buddhism and yet that it should give expression to spiritual sentiments quite different from those that move the Theravādins. For the ordinary devotee of Amida Buddha that final nirvāṇa is not of great interest compared with the joy and serenity to be experienced in Buddha's Paradise. It is an interesting problem here as to what is to count as 'another world'. The truly divine and numinous Being has the world as His screen and hence is said to dwell in another world. It is natural therefore that the going home to God which is called salvation should be a journey to that other world. Now when a Paradise is conceived as part of this world (this universe) and yet far removed from earthly or even heavenly regions, it comes very near, we may say, to being another world. Where here are we to draw the line between the literal and the analogical? It seems that, from the point of view of spiritual experience, the Pure Land far far to the West, the Buddha's Paradise, is truly another world; and that Amida Buddha is genuinely screened by phenomena; whereas, if the Pure Land doctrines are to remain orthodox, that Pure Land must be conceived merely as a higher compartment of this world. It is therefore only with difficulty that the School can serve both masters.

It is interesting to compare the personalistic view of the eternal Buddha in the Pure Land School with the impersonalistic account implied by the usual interpretations of the Mahāyānist 'Three-Body' doctrine. According to this, the Buddha is seen in one (the highest) aspect as the underlying Reality. This is the Buddha's *dharma-kāya* or 'Truth-Body'. But the Buddha-nature is also manifested in celestial glory, revealing wisdom and power, as in the shape of Amida Buddha. This is the *sambhoga-kāya* or 'Enjoyment-Body'. Finally there is the historical Buddha (and forerunners). This is the *nirmāṇa-kāya* or Transformation-Body'. In this way a fine interweaving is achieved of (i) the mystical strand with the concept of an Absolute; (ii) the numinous, with the objects of adoration and worship (the celestial Buddhas, etc.), and (iii) the incarnation strand, with the historical Buddha elevated to the status of manifestation on earth of the Divine. But it is to be noted that the *dharma-kāya* is held to be the ontological ground of the other two in the Trinity; and that in highest truth is *dharmatā* (*tathatā*, etc.). On the other hand, and in opposition to such schools as the Tendai, the Pure Land School holds that the personal manifestations of the *sambhoga-kāya* must represent something fundamental in the Buddhahood.

It is convenient to tack on at this point a few remarks about a rather different example of a priority decision affecting the mystical strand. Doctrinally, Ṣūfism was something of an explosive force in Islām, with its tendency to speak of union with Allah. Nevertheless, place for it had to be found, since the experience of the Ṣūfī mystics was hardly to be gainsaid. It is an interesting sidelight both upon the way religious thinkers wished to leave room for mysticism within a predominantly monotheistic faith and on the concern felt lest God should be brought away from the unapproachable glory proper to Him that there should have arisen such a sect as the Mohammedīya Tarīqa. This was founded by a man of remarkable intellectual and spiritual power, Ahmad ibn Idrīs, some century and a half ago. He protested against the notion of union with Allah, but replaced it by that of union with the spirit of the Prophet. In this way the exalted stature of Allah is preserved, and yet there remains room for a mysticism fortified by devotion to Mohammed. In priority, this mystical goal is far behind the fundamental duty to serve and to worship God; for one becomes, in attaining the goal, united with the Prophet who himself is but a servant, albeit the most illustrious, of Allah. The Mohammed-mysticism of this sect is therefore quite different in status from the Christ mysticism of certain Christian saints, since of course Christ is co-equal with the Father; and communion with Christ is communion with God. An orthodox Muslim, on the other hand, would find an elevation of the Prophet to divine rank blasphemous, despite the high esteem in which he holds the Prophet.

X. THE IMPORTANCE OR THE UNIMPORTANCE OF THE INCARNATION STRAND

It remains to consider the priority decisions as between the incarnation strand and the two others, singly and together.[1] It will

[1] Actually, there seems to be no case of the incarnation and mystical strands interwoven by themselves, without any admixture of the numinous strand. This is explicable in that, strictly, incarnation presupposes the existence of a deity to be incarnated. Moreover, incarnation is a limiting case of the ascription of holiness interwoven with doctrines about a deity; and there are, of course, cases where we have belief both in very holy men and in a mystical goal—it is natural and even necessary for the two to go together, since, for the many, the goal is seen in the transformed behaviour

have been seen, in the example already given of a Mahāyānist doctrinal scheme—that of Tendai—that some schemes place an historical incarnation or incarnations in an inferior position relative to the Absolute. Part of the reason for this, in the case mentioned, is that the basic doctrines about the world and about that which is beyond the world are somewhat idealistic: for the ultimate truth lies in the indescribable Something (*Tathatā*—'Suchness') lying beyond the phenomenal world, not in the appearances which confront us in ordinary life. Consequently, the life of Gotama himself is affected by this lack of value: and the appearance of the historical Buddha counts as but the most important phenomenon in an insubstantial world.

We have already touched on another reason for the lack of importance of the incarnation strand in theistic faiths: namely that it appears blasphemous to regard any human as God. Hence the unitarianism of Islām. But this principle may be generalized: that (to some) it appears blasphemous to count any other being as identical with God; for such an identification seems to involve a modification of monotheism. For this reason we have, in the early history of the Christian Church, such heresies as docetism on the one hand (by making Christ merely an appearance, there is less suggestion of the Two in the Two in One) and Arianism ('There was when He was not': hereby is expressed Christ's lower status as compared with the Father).

XI. THE JUSTIFICATION OF PRIORITY DECISIONS

It remains to consider the justifications which can be adduced for different priority decisions. And first in this connection it is useful to recall the general formal point respecting simplicity already touched upon. It was said that a formal advantage possessed by a monotheistic faith, as against a polytheistic one, is its simplicity (it will be remembered that this remark does not commit us to monotheism, since the facts of the case, so to speak, might not

of the few. Thus, where mysticism is strong, so also is the tendency to ascribe holiness and mystery to those who are supposed to have gained the goal; and Teachers who point toward the goal have a specially elevated (though hardly divine) status—e.g. Mahāvīra and the Buddha. Putting it succinctly: incarnation cannot by definition occur independently of the numinous strand; but the somewhat numinous human being can so occur. However, there are, so far as I know, no cases of human divinities (such as deified emperors, etc.) who are connected doctrinally with the mystical goal.

warrant belief in one God: the situation might be altogether more untidy). Such a formal criterion used within one strand has its analogue in regard to the blending of strands withing doctrinal schemes. To illustrate: we have, as has been said, to choose between the comprehensiveness of, say, Brāhmanism or Christianity and the simplicity of Southern Buddhism or Islām. Thus a doctrinal scheme containing mainly but one strand has one sort of advantage; one which contains a rich weaving together has another. In effect we are here dealing with a limiting case of priority decision. The more moderate type is that where, though two or more strands occur, they are ordered. Yet how are such decisions justified?

Now when I speak here of *decisions* I do not wish to give the impression that one, either in propounding or accepting a doctrinal scheme, sits down and counts off the pros and cons of different combinations and orderings. First, because there is no such highly deliberate institution of doctrines; and second, because accepting a faith is in some ways a much more complicated matter, in others a much simpler one. The evidences for the truth of the doctrinal scheme may differ from the reasons an individual has for choosing it—without this always being harmful. Nevertheless, if there are different weightings as between strands, then there will presumably be reasons of some sort to be given on one side or the other. If not, then all schemes will be equal and one would be permitted to go to the extreme of existentialism and toss up to decide between them. Since, however, it would be unrealistic to suppose that differences in doctrinal schemes do not signalize profound spiritual cleavages, we may take it that there are general considerations to be advanced on behalf of the choices.[1]

Nevertheless, these considerations are sometimes so general that they are difficult to describe. For example, the omission of the numinous strand may reflect this: that the founder and his adherents are no longer persuaded by the evidences for the Creator—no longer see God's glory shining through the world and history, and no longer find any guidance from a mysterious Being. Yet this itself may require further explication. Again, and even more generally, the feeling for simplicity may be so strong that the

[1] At the present time, the notion of deciding between one scheme and another has become much more live; since there is first much better mutual understanding between adherents of different religions, and second quite a large educated public who have some idea of what other religions are like. It may well be therefore that questions such as 'Which is the best religion?' will become more realistic than heretofore.

founder will concentrate on what he believes to be the core of the spiritual life without reference to the rest: when you are struck by an arrow, as the Buddha said, you do not pause to ask the name of the man who fired it. The justification for this simplicity will be found partly, of course, in its own appeal, but partly also in the difficulties to be seen in a complicated creed: difficulties such as the paradoxicality required there and the tendency for it to be misinterpreted superstitiously.

Yet on the other hand one may argue in the opposite direction. It will be held that a complicated creed does achieve a degree of comprehensiveness which the simpler ones do not. For instance, Brāhmanism has the advantage that it welds together both the activities of sacrifice and those of asceticism; and the Ṣūfī movement transformed Islām in such a manner that it became clear that one could love Allah with two loves:

love of my happiness, And perfect love to love Thee as Thy due.[1]

Thus the simplicity versus complication dispute is far-reaching and highly generalized; but it seems that considerations such as those hinted at above are important. There is, however, so much room for manœuvre, and such obscurity in spiritual matters, that the advancing of such considerations will be hardly likely to *resolve* differences of opinion; yet they are not for that reason to be neglected. For they adumbrate the insights born of the fire of religious life.

Again, the reasons for weighting one strand more heavily than another in a scheme containing both are difficult to describe. How for instance are we to choose between Śaṅkara's assignment of weights and Rāmānuja's or Madhva's? The question perhaps again seems unrealistic—we need conversion here, not intellectual persuasion, it may be said: a half-truth, since the so-called intellectual operations involved in arguing about doctrines find their source in the heart. In any case, some reflections on the matter are not out of place, since they refer to wide features of doctrines which in some measure constitute their power to convert.

(i) A general pragmatic point. Since religion (if it has broad claims, and this is characteristic of the more progressive faiths) tries to cater for all men, a strong emphasis on the mystical strand is liable to lead to self-stultification, since it appears that all men

[1] Trans. R. A. Nicholson, *Literary History of the Arabs*, p. 234, and quoted by H. A. R. Gibb, *Mohammedanism*, p. 103.

are not equally suited for the ascetic or monastic life. Consequently, if this is the principle way of salvation a certain type of temperament will be greatly favoured; and this may be held to offend against the principle of equal religious opportunity for all. Moreover, as it happens, rather few are called to this way of life; and this makes the tension more acute. It is true that in Indian religions the doctrine of rebirth serves to mitigate the difficulty and thereby indirectly to assist the growth of mystical doctrines (few, that is, may have a real chance of liberation in the present incarnation, but all can hope for a chance sooner or later in the cycle of rebirth). But the point remains a serious one, at least in practice, and one may not unreasonably consider the differing emphasis placed on the mystical path in different religions and different sects as in part attempts to compromise on this issue. However, this way of deciding matters may seem unduly pragmatic to some—and the appearance remains even if appeal is made to principles such as that salvation ought to be readily accessible to all men. Such a principle, it is true, seems equitable, but to be convincing in a doctrinal context it would have to be shown to flow, for instance, from the divine nature as revealed in the basic evidence. Yet the pragmatism is perhaps not too wide of the mark. For it will in part be by the evaluation of the different activities of worship and asceticism that one arrives at an appreciation of the different weights to be attached to the doctrines springing from them. This leads to the second main point.

(ii) The strength of a strand ought to rest upon the strength of its bases. A limiting case of this has already been noted: when the bases upon which rest belief in the Creator seem very weak, the strand is cut out altogether. But perception of the strength of the bases depends upon religious experience. The ordinary man, perhaps, will not be able to gain more than an inkling here; only the truly saintly and prophetic will be able to express such judgments of strength in new doctrines. At any rate, persuasion will have largely to come from the conduct on the one hand which enlivens and lies behind the doctrines; and from the religious eloquence which points to the bases upon which faith in these matters must rest.

But it is not surprising, in view of our earlier insistence on the *organic* nature of doctrinal schemes, that it is difficult to disentangle general considerations (depending upon the way matters strike us in spiritual experience) from the subtle interplay of appeals from one part of a scheme to another; hence, though the points we have noticed are of some importance, they are usually presented in already embellished doctrinal disguise.

For these reasons, the analogy with aesthetics again has some point (with the provisos mentioned before). Illuminating the important features of a piece of music is a task which depends upon insight and is hard to make decisive; so much more difficult then is the task of showing in what respects one doctrinal scheme is superior to another. However, it is by no means true that nothing can be done here; and the pattern of basic, organic and formal justifications, together with the rather vaguer justifications of priority decisions, give one the material for reasoning (in a special sense of reasoning) about religious matters.

VI

Some Epistemological Concepts

I. THE NEED TO INVESTIGATE CERTAIN CONCEPTS

OUR last remarks lead naturally to a discussion of certain concepts which are of some epistemological significance in spiritual matters—concepts such as *revelation*, *belief*, *faith*, *conversion* and *knowledge*. For although we have given a sketchy outline of the composition of spiritual doctrines and of the bases upon which they rest, there has been little emphasis on the way in which doctrines enshrine revelations. This procedure was not entirely incorrect, as we shall see; yet it would be misleading to overlook the fact that spiritual doctrines are often (though not always) held to be revealed—rather than, say, discovered. They are, that is, often thought to be revealed *to* men rather than discovered *by* men: a notable counter-instance here are the doctrines of early Buddhism, which were discovered by the Buddha. Again, it would be wrong to neglect the point that an important spiritual attitude to doctrines is that of *faith*, and that this is faith gained, in many typical instances, by *conversion*. And an investigation of these concepts will help to correct some of the errors that no doubt have crept in through our somewhat cavalier treatment of religious doctrines. For the very fact that, in order to gain some insight into the structure of religious discourse, we have been engaged upon dissecting doctrinal schemes—and that too crudely and without always being able to cut at the well-concealed joints—is bound to give an impression which we have always wished to avoid: the impression, namely, that by taking sufficient thought one should be able to work out the best kind of religious picture to suit the needs of man and the situation in the cosmos. But on the contrary, it is only because we have at our disposal the utterances of famous and holy men and the conduct that has illustrated these words that we have been able even to start discussing and comparing religious creeds; and any conclusions reached are, so to speak, *ex post dicto*. If anyone wishes to improve upon any or all of the religions that have been, his course will lie in a very different direction from that of a comparative study such as this; all that comes here (if indeed that) is a hint or two as to the nature of religious doctrines—much as the critic can sometimes illuminate the nature of tragedy. But saints and prophets are of a different stamp. Therefore, the way we have dissected should not be misconstrued; and the present task of investigating the concepts mentioned above will serve to obviate such misconstruction. For here some hints will be given as to what can briefly be called our grasp of religious truth.

To begin with, the concept *revelation* is useful, since here is signalized an important difference between many religious propositions and most of those in other frames. For there is little cause to use this notion in everyday affairs nor in science; and it already has the special flavour of the spirit about it. Why should it be that in religion almost exclusively we have this situation, that to get the truth one must accept a revelation? And why do religious books have a tendency to become *canonical* (and indeed to become *sacred*)? Even, it seems, in Buddhism, where the Founder teaches men to be lamps unto themselves and to seek their own way to truth, we discover this phenomenon. The Bible, the *Vedas*, the *Bhagavadgītā*, the *Tripiṭaka*, the *Lotus Sūtra*, the *Tao-Teh-Ching*—these are in different measure authoritative and upon the adherent is laid the obligation of studying such scriptures.

II. THE IMPORTANCE OF THE CONCEPT OF REVELATION IN RELIGION

Two connected points about revelation can be disentangled. (i) Why is it that the notion of revelation is important in religion? And (ii) why do religions make appeal to an established body of scripture? The questions are connected, because the answer to the latter in large measure depends upon the answer to the former: but can be disentangled because in the primary sense it is religious entities (not truths about these entities) that is revealed, as has been made plain in recent theological discussion[1]—though we may add that the distinction, though just, is not hard and fast, since, for example, the words of an Incarnate Deity will be as much part

[1] For a useful survey of modern views on this see John Baillie, *The Idea of Revelation in Recent Thought*.

of the revealing behaviour as other actions. If, then, this distinction can be made, it will be probable that the scriptures will gain their importance from the fact that they describe or express the primary revelation, and it is for this main reason that it has been remarked above that the second of the two questions has to be answered in the light of the reply to the first.

As to the first question, it is very important to remember that the concept of revelation has its typical use in the numinous strand. For it will be recalled that the manner in which the transcendent object is pictured is this: that the Creator lies beyond phenomena and occupies 'another world'. But even in this world there are signs of this object of worship, described, for instance, as traces of the divine or as instances of His handiwork. It is among these that the divine is, in a special sense, seen; so that these signs play an indispensable role in the epistemology of the worship strand. Given, then, the concealment of the divine and the way in which traces of the holy are found about us, the concept of revelation falls naturally into place. What is hidden is now revealed; we are afforded a glimpse behind the veil (or more correctly, perhaps, through the veil). Analogous to this is the way in which the divinity of the God-Man is revealed: His actions are signs of His underlying glory. It is appropriate to speak thus of the divine human for two reasons: (i) because He is supposed to be identical with God, and the notion of revelation is applicable to the way God appears; and (ii) because the concept has a fairly natural use with regard to certain features of human conduct. That is: just as we betray or reveal our feelings by behaviour, so too deep spirituality is revealed in behaviour: the actions and gestures of saint and prophet betray their religious experience and wisdom, and the Transfiguration is an intense example of the display of religious power.

Briefly, then: the concept *revelation* is a natural adjunct to the model of the divine as concealed by phenomena (which is the core of the doctrines of the numinous strand); and this concept is employed in an extended way (though again not unnaturally) of the incarnate God.

In order then to be acquainted with the revelation of the divine one must see a sign or signs. Something has been said on the point that this seeing of signs is not a simple matter of looking, since propositions about the divine are not merely empirical assertions. It is not sufficient that one should go out and look (even if it were sensible here to speak of a determinate direction or directions in which to look). But rather one must be roused (in most cases); and often the seeing will not come without guidance (of which more later). There are these exceptions: where an overwhelming theophany occurs; third-person rousing would not be needed here —but in either case, directives on where to look, such as might be useful if someone were in doubt as to whether there were any angel-fish in existence, would not be apposite. This is one of the reasons why God is not *observed*, but instead is held to reveal Himself. The second main reason for this, it may be added, is connected with the abasement of the worshipper. It expresses well God's due exaltedness to say that even the recognition of this greatness depends not upon the worshipper but upon the divine. From this is expanded the notion of grace: where a man only gains faith through grace. It must be noted that this principle is applied in a much more comprehensive manner than is the conception that the recognition of natural signs of the divine depends on the latter. For the efficacy of the practices which precede and reinforce true faith (such as prayer) is also ascribed to the divine.

III. WHY SCRIPTURES BECOME CANONICAL

Some of the important revelations of the divine will be described or expressed in scriptures. The reasons why these should swiftly and easily become canonical are perhaps not hard to outline. There are indeed serious religious causes of this situation as well as the less savoury ones sometimes alleged. For although it is no doubt true that the credulity of men and the jealousy of priests in guarding authoritative documents which strengthen their position are potent sources of the adoration of strange books, there are other reasons for religious conservatism in these matters. (i) Religious doctrines tend to be somewhat opaque, a feature which serves, among other things, to delineate the mysteriousness and incomprehensibility of the divine. But it is not just a sign of this (for if it were so, one might object that any way of doing this would do), but of the depth of religious discourse, which is not to be exhausted by such facile translations as we may attempt in order to express part at least of the meaning of a doctrine or set of doctrines. This is connected with what was said earlier: that though dissection may be to some extent illuminating, one cannot simply prescribe ways of constructing doctrinal schemes. And anyone who is to have anything like a good claim to be in a position to set forth doctrines (either in his own name or as a mouthpiece of the divine originator) must be a man of deep insight. A scheme will have, so to speak, its own stamp, and although we may understand much, there will most probably be much which we do not see the point of. Consequently the scriptures which enshrine much of the doctrinal scheme will be preserved in a special manner: since (*a*) they will continue to be useful to adherents of the faith who by reading and re-reading will hope to gain greater insight into the doctrines; and (*b*) the ordinary man will not be trusted, in view of the opaqueness of doctrines and of the spirituality required for innovation, to reject parts of the revelation. This scriptural conservatism is reinforced by another and rather obvious one:

(ii) People of deep insight and conduct are rather few, and it will not be surprising if the products of these men (or rather, perhaps, the products of God via these men) will be specially revered.

(iii) One should mention too that it is usual for anything associated with the numinous to be regarded as holy or sacred. Hence, the book or books which enshrine the revelation are thought sacred. This, of course, conduces to conservatism and lack of criticism of the scriptures, since to treat them otherwise will tend to be accounted blasphemy or sacrilege.

(iv) Yet these reasons are linked to another which, together with these, sets a firm seal upon the scriptures. As we have pointed out, it requires one of deep insight to propound fresh doctrines; and this insight is of course intertwined with the saintly character of the founder of a faith (if there be such). Consequently, even where (as in Hīnayāna Buddhism) there is nothing corresponding to salvation by gesture, the life of the founder will be of remarkable and lasting interest to the faithful, as an illustration—the supreme illustration—of the path along which they have to walk. And not merely as an illustration which would be superfluous (like the illustration of a novel), but as a constant source of insights about the meaning of the doctrines propounded. And all this apart from the obvious fact that the faithful will be at the greatest pains to have a detailed record of the important utterances of the master. As a result, the tendencies we have already noted as leading to conservatism over the scriptures are capped by the need to have an account of the words and lives of prophets and founders. Especially great is this, of course, if the founder plays a special historical or cosmic role. From these points, then, flows the scriptural conservatism of religion.

Similar considerations conduce to the dogmatism of religious preaching. The doctrines are presented and men are asked to accept them, often with little or no argument: men are asked to *believe* and to have *faith*.

IV. THE NATURE OF BELIEF IN

Just as the primary sense of *revelation* is with direct reference to God, not the spiritual propositions about the divine, so too the primary sense of *religious belief* is belief in religious entities, not in doctrines. For we are asked to believe *in* God, Christ, Ahura Mazda. And *belief in* differs from ordinary belief. Though there is a formal resemblance between believing a doctrine to be true and believing some other sort of proposition to be true, belief in God, etc., does not simply involve believing a number of doctrines about Him. Now the way in which religious belief *in* differs from ordinary belief will help to illustrate the point that religious belief is not just like blind or inadequately-grounded acceptance of dogmatically given propositions; and that this belief is not contrasted to knowledge in the manner in which the two concepts are customarily contrasted in more mundane contexts. A discussion of this will in turn expand what has been said about revelation.

Of course, we are already familiar with expressions such as these: 'belief in Socialism', 'belief in fairies', etc. And at first sight 'belief in God' might seem like one or other of these or both. Thus belief in God can be construed as belief that He exists, just as belief in fairies is the belief that there are fairies; and again it is like belief in Socialism—for both God and Socialism are supposed to have a certain efficacy. So both the existential and the efficacial senses of 'belief in' seem to blend together in the religious use. Such a suggestion is not too far wide of the mark, but requires modification.

For (i) whereas the status of existential propositions about fairies or zebras is clear enough, propositions about the existence of religious entities are not so easily described. That these are not ordinary existential assertions is seen from two facts. (*a*) The concepts alluded to in such propositions as 'God exists' and 'There is only one God and Mohammed is His Prophet', etc., are embedded in doctrinal schemes. They are not, in one sense of 'simple',

simple concepts, since to understand them one has to pay attention to many, if not all, of the major assertions of the doctrinal scheme. (There is another sense, perhaps, in which they would be simple concepts: for it would be claimed that God is simple, i.e. not complex, and some might think that this warranted the further claim that the concept *God* must be simple too—for that which is itself simple ought to be represented by something simple. But maybe the use of 'concept' is confusing here; the word 'God' stands for God and is as simple or complicated word as you may judge; but this does not affect the main point, that the explanation of the expression requires recourse to the propositions of the doctrinal scheme in which the word is centrally employed.) In this respect, then, existential questions about religious entities will be more like their counterparts in science ('Do genes exist?' etc.) than like the simpler existential questions of the nursery or safari. (*b*) The existence of a fairy entails that there is an object having a certain position, etc., for it is sensible on being told 'There are ——' to enquire *where* they are (and this too, in a more complicated way, with the theoretical entities of science); but spiritual entities are not localizable in this fashion. Briefly, then, belief in God involves adherence to a number of doctrines; and it is not an ordinary empirical belief.

(ii) It also, as has been said, is like an efficacial belief; but this, as it turns out, is a by-product of a more fundamental, though not dissimilar, feature. For belief in God involves the expression of a worshipping attitude towards the divine—submission and abasement. It would, as has already been remarked in Chapter I, be inconsistent both to believe in God and not to recognize an obligation to worship Him. Thus the form of words (which is the most typical use of belief-words in spiritual contexts) 'I believe in God' expresses a commitment of submission to God. Given this submission, then the efficacial belief follows, since God's actions will be accepted as for the best (Job's experience provides a good illustration of this).

Thus the expression 'belief' is used of religious faith not to show that something short of knowledge is all that is to be had; but rather because the notion of trust is involved: one would not wish to rewrite the Creeds, so that they began 'I know that there is One God . . . etc.'. The doctrines taken as true serve to shape the trust, to give it its direction; and even if they were known to be true it would still be appropriate to speak of *belief* in God.

Nevertheless, we also wish to say that doctrines are merely believed, rather than known, to be true. Now this is partly because they are secondary to the entity behind them; because, that is, the use of 'belief' here reflects its use as in 'belief in'. But it is also because of the doubting that often afflicts the spiritual person. It is notorious that deep religious belief requires continual bolstering; and we hear so often of men being afflicted by religious doubt. As the prayer puts it:

> Lord, I believe: help Thou my unbelief.

And the *Ṛg-Veda*:

> O faith, endow us with belief.[1]

The sources of this situation are at least threefold.

V. BELIEF AND RELIGIOUS DOUBT

(i) Much has to be taken as it is given dogmatically (for reasons which have already been outlined). It is natural, however, for the adherent to attempt to relieve some of the opacity of doctrine and this leads him to questionings which are, as regards the numinous and incarnation strands at least, in danger of becoming blasphemous. Therefore, in so far as the questioner is operating within the orbit of worship, his sense of wonder and abasement is likely in some degree to be weakened. A doubt is in part a failure to express worship. But further, in this connection, spiritual doctrines have frequently been mixed up with other families of propositions, with those of science, for example, and the same mistake which leads dogmatists to hitch their wagon to scientific assertions, many of them false, leads the doubter to reject the religious beliefs because he perceives that the mixed-in non-religious assertions are false. A notorious instance of such a case is seen in the disputes about evolution during the last century.

(ii) Religious doctrines, at any rate in the numinous and incarnation strands and to a lesser extent in the mystical strand, are of their nature bizarre—since, for instance, the claim that there is a God is a wonderful and marvellous claim: the claim has to be astonishing to be an adequate expression of the numinous strand. But amazement before the divine, though it is partly how

[1] X.151.5.

belief in God is constituted, can be ambivalent: that which is too astonishing is easily doubted.

(iii) There is an important need for doctrines to be brought alive to the ordinary worshipper. This is done not only in the ritual, sometimes colourful, which expresses worship, but in the daily meditations and prayers which are recommended to the individual. The need for this arises from the fact that religious doctrines are, by the nature of their evidence, somewhat remote: that is, though we may see the hand of the Creator in certain aspects of the world and of human life which strike us from time to time, God is not seen in the way people who are important in our daily lives are seen. To live *sub specie aeternitatis* requires quite a considerable imaginative effort. True, pageant-like ceremonies, festivals, road-side chapels, the temple gong and the like help people to keep their religion in mind during their daily life; but these aids have a certain tendency to turn back on themselves unless illuminated by other-worldly living, since religion loses its awesomeness and strangeness when it is made normal. Consequently, belief has to be nourished by continued meditation and imaginative practice; and in this way doctrines will be kept as much alive as an important personal fact. That is, a man's actions will be affected by his doctrinal belief in much the way they are affected—almost automatically—by the knowledge of some important fact about his own life. In view, then, of the effort needed to keep one's faith truly alive, it is not surprising that doubts should spring up like weeds through the cracks in the religious life.

Connected with this is a point which throws religious belief into a seemingly poor light. Often, if someone begins to doubt a doctrinal scheme, he is asked by his adviser to go on even more assiduously with the practices associated with that scheme—practices such as worship and meditation. And it is not uncommon to hear that it is by practising one's faith that one gains true belief. Now at first sight this does not look intellectually respectable: surely lack of belief in the doctrines would be a bar to sincere worship, etc. It would seem to be scarcely honest to indulge in religious practices without having any conviction of the truth of what lay behind them.

It is useful here to distinguish between assent and conviction. It would be wrong to practice a faith unless one had assented to the main articles of faith; but one might nevertheless, without forfeiting the right to worship, lack conviction. The claim that justified the advice to go on worshipping, even if one's faith were weakened or in doubt, would then amount to this: spiritual practices nourish conviction. Belief, so to speak, has a snowball effect; for belief leads to practice and practice to conviction.

The cause of this situation can be explained as follows:

(i) With respect to the numinous strand, the practice of the public and private rituals which express abasement and awe helps to give one an increased sense of humility and wonder; and as a result the evidences of the central propositions of the numinous strand will become more obvious—the worshipper will be more open to signs of God's handiwork, etc.

(ii) The worthwhileness of the mystical path will by no means be brought home to the beginner, but provided he is willing to risk assent to the claim made by the mystic he will find increasing evidence to back the claim (provided also, that is, there is such evidence). It is in the nature of the claim that the fruits cannot be seen directly beforehand—one would be somewhat in the position of the graduate student uncertain whether to take up symbolic logic seriously or not. The proof of the pudding is in the eating. And before the eating one has to go on hints and the advice of others. And in general, it will be likely that since the doctrines draw their life and sustenance from the practices, the practices will give greater insight. Such beliefs, the evidence for which will produce conviction only or mainly after assent, may be named *ulterior beliefs*.

Nevertheless, even with ulterior beliefs one requires some evidence to go on beforehand. The balance has to be tilted in some manner initially. This tilting will be much the more alarming in a religious context than it would be elsewhere, since the claims of religion are so great, its entities so stupendous. Thus though the assent to the proposition that mathematical logic is an important pursuit might commit one to long training in a field which one might still have one's doubts about, the extent to which one would be morally committed in the matter of religion would be far far greater. For doctrines are supposed to touch all areas of a man's life in one way or another. Thus the significance of the initial tilting of belief will be profound, and it will not be surprising that in some cases the change is violent. This change is commonly called *conversion*. For it, there is needed some experience of a sign or the accumulation of signs which will serve to give the converted man a strong intuition that the doctrines to which he is turning are true. It may be noted too that there is also a sense in which someone who has already formally assented to a creed (sincerely enough) can be converted (to that same creed). Thus he may accept the propositions as true, but they are scarcely alive to him; they do not affect his conduct or his ways of thinking. This is an understandable phenomenon in view of what has already been said about the need for the guidance of the imagination in imprinting religious beliefs.

Religious belief involves trust, then, in two main connected ways. First, belief in Allah, etc., involves worship of and abasement before the object of worship, and this entails trust that the actions of the Divine Being are for the best. Second, religious belief involves trust that the commitment will be justified, though this is by no means assured on the initial evidence. Thus: it involves the ulterior belief in and trust in a divine entity given in a doctrinal scheme; save in the case of the purely mystical faith, where it simply involves the ulterior belief in the worthwhile character of the goal.

VI. BELIEF AND KNOWLEDGE

The appropriateness of expressions such as 'belief' and 'faith' to stand for spiritual attitudes towards the divine or towards doctrines arises in a different way from that in which it is deemed correct to use 'belief' (rather than, say, 'knowledge') in certain everyday contexts. For sentences in the spiritual frame of the shape 'I believe . . .' are not typically used, like their counterparts in the discourse of exchanging information, to signalize a lack of clinching evidence such as would justify the claim 'I know . . .' Nor does the religious utterance 'I believe in . . .' necessarily signalize a lack of certainty. Thus it is not helpful to distinguish between the status of spiritual propositions and others (of certain frames) by saying that the former are recognized as true through faith and are cases of belief, while with the latter we can have knowledge. For (i) there is a use for the concept *knowledge* in the spiritual frame, as we have seen; and (ii) the distinction smacks of the suggestion that we are, so to speak, just *contingently* worse off as to evidence in the one realm than in the other. It is not the case that religious propositions are of the same kind as others, except that we have not the facilities (at the moment, in this life) to show them to be true as we might show propositions about moles or men or tomorrow's sunrise to be true. But the difference in situation is not merely contingent (though this point is perhaps obscured in the more numinous faiths by the 'contingent' atmosphere that they possess); and the importance of faith in one context and its unimportance in another is the product of a whole range of divergencies which demarcate spiritual discourse as having a characteristic style. Thus the procedure adopted here, of discussing the different strands of religious discourse and depicting their style, was essentially correct—for unless the nature of religious propositions is recognized, discussions as to the role of faith and reason in religion will tend to be nugatory. And as it is, discussion of these 'epistemological' concepts does little more than remind us that religion is not science or art, etc. (broad slogans these).

But further, as was remarked under (i) above, *belief* is not master of the whole field here—as though its applicability depended upon the extrusion of the concept *knowledge*. Nor is the old contrast between faith and reason (and their analogues) exclusive. For both the concepts of knowledge and reason have some application in religious discourse. But excessive concentration upon such contrasts can lead to distorted views: for instance, because religion may be considered *irrational*—a view which has the demerit of distracting attention away from the manner in which a doctrinal scheme may be justified; indeed, extreme irrationalism is for this reason self-defeating, for if anything or nothing were to count for or against the truth of any religious proposition, it would be vacuous, and this is hardly the intention of theological irrationalists. Again, the suggestion that only belief is to be had in matters of the spirit leads to the thought that there is something defective about theology, as compared with, say, science—there may be such defects, but not for this reason. Therefore it is well to see how the concepts *knowledge* and *reason* have application in religion.

First, it should be noted that some of the difficulties which attend the aforementioned contrasts are due to the fact that it is not realized that the standards which religious propositions are thought not to satisfy are inappropriate ones. That is, a model of rational method is set up, and enquiries which fail to resemble the model are condemned as inadequate: this philosophical move is one which leads, for instance, to scepticism—because propositions about tomorrow's sunrise are neither as certain as nor established in the same rigorous manner as mathematical truths, they are sceptically regarded as lacking certainty or rational justification; but then a standard is being imposed which hardly applies. Such a tendency is, of course, fostered by the hypostatization of faculties such as 'faith', 'reason', etc., whereby we are tempted to distribute the various intellectual organs among the various intellectual jobs.

Thus, if mathematical reasoning is taken as the paradigm for the employment of reason, we shall have to deny that there is (except trivially) reasoning in religious matters. And if it is not reason we use, it must be something else—faith, perhaps. But of course there is no need to have such a central model, divagations from which are to be signs of imperfections. It is the mark of the educated man, as Aristotle said, to expect that degree of exactness which the subject-matter allows. And we may add that lack of exactness is not properly a defect except in comparison with the maximum possible in the field in question. Consequently, there is no *immediate* need to deny, because religious discourse is not precise like that of mathematics or even physics, that in some sense of 'reasoning' there is reasoning in this field. But the canons of correct reasoning will of course differ greatly from those in other realms.

What *is* true, seemingly, is that the truths of religion are not *discovered* by reasoning (though they are in good company here), whereas the truths of mathematics and certain theoretical truths in science are so discovered. One cannot, as has been repeated above, work out the correct doctrinal scheme by cogitation. Nevertheless, it is obvious that in a doctrinal scheme some of the propositions are more central than others so that it is not absurd to say that the latter depend (albeit loosely) upon the former; and there are applications of central propositions to matters not immediately treated of in the initial revelation. Consequently, one may legitimately speak of religious inferences, conclusions, etc.; and therefore of theological reasoning. Indeed the framing of a doctrinal scheme, that is a compendium of central propositions, out of the materials given in the scriptures, etc., is an important employment of reasoning in the theological sphere. In this sense, it is somewhat misleading to oppose reason and revelation.

In actual practice, however, such an opposition arises mainly from a dispute as to the validity of certain arguments, namely those which purport to demonstrate the existence of God. Thus, to say that reason plays no role in religion is often no more than a shorthand way of saying that these arguments are invalid. The arguments, which depend upon very general premisses (or necessary ones), have a mathematical appearance; and if valid would seem to establish the claim that by general and precise reflection one may arrive at spiritual truths. That such a claim is suspect is clear from the following considerations.

(i) The concept *God* and its analogues are precipitated out of doctrinal schemes; and therefore a simple single-track argument is hardly likely to establish that there is an instance of such a concept.

(ii) The entities shown to exist (such as Prime Mover and Necessary Being) do not obviously resemble an object of worship, etc.

(iii) A conjunction of such arguments will not be persuasive, since it is by no means obvious that there is an identity between the conclusions.

(iv) The common methods of religious persuasion are by preaching and example, and these arguments are therefore remote from ordinary spiritual practice.

(v) In other respects, spiritual discourse seems to differ profoundly from that in the mathematical and scientific frames. It would hence be surprising if strictly deductive methods of argument as displayed in these alleged proofs were applicable.

On the other hand, there is no doubt that some of the 'Proofs' are suggestive. For example, the Argument from Design certainly sums up some of our grounds for believing in a Creator; but the summary constitutes neither a proof nor a persuasive argument. It is not a proof, because this notion is only applicable strictly in mathematics; and it is not a persuasive argument, because one cannot by repeating it gain someone's assent to the conclusion. To show that there is a Creator requires a much richer type of persuasion: one must point out in forceful and illuminating manner the glories and mysterious beauties of the world which suggest God's existence; one must bring someone to begin worshipping by inducing awe and wonder. Thus the so-called Argument from Design is merely a summary of one method for converting someone to belief in a single Deity. Again, the Cosmological Arguments succeed in expressing our astonishment that there is anything at all, but can hardly count as a scientific argument, since the question is necessarily extra-scientific, nor indeed is it in any straightforward manner empirical. The question: Why does anything exist at all? is already a religious one, for we are not content with positive answers other than such as this: Because God created the world. Acceptance of the force of the Argument will depend mainly on whether one has the required feeling of astonishment, a feeling which is not necessarily or even perhaps at all induced by backing the argument with metaphysical subtleties or by clothing it in the appearance of a scientific proof.

Thus, in so far as these 'Proofs' are impressive, it is because they express something richer and deeper than appears on their desiccated surface; and the more we reflect on this, the more we are driven to distinguish between such 'arguments' and mathematical or scientific ones. Slowly the contrast between revelation and reason evaporates. Replacing it, perhaps, is rather a different distinction, namely that between general and special revelation. That there is something like the former appears from the following points. (i) There are general similarities between independently consolidated faiths, or at least between different manifestations of the numinous strand. (ii) Unless men had already a glimmering of understanding of religious matters, preachers would have nothing to appeal to when they delineate more clearly the features of an unknown god. (iii) Unless there were some broad canons for determining the truth of religious doctrines, they would be vacuous.

It may be added that sometimes certain doctrines are regarded as more philosophical or metaphysical than others. Thus it is sometimes said that one may supplement theology by philosophy, and the presumption is that some doctrines are based upon rational speculation, while others are not. Two points about this are to be made. (i) It is commoner, as we have said, for the concept *revelation* and its analogues to occur in the context of worship; and so the contrast will tend to develop as one between two types of doctrine (respectively enshrined in worship and mysticism). Thus many of the doctrinal schemes that have been given the title of 'philosophies', such as the Neo-Platonism of Plotinus, the idealism of Śaṅkara, the speculations of Nāgārjuna, etc., are in reality expressive of a mystically based world-view. Again, ontological concepts, as we have remarked, have a peculiar fittingness for expressing mystical experience; and these words are counters traditionally used in philosophy. That philosophers have tended to operate with them is due to these causes: (*a*) they are, when interpreted in everyday contexts in a manner which is inappropriate (when for example they are looked on as ordinary predicates, nouns, etc.), sources of perplexity and give rise to logical problems; (*b*) philosophical enquiries have only with difficulty been separated from other investigations, such as science and theology—and consequently, conclusions which are important in religion are likely to turn up in the midst of extraneous argumentation. One would not wish that this situation should be perpetuated; but it accounts for the way in which certain types of spiritual belief have been thought specially *philosophical*. One may add too that the feature of mystical doctrines to which we drew attention earlier, that is the tendency to picture the cosmic situation as *necessarily* evolved (not the result of contingent action on the part of God, Satan or man), helps to give them a 'metaphysical' air. A corollary of this (and of the point about ontology) is that the structure of reality is not depicted in personal terms: the psychological attributes of the divine are played down—and so the doctrines have an abstract look, a look thought to be typical of metaphysics and philosophy. For all these reasons, then, the distinction between theology and philosophy, metaphysics or ontology, and between two sorts of doctrine is often at bottom a contrast between the propositions thrown up by the numinous strand and those thrown up by the mystical strand. It is not necessarily a contrast between revelation on the one hand and rational speculation on the other, still less a contrast between the objects of faith and reason.

(ii) However, it is true that there is a greater amount of open-mindedness among the exponents of mystically-tinged doctrines, a good deal less conservatism and a greater tendency to tolerance and even syncretism. The reasons for this state of affairs are not far to seek. (*a*) There is a sense in which mystical religion is 'experimental': one can, like the Buddha, test different ascetic prescriptions. (*b*) The practices of the mystic are individually performed (by necessity), in isolation, whereas the rituals of worship tend to be communal and public. Hence, sacerdotal conservatism will be more in evidence in a worshipper's religion. (*c*) The claim to have personal experience of the divine—an experience which is alarmingly direct, gives the mystic a sense of entitlement to express doctrines in his own idiom; a right which would gain some force from the spiritual behaviour of the mystic. (*d*) The conflict between the seemingly blasphemous mystic and the exponent of a faith of worship will cause a certain rebelliousness in the mystic towards authoritarian conservatism. (*e*) The doctrine that one can gain even in this life direct access to the divine will make the mystic look favourably upon those from other folds who in adopting similar prescriptions tread the path towards the Ineffable; and this, together with the tendency to rift aforementioned, will make him more tolerant and even syncretistic.[1]

For these reasons the mystic will tend to have a greater love of doctrinal innovation and so of so-called philosophical speculation. It is not surprising therefore that the contrast between two types of doctrine should often be misconstrued as a conflict between theology on the one hand and philosophy on the other.

The appearance of rationality which is conferred upon certain sorts of doctrine by these facts is reinforced by another and not totally unconnected one, namely that the notion of knowledge plays a greater part in mystical religion than elsewhere. For somehow one gains knowledge, as we have said, in this contemplation. Incidentally, the contrast between the practical and the theoretical has undertones of a religious distinction, since theory is originally contemplation; thus we have an analogy between the contrast of theory and practice on the one hand, and that of contemplation and works on the other. The latter is explained as follows: a feature of theistic faiths is an emphasis on the active fulfilment of God's behests—what we have termed spiritual realism; but this contrasts with the tendency to self-centred (though not selfish in an ordinary sense) quietism among the mystics, for the love the mystic may display in action towards his fellow-men flows from his prior interest in the beatific vision, much as the practical fruits of science flow from a prior preoccupation with useless theorizing. Thus the religious contrast is somewhat analogous to the other one; and this helps to account for the way the love of wisdom, i.e. philosophy as once understood, is

[1] The independence of the mystic is well brought out by a remark of Śaṅkara's (discussing the different canons to be employed in the enquiry into Brahman (Comm. on *Vedānta-Sūtras*, I.1.2): 'Scriptural text, etc., . . . are not, in the enquiry into Brahman, the only means of knowledge, as they are in the enquiry into active duty, but scriptural texts on the one hand, and intuition, etc., on the other, are to be used according to the occasion.' By *intuition* here is meant the so-called *sākṣātkāra* or realization of Brahman. The 'etc.' comprises inference, and so on. Thus in this dual-strand religion, with the mystical predominating, although there is considerable scriptural conservatism, it is allowable to appeal to the knowledge yielded in the direct experience of Brahman. The more rigid dogmatism of Christianity, on the other hand, backed as it has been by a powerful ecclesiastical organization, has severely limited the freedom of the mystic to express himself as he wishes to.

associated with the love of spiritual insight. Since we have already sketched the nature of mystical knowledge, all that need be done here is to enter a reminder. The knowledge of the divine (which is a kind of knowledge of what something is like) may be called 'indescribable knowledge by experience', and for it we find, in different faiths, special terms, such as *gnōsis*, *ma'rifat*, etc. We may call the knowledge yielded by this experience, the knowledge that the world is impermanent, unreal, etc., 'certitude by experience'. Both these types of religious knowledge are to be distinguished between knowledge of the facts of the faith (theological or doctrinal knowledge: this is open to believer and unbeliever alike—that Christ was born in Palestine is an item of knowledge about the Christian faith that anyone is capable of grasping) and practical knowledge on how to achieve the spiritual goal (spiritual expertness).

The common contrasts, therefore, are too facile, though they do bring out two important points which must once again be insisted upon. (i) Doctrinal speculation is not open to the individual except upon very strict conditions: conditions, one might say, of character. For even doctrinal understanding depends upon a certain acquaintance with the practices which give religious propositions their life; and therefore the profound understanding of matters of the spirit which would be a prerequisite of religious discovery must flow from a considerable depth and holiness of character. All this should serve to militate against an over intellectualist view of religious thinking. It is not of course suggested that there cannot be sound conclusions drawn from ratiocination upon doctrinal premisses, even by men to whom we might be chary of ascribing the highest spiritual character; and indeed if the strict requirement outlined above were to be applied in the case of every theological thinker, it is doubtful whether all would survive so rigorous a test. But the framing of theological conclusions upon revealed premisses and the arrangement of given doctrines in a coherent scheme are not activities which call for too penetrating a spiritual insight. For this penetration is needed, but not of that depth required for major doctrinal innovation. Of course, the distinction drawn here between major doctrinal speculations, etc., and minor ones (for the most part consisting in elaboration and interpretation of what has already been given), is not easily defined, and will partly depend on the sort of doctrinal scheme with which we are concerned. On the whole, for instance, there will be less latitude in claiming something to be a revelation in the numinous strand than there will be in claiming something to be the highest truth in the mystical strand. In addition, where there is a doctrine of incarnation, a single incarnation will leave little room for doctrinal innovation, whereas a belief in many incarnations will allow of much more doctrinal development and change.

(ii) The second important point alluded to above, as being signalized, albeit obscurely, by the common 'epistemological' contrasts, is that spiritual propositions have an opaqueness not to be dissipated by translation into easier language. This is not to suggest that attempts to do this are misguided, for if this were so, half the sermons and commentaries directed at the faithful would have to be jettisoned. Certainly the desire to gain a clearer understanding of doctrines, in which such translation plays an important part, is legitimate and indeed required; but at the same time, it would be wrong to suppose that the force of doctrines will ever be perfectly clear, prior at any rate to profound experience, and even here their import would be by no means fully explicable in words.

VII

Moral Discourse and Religion

I. MORAL DISCOURSE MAY BE REGARDED AS A STRAND OF SPIRITUAL DISCOURSE

It is now in place to consider the relation that moral propositions bear to specifically religious ones, i.e. to those propositions which express the numinous, mystical or incarnation strands. It is, of course, somewhat artificial to make such a division, for two reasons. First, in developed doctrinal schemes moral assertions are already incorporated into the pattern of belief—as when God is said not merely to be all-powerful and all-holy but supremely good. However, this incorporation may be regarded for our purposes as a case of weaving-together such as we have discussed with respect to the specifically religious strands. The point of so regarding it will be elucidated below. Second, claims such as that nirvāṇa is the supreme good are formally straightforward practical assertions on a par with mundane value-judgments: so that we may say that in certain cases at least it is not right to view moral propositions as somehow extrinsic to specifically spiritual ones and therefore in need of weaving together with the latter. For these reasons then the procedure proposed here, namely to regard moral beliefs as representing an independent strand of discourse which is then combined with the other strands, is going to look even more artificial than our previous dissection of spiritual discourse. This impression may be enhanced further by a particular view about morality held by some religious people, namely that moral commandments are derived from God. This suggests that moral propositions are not logically independent of religious ones. It is therefore necessary first to explain the reasons why moral propositions can be regarded as extrinsic to religious ones.

The rationale for dividing the different strands of religious discourse lay principally in the diversities of basis for the propositions in doctrinal schemes. Hence the main way of showing the independence of a substantial part, at least, of moral discourse would be to show that the basis for its propositions is not specifically religious. For the purposes of what will inevitably be a highly schematic account of moral discourse I propose to consider the latter under the following heads: (i) moral rules (such as 'It is wrong to steal', etc.); (ii) statements of particular duties (such as 'It would be wrong for me to tell a lie to cover my embarrassment over my failure to send him a present', or 'It was wrong for him to be annoyed'); (iii) practical value-judgments (such as 'The best things in life are free', or 'Health is a great blessing'); (iv) moral judgments (such as 'He is courageous' or 'He is wicked'). The relationship between (i) and (ii) is fairly clear, for the moral rules are held to be true if they state correctly what particular duties are *in most cases*. Thus it is correct to say that stealing is wrong because in most relevant particular situations the agent should say that it is wrong for him to steal. Thus the justification of rules and of duties falling under those rules makes appeal to the same kind of consideration, with the simple difference that in justifying a rule one would be making a widespread claim, though it should be noted that the notion of justifying a particular duty acquires a certain bias because normally it is only necessary to justify a duty where there is a possible conflict with the general rule. What, then, is the kind of consideration appealed to in justifying rules and duties? Very generally: the prevention of suffering and the enhancement of natural goods. Thus: civilized society, i.e. a society in which men have on the whole a good chance of not being destitute and utterly miserable, and in which there is the possibility of achieving more than the mere supply of basic physical wants, could not exist without a general adherence to such rules as 'It is wrong to steal', 'One ought to keep promises', 'It is wrong to lie'. These may be described as socially necessary rules. Again, there are others which are hardly necessary for the existence of civilized society but which conduce to the betterment of life within such a society, such as may be claimed for the rule of monogamy with its attendant rules such as that it is wrong to commit adultery. Monogamy is correct if it is true that it raises the status of women, conduces to greater happiness in the offspring, prevents more suffering than it brings, etc. Thus the justification of socially necessary and ameliorative rules is utilitarian, appealing to the consequences as evaluated by practical value-judgments. It may be remarked that the negative formulations of utilitarianism

('Prevent suffering') are more immediately convincing, though not always adequate, simply because it is obvious that certain situations bring suffering, but there is less agreement—and urgency—about positive values. Similarly, where there is a conflict of duty with a rule, this is because the consequences of obeying the rule will be more evil than the consequences of disobeying it in a particular way: for example, where telling a lie will cause suffering. This may outweigh the loss of trust occasioned by the infringement of the rule. It can be seen that in the main it is unnecessary to appeal to any specifically religious premisses to justify rules and duties, *provided* that the practical value-judgments are not dependent upon religious premisses. (Exceptions to this generalization will be discussed later.)

Now one main ground for supposing that value-judgments are not so independent is that we wish to ask limiting questions about these, namely: Why should suffering be prevented as far as possible? Why should we promote happiness?—or more generally (since moral argument is neutral as to persons): Why should we treat others with compassion and benevolence? There are two sorts of answers that might be given to these: first, looking at them as genuine questions, by finding a higher ground for these principles and saying such things as 'Because it is God's Will' or 'Because man is made in the image of God', etc.; or second by implicitly refusing to count them as real moral questions and saying something like this: 'Well, that is the basis of morality', or 'If anyone fails to see why suffering is wrong, he is just amoral', etc. Roughly speaking, it is those who give the first sort of answer who claim the essential dependence of morality upon religion, those who give the second sort who preach the autonomy of ethics. There are two apposite comments on this situation. (i) The possibility of the second kind of reply to these limiting questions itself allows us to treat moral argument as independent of spiritual premisses. (ii) Limiting questions are such that we have no real guidance as to whether to answer them or not, except by considering whether it makes any substantial difference as to whether we use the principles as principles or climb higher. And I think it can be claimed that (with exceptions noted below) appeal to God's Will or to the doctrine that man is made in the divine image will not yield any different result from simple appeal to the principles that suffering is an evil and that men are to be treated compassionately and benevolently. It is therefore not implausible to treat moral rules, duties and valuations as justifiable independently of spiritual premisses. Finally, we turn to moral judgments.

In saying of someone that he is good or bad we are of course (among other things) praising or blaming him. One main function of praise or blame is to get people to do the right things and to refrain from the wrong things: it is then a form (usually but not always the mildest form) of reward and punishment. As such its purposes are controlled by the rules and valuations held to be correct. Hence moral judgments hold, in this respect, a subsidiary position in moral reasoning. But on the other hand, the commending of someone to a third person often plays a vital role in moral education: examples for us to follow are often not merely inspiring but also illuminating. This is partly because of the immense complexity of life. The consequences of action appear inscrutable, hard to evaluate, full of subtlety. And worse, they are often screened from us not merely by such darkness but also by our own desires, our own lack of candour and perseverance in considering them. Hence, since the rules are not always satisfactory guides to conduct and valuations often hard to apply, moral examples are good to follow and are indeed often a source of moral insight. (Hence the key place frequently held by the profoundly good man in advances in moral thinking.) However, it does not seem to be the case that moral examples of this sort need be also religious ones: that is, it is by no means self-evident that profound moral depth of character can only be achieved by believers; and in any case the reasons for their being right in what they do will be as described above (with regard to moral rules, duties and valuations).

For these reasons, then, it seems not inappropriate to treat moral propositions as logically independent of religious ones, except in the sense that by becoming incorporated into doctrinal schemes they acquire the status also of being religious propositions. Hence, from our point if view, they may be considered as constituting a separate strand of discourse within doctrinal schemes. I therefore propose to discuss this strand first in its association with the numinous strand, then in its association with the mystical strand and then in relation to incarnation.

II. MORALITY UNDER THE AEGIS OF THE NUMINOUS STRAND

We can best understand the way moral and spiritual beliefs are welded together in a numinous faith by attending to such central activities as worship and sacrifice. Commonly these are communal rites: but it is noteworthy how the concepts undergo an extension. Thus private prayer is held to count as worship of the Divine Being, and in this way the activity of worship comes to permeate life more fully. This spread of a spiritual activity from the formal to the informal we may describe as *intra-spiritual* extension. But there is a further spread which is more germane here, namely when a spiritual concept is, so to speak, superimposed upon a non-spiritual one, as in the following:

> The sacrifices of God are a broken spirit: a broken and a contrite heart, O God, thou wilt not despise.[1]

And more clearly still:

> Work shall be prayer, if all be wrought
> As thou wouldst have it done,
> And prayer, by Thee inspired and taught,
> Itself with work be one.[2]

In such examples we find that duties, etc., are regarded as sacrifices or prayers or worship. This we may describe as *extra-spiritual* extension. Thus the performance of a duty is regarded in a new light, but yet also remains a duty justifiable in the ordinary way, and this is the ground for saying above that spiritual concepts are, in this sort of case, *superimposed* upon moral ones. Briefly, then, the way that the numinous strand incorporates fully the moral strand is through superimposition. Our lives are a sacrifice to God: each action a prayer: the daily round a continual worship of the Lord. Thus too moral rules are viewed under the guise of commandments, for submission to them is a form of the submission to the Will of God. Moreover, in being sinful creatures who yet strive after the holiness of the divine, we are in a position to view such good actions as we may perform as in a small way going towards the expiation of our uncleanness. Thus the activities of worship and sacrifice are no longer isolated performances, but become the nucleus of an extended activity of worship.

[1] *Psalms*, li.17.
[2] *Church of Scotland Hymnary*, Hymn 356.

Yet it may well be asked how such an extension may be justified: why should it be plausible to count daily conduct of a certain sort as being a kind of worship? We may answer this in two parts, first by considering why the superimposition works this way round, and second by considering the supposed solidarity between morality and numinous religion.

(i) Why is there a superimposition of numinous concepts upon moral ones and not vice versa? In fact, the question is a little misleading, for in reality it is perfectly possible for moral concepts to be the preponderating ones as when it is said that true religion consists simply in loving one's neighbour or when someone speaks of faith in humanity. However, this situation is one where rites and their extensions are thought to be of hardly any independent importance, and where in fact it might be incorrect to talk of religious discourse at all. Thus it is perhaps a matter of simple definition that where there is superimposition in a doctrinal scheme containing the numinous strand, the numinous concepts are superimposed. But it may be worth remarking that the activity of worship, in a numinous religion, is considered of such great importance and the object of worship of such vast holiness that worship naturally comes to be thought of as the central point of life. Moreover, as we have seen earlier, the transcendence of the divine is such that sinful man gladly extends his expiations beyond mere words of praise and bought burnt offerings in order more adequately to express his submission. Thus the concept *worship* is likely to spread and formal worship is likely to remain at the centre.

(ii) We now come to the more vital question as to the supposed solidarity between numinous religion and morality. First, worship involves abasement before the Holy One, and this has a moral analogy in the disposition of humility. This latter has rather a central place in the good character, not merely because boastfulness and self-glory infringe the spirit of the commandment 'Thou shalt not lie' but much more importantly because by removing concern about oneself one makes a place for a concern for others which is demanded by the fundamental feature of moral reasoning: that it should be neutral as to persons. Thus religious and secular humility are both central in their own spheres. Second, abasement before the Holy One contains a recognition by the worshipper of his own profanity and a desire to reduce his sinfulness. By sacrificing himself to the Divine Will he may make some expiation for his sins. But why should virtue be like a sacrifice? A hint is given in the following passage:

> I beseech you, by the mercies of God, that ye present your bodies a living sacrifice, holy, acceptable unto God, which is your reasonable service.[1]

This illustrates, of course, only a particular application of the notion of sacrifice. There are two sides to its use here. First, a sacrifice is holy, that is to say it is, in order to be associated with the Divine Being, consecrated, and in the extended sense of 'sacrifice' this means, in this particular case, that one's body must be kept pure (again this is not literal speech, but is a shorthand way of saying that the improper expression and satisfaction of the so-called physical desires must be avoided). But second, and more importantly, this control of desires self-evidently involves failing to satisfy desires and this is giving up something. In an extended sense, then, it is a sacrifice. And in general moral struggles self-evidently arise from conflict between duty and self-satisfaction or self-interest; and thus, though perhaps it is true that the majority of conduct in conformity with the dictates of conscience is performed unthinkingly, without struggle, yet first, there are important occasions where a real struggle is involved, and second, the attempt to conform all one's conduct to a correct pattern of life would for most if not all people mean a struggle. For these reasons, then, the performance of particular duties may be regarded as the giving of sacrifices, as gestures which in some measure help to make the gap between man and God tolerable.

With this extension of the notions of sacrifice and worship there is, naturally enough, a corresponding spread of the idea of sin. This is no longer a simply religious concept, but one which includes a strong moral element: sinfulness is not merely uncleanness before the All-Holy but also moral inadequacy viewed as the failure to conform oneself to God's Will. No longer is it possible to make any simple distinction between holiness and righteousness.

The completely successful superimposition of spiritual upon moral concepts is made possible doctrinally by the principle that God is perfectly good: thus there can be no conflict between our duty and God's Will. But this principle also illustrates the effect which the weaving-together of the numinous and moral strands has upon the former. Any supreme object of worship, having, as

[1] *Rom.*, xii.1.

we say, supreme mystery-value, must necessarily, it is thought, be utterly good; and the claim that this is so is to be justified in some such ways as the following. (i) The All-Holy one, being the fount of man's salvation, provides the greatest possible blessing, and so can be described as supremely loving and benevolent. (ii) The doctrine of creation pictures God as the cause of the world and hence of any non-spiritual goods in life (but hence also the problem of evil). (iii) The analogies which go towards justifying the superimposition of numinous upon moral concepts and which point thereby to similarities between moral inadequacy and religious impurity also by reflection suggest that the utterly holy is also utterly good.

The fact that we have two strands woven together is well illustrated by the doctrine of Original Sin, which is partly a straightforward mundane thesis about men's nature and partly a supramundane one about men's relation to God. For on the one hand it points to the general fact that men pretty consistently fail to live up to the best ideals—men are as a matter of empirical fact (given, that is, certain moral standards wherewith to evaluate the data) constantly failing to be virtuous; but on the other hand the doctrine is clearly not just such a straightforward thesis. For instance in imputing universal inadequacy to be traced to the Fall of Man it suggests that men should feel remorse for something which is inherited and so not strictly imputable to the individual.[1] But the shame men should feel is shame before God, and so we are beyond the sphere of ordinary moral responsibility. Our impurity comes from our not being divine, one might say—or more precisely, from our no longer being close to God (here again the numinous strand displays its predilection for contingency: man's separation from the divine object of worship is best expressed here in story form, as being due to an historical choice).

It is interesting also to notice how the tension between the two strands occurs over doctrines of faith and grace. It is of course perfectly in accord with the spirit of the numinous strand to ascribe to the Supreme Being credit even for what otherwise might be described as our own moral successes. On the other hand an exclusive insistence on the part God plays in such matters leads to deleterious consequences from the moral angle: it is likely to cause passivity in the adherent and the feeling that faith alone

[1] Argued, for instance, by Professor H. D. Lewis in his *Morals and the New Theology*.

matters and that conduct is not to be worried about. Hence we find disputes about the role of grace in the religious life, strikingly exemplified by the opposing two schools of Vaiṣṇavism—the one holding the *mārkaṭa-kiśora-nyāya* or 'monkey-offspring-method', the other holding the *mārjāra-kiśora-nyāya* or 'cat-offspring-method'. On the one doctrine God leads men as a mother monkey leads her young: the little one needs to make an effort himself, though he could not of course get from A to B without the guiding hand of his mother. On the other view, God brings men to salvation as a cat transports her young: here the kitten is quite passive, merely being taken from A to B by the scruff of its neck.

So far our account of the relation between the two strands has suggested that in point of content moral beliefs are unaffected by their association with religion, though the spirit in which one performs duties and so forth is of course greatly altered. It is as well, however, to append here a few remarks about certain alterations in content which do in fact occur (though secular and numinous morality will remain in the main coincident). First, there are certain rules which arise directly from spiritual beliefs and which are, in doctrinal schemes, placed on a par with secular moral rules, i.e. such rules as that it is wrong to steal. For example, it is wrong to blaspheme, since this infringes in a terrible way the duty to worship God; and it is similarly wrong to damage or affront things or persons specially connected with the divine, e.g. it is wrong to plunder churches or to revile priests. All these rules are derivable, as indicated above, from the prime requirement that 'Thou shalt worship the Lord thy God', which itself needs no extrinsic justification, being a specifically religious duty arising, so to speak, out of the religious situation: hence it is in a sense analytically true, since it presupposes the existence of God and a God is by definition to be worshipped. Second, the existence at the centre of life, so to speak, of specifically religious activities involves some reappraisal of ends—for clearly the ends which a man ought to set himself, on a religious view, and which have to be harmonized into a pattern of conduct, will differ in this vital respect from the ends set before the secular man. This may, under certain difficult circumstances, lead to choices of action quite different from those of the non-religious, as when for example a man finds it to be his duty to witness to his faith through martyrdom. This would, from the formal point of view, have a parallel in a man's sacrificing his health and ordinary happiness for some special non-extrinsically justifiable cause, such as the composition of music—as did Mozart; but I am not implying here of course that such causes as music are to be matched with religion in point of value, for obviously, if the claims of religion are correct, the importance of serving God will be of vastly more immense value than even the creation of masterpieces—though in any case some may regard the contrast as artificial, since many of the latter have a religious inspiration or could be interpreted as so inspired. Third, the superimposition will affect the content of moral beliefs in a somewhat circuitous way since moral rules, by being described as the laws of God, will gain the protection of doctrinal conservatism (the reasons for which have been examined in the previous chapter): consequently the weaving together of moral and numinous discourse will tend to make the moral views of adherents more old-fashioned than their secular counterparts, and this may be sometimes a good and sometimes a bad thing, though it is not in place to discuss that here. Fourth, on the broader political plane, such doctrines as that of Original Sin, any view, that is, implying man's inherent sinfulness—and such a view is naturally characteristic of the numinous strand, militates against hopes that man can by his own efforts create a heaven upon earth and will therefore tend against political utopianism. Fifth, the belief that man's main goal is a supernatural one may result in a sharp divergence from secular morality where a decision hinges on the weight to be assigned to goods in order to determine the direction of benefaction. For example, euthanasia, if ever to be justified, would be justified by the fact, in a particular case, that a man is in unsufferable pain, without hope of being able to achieve any normal goods; but it might nevertheless be held that he was capable of spiritual consolation and salvation—and so it would be utterly wrong to cut him off from these by premature death.

So much then for the general effects of numinous upon moral discourse. There is one other which deserves mention but which will be dealt with later, in the discussion of the incarnation strand, namely the fact that in the religious view the type of man held up as the best example of humanity will be religious—this will serve to reinforce the point already made, that specifically religious interests and activities are at the centre of life.

III. MORALITY UNDER THE AEGIS OF THE MYSTICAL STRAND

It has already been noted that the main claim of a mystical religion amounts to a straightforward practical value-judgment: for instance, the claim that nirvāṇa is the *summum bonum* shows what the main goal of existence is. In fact, however, the scope of such a claim is limited in practice, as a natural consequence of the empirical fact that not all seem well suited to attain such a goal. In the Indian religions there is little difficulty accruing upon this limitation, simply because of the doctrine of rebirth: thus nirvāṇa or *mokṣa* (etc.) can be everyone's ultimate objective, even though it is to be hoped for in this particular birth by only the very few. And in the Judaic religions it is generally held (wherever the mystical path is recognized as leading to God) that there are different ways to communion with the divine, that it is not everyone's calling to forsake the world for the spiritual blessings of seclusion. Some have to remain 'in the world', to fight God's fight there. But in any case these are faiths whose doctrines are far from being compounded merely out of the mystical strand.

However, despite the limitation, the mystical claim is that a certain goal is of overriding importance. It is, of course, a peculiar goal in that its pursuit involves giving up a large number of the goals men commonly prize: it usually involves celibacy, a fair degree of abstention in the matters of food, drink, etc., seclusion from the interesting bustle of everyday life, the renunciation of political, administrative or financial power—and so on. Its hallmark is, as far as wordly enjoyments are concerned, austerity. Whether the pursuit of this goal is in fact to be justified is not for us here to argue, but it is worth pointing out that a decision on this issue is hard, since one could only be sure that it is a worthwhile pursuit after tasting the fruits thereof. (Though one must make this qualification, that where the mystical goal is described as union with God or Allah, etc., its pursuit then is self-evidently worth while—the dispute then shifts its centre to the question whether such mystical experiences are in fact cases of coming into contact with the divine, and if so whether or not there are other paths leading to the latter.)

But it is clear that the moral rules associated with the mystical strand will be regarded as conducive to the all-important spiritual goal. This in fact seems to be the case with regard to the purely mystical religions. For example, the second section of the Noble Eightfold Path summarises the main principles of morality (right speech, right activity and right livelihood): their position in the Path is a clear indication of the way they fit into the mystical endeavour towards nirvāṇa. Thus the *summum bonum* (since it is in effect defined by the procedure for attaining it) is, so to speak, moralized—nirvāṇa is not merely the state a man may reach, but is the state a good man reaches. At the same time, there is a solidarity between asceticism and morality, since the capacity for good conduct is largely consequent upon training in self-control, and we may compare what was said earlier about sacrifice. The neat coincidence between self-control, asceticism and sacrifice is well illustrated in the following passage, which represents the position of a complex mystical-numinous doctrinal scheme of course:

> Hunger and thirst and abstention from pleasures, these are the initiatory rites. And when one eats and drinks and enjoys pleasures, these are the *Upasada* ceremonies . . . And austerity, almsgiving, uprightness, non-violence, truth-telling, these are the offerings for the priests.[1]

Again (to broaden the range of these remarks), the solidarity between morality and asceticism is seen in this: that on the one hand the highest moral conduct involves unselfishness and on the other the mystical path requires self-abnegation. That is, we have on the one hand the disregarding of one's own desires and interests where these conflict with the highest good, and on the other the sacrifice of selfish aims (or more precisely of the aims of the non-spiritual self) in order to gain a higher blessing. Nevertheless, it is a common charge against mystics that they are essentially self-centred, in that although they do not seek common goods such as most men selfishly compete for, yet they still seek a state of bliss: they differ from the ordinary selfish man merely in having a different appraisal of the relative worth of different satisfactions. And it was in large measure the reason for dissatisfaction with Lesser Vehicle Buddhism that it was selfish in aim—whereas Mahāyāna not merely offered a wider basis for religion but stressed more emphatically the importance of *karuṇā* or charity and compassion, through the examples of the *bodhisattvas* who sacrificed even their highest spiritual attainment in order to help

[1] *Chāndogya Upan.*, III.17.1–4 (3 omitted).

others thereto. Similarly, the self-centred quietism of Brāhmanistic religion as expressed in certain of the *Upaniṣads*, with its insistence that engagement in works is itself contaminating and so conducive to rebirth, was considered unsatisfactory by the author of the *Bhagavadgītā*, who emphasizes the point that provided works are performed in a spirit of detachment (so that their fruits are rejected) they do not ensnare:

> Whatever thou doest, whatever thou eatest, whatever thou offerest, whatever thou givest, whatever austerities thou performest, that do as a gift to Me. Thus thou shalt be freed from the bonds of action and its good and bad fruits.[1]

This latter idea opens up the possibility of a variation upon the training recommended in the mystical path: the discipline is attained not merely by yogic practices but by the daily performance of tasks in the right spirit. This is not unlike Brother Lawrence's Practice of the Presence of God, nor is it far removed from Zen methods—where the acquiring of a mundane skill such as archery or flower-arrangement is itself turned into a type of mystical training. It is in such ways as these that the affinity between morality and mysticism can be consolidated, despite the tension which accrues upon the self-centredness (albeit of a higher kind) of the mystic.

The mystical experience, furthermore, being of an overwhelming and glorious nature, is held to transmute the moral capacities acquired through the discipline of the path and to be a source of depth and power of character such as are rarely found —if at all—in ordinary men. This was one of the grounds for calling the mystic 'holy' and also for regarding the source thereof as holy and thus in a respect like the divine. If the claim that the experience does give this power and does conduce to saintliness, this would be a good reason for the claim found in mystical religion that only (or mostly) in mysticism is the highest morality to be found: it is here that we look for that transcendence of ordinary virtue which distinguishes the most glorious examples of human character. But whether or not the premiss upon which the claim rests is true is not for us to argue here.

It is, incidentally, because of the supposed transcendent character of the mystic that such assertions as the following are made: that the perfected man is beyond good and evil.

[1] ix.27–8.

> Give up good and evil, truth as well as untruth. Having given up truth and untruth, give up the consciousness that you have given them up.[1]

A man of such deep insight who is already trained in good conduct is no longer concerned with self-examination or deliberation. And further, such a man 'beyond good and evil' is likely to be the ideal in a mystical faith; and this fact is enshrined in the moral judgments found there, expressing the respect in which the spiritual master is to be held.

We may sum up, then, the effects of mysticism upon moral attitudes as follows. (i) One special goal of human endeavour is prized above all others. This is, however, a peculiar (and hence unworldly) objective. (ii) Since the attainment of this goal requires at least a moderate asceticism, obedience to moral rules will tend to be regarded not merely as conducive to the general benefit but also as good training in self-control (hence the inclusion in some cases of austere rules in codes of morality prescribed to adherents, e.g. the prohibition of intoxicants in Buddhism). (iii) Moral judgments will be coloured by the raising of the spiritual man to the highest place of honour. And notably this quietistic ideal will conduce towards such principles as *ahiṃsā* or non-injury.

At the same time, it should not be forgotten that mysticism is itself influenced by independent moral beliefs, so that, as we have said, such goals as nirvāṇa are moralized: the achievement of the goal is set at the end of a path which regulates the pattern of life and which includes the performance of one's duties towards others in a pure and benevolent spirit. This militates against the tendency towards complete withdrawal from the active scene which characterizes an extreme mysticism.

IV. MORALITY UNDER THE AEGIS OF THE INCARNATION STRAND

Since the notion of incarnation presupposes that of a God in another world, the superimposition of numinous upon moral concepts will already obtain in a faith containing the incarnation strand. But the doctrine of an incarnation will alter the situation somewhat. One obvious effect is that the incarnate deity is likely to serve as a brilliant moral example for the daily guidance of the

[1] *Mahābhārata*, xii.337.40, quoted by S. Radhakrishnan in *Eastern Religions and Western Thought*, p. 102.

adherent. (This is not always so, as the instance of Krsna's youthful career as a rural Romeo indicates; but of course a doctrinal scheme allowing the possibility of many incarnations has a greater flexibility and can, in effect, be more easy-going.) Where, as in Christianity, there is but one Incarnation, the Divine Human will naturally be the supreme moral paradigm.

There are two comments to be made here. (i) Having but one supreme example is an advantage and a disadvantage. On the one hand, the concentration of devotion and meditation upon one figure is likely to cause people to have always before them a morally inspiring example. This is conducive to persistent reflection upon their conduct, which in turn will result in earnest striving to conform their lives to the highest ideals. Putting the advantage more succinctly: the machinery of meditation and devotion is here geared to moral endeavour. Provided, of course, that the Divine Human really does display great insight and moral heroism (a fact to be determined by recourse to the evidence about his life), the attempt to imitate his conduct is likely to have good consequences. The perceptiveness of the adherent in moral matters is, because of the reverent attention paid by him to the paradigm, likely to be heightened. But on the other hand, a religion allowing but one incarnation has the possible disadvantage that it restricts very considerably the range of moral examples which adherents are to look to. A result of concentrating attention upon one supreme example is that the insights to be gained from contemplating the divine career will not always be easy to apply to one's own conduct. Further, the very fact that the human paradigm is given the attributes of deity may seem to make his life somewhat remote from that of the ordinary man: after all, it may be felt, a Messiah's career is of a very special nature. By making the Incarnation unique, the Christian doctrinal scheme runs the risk of making the moral lessons taught by Jesus' life less effective. On the other hand, this disadvantage—even if real—may be outweighed by the great intensity which a single paradigm is likely to have for the reasons mentioned above.

(ii) In order to be identical with the All-Holy, Jesus needs to be sinless. Now if in fact he was so, then he displays an example of complete purity which should give the ordinary adherent an objective to strive for. One cannot simply, under these circumstances, count sinfulness as an ineradicable property of human kind and so have a 'realistic' ethics which abandons the ideal of complete purity. Thus the effect of the doctrine of Incarnation at this point is that the highest possible demands are made upon the adherent inasmuch as he must attempt seriously the *imitatio Christi*.

There is another feature of the situation which stands out clearly. The life of an incarnate deity is obviously of such a nature that God is somehow revealed in it. Thus inevitably the divine human is concerned with propagating spiritual truth. Therefore, although the adherent will not be in a position to show forth the truth in quite the same way, implicitly it is his duty to promote true religion. This is of course but a particular aspect of a wider consideration that the paradigm is not merely a luminous example of goodness and heroism, but is also an example of the deeply religious life. In this respect it differs from such secular examples as may be appealed to in moral education. Similarly with the saints thrown up in the course of the faith's history—these subsidiary moral paradigms can be connected with the supreme one, since, for example, they show conspicuously Christ working in men. Indeed the life of the incarnate deity may be the best instance in which the solidarity between the numinous and moral strands is displayed, a convincing demonstration that truly God is Love. Serving God and serving man, it will be claimed, will here be seen to be closely allied. Moreover, the very fact of an incarnation or *avatāra* shows that God is concerned to reveal Himself in as obvious a way as is possible in order to establish or re-establish true religion; and thereby it is clear that He desires man's spiritual well-being. Thus an incarnation may not merely show how well moral conduct fits into religious activity but also exhibits that which makes utter coalescence possible, namely God's merciful goodness.

COMMENTS ON THE PRECEDING

The brief sketch given here, if correct, shows that it is mainly in one connection that there is likely to be dispute about the status of moral rules, etc.—namely in connection with the numinous strand. For it is here that patterns of religious discourse about morality appear to differ most in flavour from secular patterns, since, as we have endeavoured to show, numinous concepts are superimposed upon moral ones and one finds such apparently eccentric reasons for justifying actions as 'This is the Will of God'

—reasons which are not obviously in line with our more mundane justifications (in terms of mundane consequences). Unfortunately, the history of thought upon these matters has been bedevilled by two facts. First, rationality has been by no means characteristic of the reasoning of ordinary people about moral matters, and as a symptom of this state of affairs appeals to authority and to mere custom are widespread. Consequently, the present attempt to distinguish a separate strand of discourse by pointing to the proper grounds for making moral assertions may not appear to accord too well with the facts as to how religious people actually argue. Second, there have been philosophical attempts to argue that moral standards must be objective, and if objective then requiring support from outside man—a support only to be provided by a divine entity. In this manner it is claimed that moral discourse presupposes some religious truth and thus that morality is intrinsically connected with religion. We have already given grounds for rejecting this kind of view, but of course like many such positions it is incapable of clearly decisive refutation (which would in any case take up far more space than is available here). Consequently it would be idle to pretend that our sketch of the relation between the two types of discourse is an accurate account of the way in which any reflective person would view it. Nevertheless, it does seem to possess this advantage over philosophical theories which assert an intrinsic connection between morality and religion, namely that by describing the relation between the two as one in which mutual intimacy depends upon considerations which are to be appraised in an aesthetic manner (we see how the two hang together) and not upon entailments (which ought, when exposed to the light of day, to appear self-evident), room is given for disagreements upon the issue, which, though capable of resolution, is not *easily* resolved. Whereas on the philosophical theory, disagreement with the thesis has to be explained as due to lack of reflection or to obtuseness or to perversity—none of which diagnoses appears immediately convincing.

Another difficulty about the distinction is that historically moral rules and so forth have usually appeared in a religious context before being recognized as possibly independent. Thus a rule may be first obeyed merely because it is said to be a commandment of God and not for the reasons that make it a good rule (and hence, presumably, commanded by God). Thus the so-called 'weaving-together' of which we have spoken is not, it seems, something which precedes amalgamation of the two strands of discourse. However, the use of this notion in describing their mutual relation is perhaps convenient in that it draws attention to analogous ways in which different strands of specifically religious discourse are united. Moreover, although it is true that moral rules often appear in early history embedded already in doctrinal schemes, there is ample evidence of the way increased moral insight (as displayed, for instance, by the Prophets in the Old Testament) affects the religious outlook; and to this extent the weaving-together is an historical process.

A final general comment upon the relation between morality and religion as it has been described here is that it is of course highly schematic. The richness of superimposition, for example, has hardly been conveyed, especially in that we have not here dealt with the rather large topic of religious institutions which themselves have a strong influence in shaping people's conduct and which exhibit many instances of the subtle extension of spiritual concepts in those rituals which enhance the solidarity between religion and everyday life. For example, the Christian marriage ceremony, with its supposition that wedlock is a sacrament, points to the analogy between this human relationship and the divine marriage between Christ and His Church. However, the brevity with which we have dealt with these matters is not unintentional in that first we have here a specially complicated situation to describe and one that cannot adequately be dealt with summarily but would better be thoroughly treated in a separate volume; and second because the main task of the present book is to give some account of specifically religious discourse, and a lengthy treatment of morality might well convey the impression that this side of religion is the most important one to be scrutinized philosophically, whereas in fact it is the numinous and the mystical and the incarnate which most need illumination. However, it is hoped that sufficient has been said to illustrate the manner in which moral discourse fits in with that which is specifically spiritual.

VIII

Conclusion

In conclusion I wish to recapitulate fairly briefly what has been said here, in order that an outline of the woods may emerge from behind the trees. And in addition I shall try to give a short inventory of those aspects of religious discourse which have not been dealt with.

The first main contention emerging from the preceding discussion is that there is no single analysis of religious language, that it is, so to speak, logically variegated. Hence there will be no single definition of religion in terms of content, and the search for such a definition will be a snare, leading one on to lack of discrimination. And the contention is supported in detail by the attempt to distinguish different strands of religious discourse. If the distinctions are correct, then simple definitions of religion (as, e.g., 'man's relationship with the divine') are bound to issue in a distorted description of one strand or another. At the same time, there is no denying that there is a certain justification in the lack of such discrimination, and this arises from the following situation: that certain doctrinal schemes succeed in weaving together concepts from different strands. This is possible because of certain analogies which obtain between concepts such as *God* and others such as *nirvāṇa*. Nevertheless, the present contention is that these are never quite so close that it would be absurd to use only the concepts of one strand without those of the others (save in one special case—the incarnation presupposes the numinous). It is, that is to say, not absurd to have a one-strand doctrinal scheme, and this is forcibly illustrated by those of early Buddhism and Islām. In particular, since Westerners habitually think of religion in terms of a God or gods (because, as it happens, Western civilization has been dominated and shaped by polytheistic and theistic faiths), the example of Buddhism is most vital, since it exemplifies an agnostic doctrinal scheme—one where to all intents and purposes the numinous strand is absent. Those who say that the southern Buddhists, in speaking of nirvāṇa, are *really* speaking of much the same thing as Christians are talking about in talking about God, can indeed point to certain similarities between the concepts, and it has been our concern to show how weaving-together of different strands may be achieved. But the differences are equally vital for an understanding of their nature. It is for such reasons that it has been herein said that the coalescence of two strands can be justified only in a somewhat aesthetic manner, by pointing to suggestive likenesses.

The important distinction between the numinous and mystical strands has been arrived at not merely by considering certain superficial differences in the language of the two strands but by examining the spiritual activities of worship and mysticism in the light of which the concepts can be to some extent elucidated. For it is largely in these activities that notions such as 'divine' and 'nirvāṇa' find their application. The characteristic atmosphere of these activities has been used to account for various features of the doctrines associated therewith.

The discussion of these points has naturally helped to uncover the kinds of grounds which go to support claims made in the different strands. These are what we have called the *basic* justifications for such claims. In the numinous strand, basic justification involves appeal to those marvellous and awe-inspiring features of the world and of life which betray the handiwork of the divine: through these features the Holy Being reveals Himself. But in addition we must take note of certain *formal* points: for example, the simplicity of monotheism may be considered to be a formal advantage as against the untidiness of polytheism. Appeal to such formal justifications plays quite an important part in the support of a doctrinal scheme. Again, the confirmation of a mystical strand involves pointing to the behaviour and utterances of the mystic and seeing whether his life has lain along the prescribed Path, whether his character shows lucidly his spirituality, and so forth. Thus the basic justification of such a claim is rather different from that in the numinous strand. At this point, however, the situation is complicated by the fact that some doctrinal schemes are complex and so give rise to descriptions of the mystical goal as union with the divine, etc. Here, provided that claims about the Holy have been justified and provided that those about the achievement of bliss are also confirmed, the question arises: How do we know that the latter attainment is really gaining intimacy with the divine object of worship? Here the somewhat aesthetic analogies of which we have spoken are to be considered: and in so far as anyone appeals to these in order to back the contention that this nirvāṇa-like goal is really union with the Holy, he is attempting what we have called an *organic* justification. He points to the timelessness, transcendence, goodness, etc., of the nirvāṇa-like goal to show its similarity to the divine. Hence already the structure of justifications, even on this highly schematic account, is pretty complex. But in addition, we have pointed out that (i) the concepts often do not completely coalesce, for the simple reason that however similar we may show them to be the paths by which we arrive at the concepts are different, and (ii) consequently we have doctrinal distinctions between different aspects of the Godhead. A natural issue out of this situation is that one may have to decide as to how strongly one aspect is to be emphasized as against another, and such a decision is what has here been called a *priority decision*. On what grounds such is to be made is a somewhat obscure question, but we have tried to show, first, that pragmatic considerations (such as that all are not capable of mystical endeavour) play some part here; and second, that the strength of the strand ought to depend on the strength of its bases: thus, the numinous element in a doctrinal scheme ought perhaps to be given greater prominence, if the basic justification of claims about the divine appear stronger than that of mystical claims. But judging relative strengths here is a difficult matter.

Such in outline, then, is the pattern of justification of doctrinal schemes. But we have been at pains also to point out that the dissection of doctrinal schemes we have here attempted is not to be taken to imply that it is possible to excogitate a doctrinal scheme for oneself. These remarks about doctrines are only possible *ex post dicto*: we can gain insight about the schemes once they are given to us, but it does not follow that we would thereby have sufficient insight to construct a new one for ourselves. This indeed would be quite outside the spirit of religion. Nevertheless, though we may bow before revelation and be wary of penetrating too deeply the mysteries that are there contained, though we may act before the divine word with the utmost reverence, yet it must not simply be thought that there are no grounds for accepting a faith. Admittedly, these grounds may only grow clear (as clear, at any rate, as they could ever grow, for we are here seeing in a glass darkly) long after we have been taught the faith and have started practising it, but still it would be foolish to say that in these matters we are quite beyond reasoning. Foolish for two reasons: first, because the kinds of justification we have above delineated seem in fact to have a place in religious thinking, so that blind acceptance would not even be in line with religious practice; and second, because in general any claim for which there *could* be no ground would be vacuous. For this reason, proponents of extreme revelationism are unthinkingly allied to those who would assert that religious propositions are, because unverifiable, meaningless. But it should of course be remembered that the type of reasoning employed on behalf of religious claims is of a special nature, and is of course quite unlike that which is exemplified in mathematics or physics. Hence the inappropriateness of the common distinction between reason and revelation and of the attempts to prove God's existence, etc.

In the above account of the pattern of justification we have bypassed one strand of religious discourse which for various reasons has rather a special place: namely the incarnation strand. Its special position accrues upon the following facts: first, it presupposes the numinous strand and is therefore not so independent of the latter as is the mystical strand, though of course one can certainly have a doctrinal scheme containing the numinous strand which has nothing to say about an incarnation (though there may exist in such a faith prophets or saints of central importance, and, as we have seen, these persons are not sharply to be distinguished from the incarnate deity, though the latter may have an insight and purity not to be found in the normal saint or prophet—and such a difference of degree can of course be of the profoundest importance). A second point which makes incarnation a special case is that much of the evidence in support of a claim such as that Christ is God is straightforwardly historical—and this despite the fact that the investigation of it may be bedevilled by prejudices (so that it seems almost impossible to have any objective history of a divine career). But the straightforwardly historical facts do not of course by themselves guarantee divinity, since, first, the incarnate one's person must have certain resemblances to that of the All-Holy; and second, his career must fall into a convincing pattern. Neither of these requirements is to be established simply on the basis of recorded facts, however detailed these may be; for on the one hand, numinous concepts have to be introduced, and on the other one must have an eye for pattern. Thus the structure of justification here is most complex.

Finally, with regard to the way in which doctrinal schemes are composed and confirmed, we have given a sketch of the relationship between moral propositions and those which are specifically spiritual. For the purposes of the present investigation, it is possible to treat the former as constituting a separate strand of religious discourse, even though often in ordinary circumstances it would be inappropriate to treat moral utterances as being a type of religious language. There we attempted to show that there is a solidarity between morality and religion in the numinous strand, in that certain dispositions important in moral conduct (such as humility) fit snugly with the attitudes demanded in worship and that this made possible a superimposition of numinous upon moral concepts (as, e.g., in the notion of sacrifice). And further, the career of a divine Saviour helps to consolidate the alliance. As to the claims typically made from within the mystical strand, these are seen to affect moral views inasmuch as an abnormal goal is proposed as the *summum bonum*, and this of course has strong effects on deliberative decisions. Further, moral rules are given a place in the mystical Path as prescribing ways of conduct which constitute good spiritual training.

In the course of the investigation certain incidental points have been made. First, idealism can be understood by reference to the mystical goal, and this partly explains the inherent attraction of such a theory for metaphysicians. And this illustrates the more general contention that many philosophical systems have a religious element to be distinguished from the logical and epistemological theses which are the proper concern of the philosopher. Second, notions such as 'belief' and 'knowledge' have specific spiritual uses different from their everyday ones; consequently, the divergence of religious truths from scientific or everyday truths cannot simply be described by such common contrasts as those between faith and reason, belief and knowledge, etc. Indeed, the clearest way to distinguish seems to be by reference to those activities which are specifically religious, such as worship and mysticism. Only thus, it seems, can a rich enough picture of religious discourse be built up to expose the epistemological dissimilarities between religion and science or common sense. Third, there has been an attempt to show that doctrines, though they can be analysed to some extent and confirmed in various ways, are only to be discovered by those of deep religious insight and are not to be excogitated. And in general, if what has here been said about the bases of spiritual propositions is correct, it will not be hard to see that it is wrong to intellectualize religion. It will perhaps be objected that what is said above about deep insight is incorrect because there appear to be cases of doctrines propounded by those presumably without such insight, as happens in certain religious sects belonging to the 'lunatic fringe' (I forbear to mention examples, though the reader will doubtless be able to think of the kind of sect I mean). This points to an inadequacy in the present study and with it I shall begin the promised inventory of those aspects of religious discourse which have not been dealt with.

First, then, the present study is meant to cover what may be described as religious discourse at its best. There are aberrant sects where, for instance, religious discourse is taken in a purely literal sense and the same is true perhaps of certain primitive religions. If, for example, it is claimed that a certain religious teacher is immortal, in the literal sense that he will be living in this world after any date you care to mention, this claim is hardly distinguishable in type from a simple empirical assertion. It is not denied, of course, that empirical assertions come into religious discourse, but many of the more important doctrines do not appear to be of this sort at all. It is with some of these we have been concerned, not with those so-called religious assertions which are in effect indistinguishable from empirical claims except for the impropriety of the grounds upon which they are held. Thus, the present investigation by no means covers all doctrines which have or will be called 'religious'. On the whole we have dealt with such faiths as Christianity, Islām, Judaism, Hinduism, Buddhism, Taoism, etc., which have been taken to exemplify at their core the nature of religious claims. But perhaps it will be agreed that if a reasonable account of the doctrines of such faiths has been given, this is adequate to justify the hope that it is also a reasonable account of the nature of religious discourse.

Second, there are a number of topics which I have skated over or round, either because I was unclear as to what to say about them or because they did not warrant extensive treatment in such a general account as this. In the former class fall: (i) The Christian doctrine of the Holy Spirit, which does not seem to fit neatly within the picture herein presented and which seems in any case rather obscure; (ii) the important Indian belief in rebirth; (iii) the nature of beliefs about an after-life (this has only briefly been touched on); (iv) the status of belief in evil spirits, such as Satan and Ahriman. Under the second head fall: (i) the epistemology of miracles; (ii) the nature of performatory rites such as baptism; (iii) the way secondary holy objects such as the Church or holy water are related to those Beings from whom they derive their sacredness; (iv) the nature of minor numinous beings, such as angels, in a monotheistic faith. Doubtless there are many other detailed features of doctrines hardly considered here. With these qualifications and the rider that in any case this account has been schematic, it is nevertheless hoped that it gives a fair picture of the structure of religious truth.

But perhaps the neutralism of the enterprise will still seem distasteful to some, and perhaps the dissection of doctrines will appear a grossly crude and indelicate way to deal with them. To those who regard what has been written here as profoundly irreligious, I tender apologies with the weak words that it was not meant to be so. Yet it may after all be presumptuous to attempt to unfold the meaning of that which is recognized as a mystery. But if words are used to speak of this mystery there is room for philosophical analysis. And if not *this* analysis, then some other.

Bibliography

BAILLIE, J. *The Idea of Revelation in Recent Thought.* London: Geoffrey Cumberlege, 1956.

BEVAN, E. *Symbolism and Belief.* London: George Allen and Unwin, 1938.

BRAITHWAITE, R. B. *Scientific Explanation.* Cambridge: Cambridge University Press, 1953.

CARPENTER, J. E. *Theism in Medieval India.* London: Williams and Norgate, 1921.

CLARK, J. M. *The Great German Mystics.* Oxford: Basil Blackwell, 1950.

CONZE, E. *Buddhist Meditation.* London: George Allen and Unwin, 1956.

—— (Editor). *Buddhist Texts.* London: Bruno Cassirer, 1954.

COPLESTON, F. C. *Aquinas.* London: Penguin Books, 1955.

DASGUPTA, S. N. *History of Indian Philosophy,* Vols. I–V. Cambridge: Cambridge University Press, 1922–55.

FESTUGIÈRE, A. J. *Contemplation et Vie Contemplative selon Platon* (2nd Edition). Paris: Vrin, 1950.

FLEW, A. G. N. (Editor). *Logic and Language* (2nd Series). Oxford: Basil Blackwell, 1953.

GIBB, H. A. R. *Mohammedanism* (2nd Edition). London: Geoffrey Cumberlege, 1953.

GINSBURG, C. D. *The Kabbalah* (New Edition). London: Routledge and Kegan Paul, 1953.

HEILER, F. *Die Buddhistische Versenkung,* Munich: E. Reinhardt, 1922.

HERRIGEL, E. *Zen in the Art of Archery,* trans. R. F. C. Hull. London: Routledge and Kegan Paul, 1953.

JENNINGS, J. G. *The Vedāntic Buddhism of the Buddha.* London: Geoffrey Cumberlege, 1947.

LEEUW, G. VAN DER. *Religion in Essence and Manifestation,* trans. J. E. Turner. London: George Allen and Unwin, 1938.

LEWIS, H. D. *Morals and the New Theology.* London: Gollancz, 1947.

NICHOLSON, R. A. *Literary History of the Arabs* (2nd Edition). Cambridge: Cambridge University Press, 1930.

—— *Studies in Islamic Mysticism.* Cambridge: Cambridge University Press, 1921.

OTTO, R. *The Idea of the Holy,* trans. J. W. Harvey (2nd Edition). London: Geoffrey Cumberlege, 1950.

—— *Mysticism East and West,* trans. Bertha L. Bracey and Richenda C. Payne. London: Macmillan and Co., 1937.

PRESTIGE, G. L. *God in Patristic Thought.* London: Heinemann, 1936.

RADHAKRISHNAN, S. (Editor andTranslator). *The Principal Upaniṣads.* London: George Allen and Unwin, 1953.
—— *Eastern Religions and Western Thought* (2nd Edition). Oxford: Oxford University Press, 1940.
RAMSEY, F. P. *The Foundations of Mathematics.* London: Kegan Paul, Trench, Trubner and Co., 1931.
RAWSON, J. N. *The Katha Upaniṣad.* Oxford: Oxford University Press, 1934.
RENOU, L. *Religions of Ancient India.* London: The Athlone Press, 1953.
RHYS DAVIDS, T. W., and STEDE, W. *The Pāli Text Society's Pāli-English Dictionary.* London: Päli Text Society, 1921–5.
SIMON, M. *Jewish Religious Conflicts.* London: Hutchinson's University Library, 1952.
SMITH, F. H. *The Elements of Comparative Theology.* London: Duckworth, 1937.
STRAWSON, P. F. *Introduction to Logical Theory.* London: Methuen and Co., 1952.
SUZUKI, D. T. *Introduction to Zen Buddhism* (New Edition). London: Rider, 1949.
—— *Essays in Zen Buddhism* (1st Series). London: Luzac and Co., 1927.
TAGORE, R. *Autobiography,* trans. S. Tagore and I. Devi. London: Macmillan and Co., 1914.
TILLICH, P. *Biblical Religion and the Search for Ultimate Reality.* Chicago: Chicago University Press, 1955.
THOMAS, E. J. *History of Buddhist Thought* (2nd Edition). London: Routledge and Kegan Paul, 1951.
UNDERHILL, E. *Mysticism* (2nd Edition). London: Methuen and Co., 1911.
WITTGENSTEIN, L. *Philosophical Investigations,* trans. G. E. M. Anscombe and R. Rhees. Oxford: Basil Blackwell, 1953.
ZIMMER, H. *Philosophies of India,* ed. J. Campbell. London: Routledge and Kegan Paul, 1953.

Index

HORNER, I. B., 72n.

iddhis (magical powers), 106
idealism, 95 ff., 102 f., 147n., 201
Indra, 35n.
Insam'l Kāmil, 133n.
ISAAC, 121
ISAIAH, 28n., 125
Īśvara (Lord), 45, 46, 49, 107, 133, 145, 151,
Islām, 8, 12, 15, 57, 80, 110, 128, 129, 130, 152, 154, 156, 191, 197, 202

Jainism, 129
Jātaka-Nidāna-Kathā (Birth Stories), 116
JESUS. *See* CHRIST
jhāna (stage of meditation), 92, 95 ff.
JĪLĪ, 133n., 144, 145
jñāna (knowledge), 148
JOB, 28
Job, Book of, 28n.
JOHN, St., of the Cross, 55
JOHN, St., the Divine, 28n.
JOHNSON, Samuel, 101 f.
Judaic religions, 7, 112, 117, 189
Judaism, 8, 12, 110, 111, 129, 202

Kabbala, The, 31n., 133n., 146
Kandy, Sacred Tooth at, 59
KANT, Immanuel, 55n.
karma (*lit.* deed: law governing rebirth), 152
kathenotheism, 35n.
Koran, 41n.
Kṛṣṇa (Krishna), 30, 41, 108, 147, 193

LAWRENCE, Brother, 191
LEEUW, G. Van der, 34n.
LEWIS, H. D., 186n.

MADHVA, 157
Mahābhārata, 192
Mahāparinibbāna-Sutta (*The Sutta of the Great Decease*), 116n.
MAHĀVĪRA, 154n.
MAIMONIDES, 32
ma'rifat, 177
Mark, Gospel according to, 20
mārkata-kiśora-nyāya (monkey-offspring-method), 187
mārjāra-kiśora-nyāya (cat-offspring-method), 187
Martians, 49
Mātariśvān, 35n.
māyā (illusion), 33n., 36, 54
Messiah, The, 125, 193
Milindapañha (*The Questions of King Milinda*), 21n., 58, 61, 69, 71, 84, 86, 98n., 128
Mitra, 35n.
MIYAMOTO, Shoson, 56n.
MOHAMMED, 128, 130, 154, 165
Mohammedīya Tarīqa, 154
mokṣa (release, salvation), 36, 136, 189
monarchianism, 35n.
monism, 33, 35n., 113, 126
monotheism, 44, 113, 126, 155
mukti (release, salvation), 136

NĀGĀRJUNA, 33, 88, 174
NĀGASENA, 69, 71
nats (spirits), 58
Neo-Platonism, 11, 174
See also PLOTINUS
nibbāna (extinction, as of a fire), 59 f.
See also nirvāṇa
nibbuta (extinguished, released), 59 f., 76
nicca (permanent), 58
Nichirenites, 128, 152
NICHOLSON, R. A. 133n., 144n., 157n.
NIETZSCHE, Friedrich, 1
nirmāṇakāya (Transformation Body), 153
See also Three Body Doctrine
nirvāṇa, 57, 58, 59 ff., 61 ff., 65 ff., 71 f., 76 ff., 82 f., 85, 86, 87, 95 ff., 116n., 190, 192, 197, 199
Noble Truths, Four, 59, 60
non-dualism, 33, 150 ff.

OM, 28, 107
Original Sin, 186, 188
Orphism, 103